UNPUNISHED

Center Point
Large Print

Also by Lisa Black and available from Center Point Large Print:

That Darkness

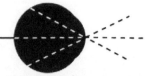

This Large Print Book carries the Seal of Approval of N.A.V.H.

UNPUNISHED

Lisa Black

CENTER POINT LARGE PRINT
THORNDIKE, MAINE

Library of Congress Cataloging-in-Publication Data

Names: Black, Lisa, 1963– author.
Title: Unpunished / Lisa Black.
Description: Center Point Large Print edition. | Thorndike, Maine :
Center Point Large Print, 2017.
Identifiers: LCCN 2016056315 | ISBN 9781683242963
    (hardcover : alk. paper)
Subjects: LCSH: Women forensic scientists—Fiction. | Murder—
Investigation—Fiction. | Large type books. | GSAFD: Mystery fiction.
Classification: LCC PS3602.E283 U56 2017 | DDC 813/.6—dc23
LC record available at https://lccn.loc.gov/2016056315

This book is dedicated to
the newspapers of America.

I will miss you if you leave us.

A false witness shall not go unpunished,
and he who speaketh lies shall not escape.
—Proverbs 19:5

Chapter 1

Jack eyed the kid as his partner continued the questioning, noting how he had perfected the adolescent sprawl, head lolling, face bored nearly to a coma, arms and legs splayed in a show of utter contempt for both his surroundings and the two men present there—or at least as splayed as he could get with one hand cuffed to the table. Jack watched, and waited, and worked to resist the overwhelming desire to smack the kid out of his seat.

"Ronnie—" Jack's partner, Riley, began, loose tie flopping over a wrinkled shirt and red hair askew.

"Reign," the kid corrected him. "They call me Reign."

"My mistake," Riley went on. "Ronald—"

"*Reign.* 'Cause I'm the king."

Jack straightened his long frame from where he had been standing with his back against the cool concrete wall of the interrogation room— perhaps a mistake, because he needed coolness. "Can you even *spell* 'reign'?"

Ronnie Soltis swiveled his head to take in Jack as if he had only then noticed the man's existence, as if they hadn't been at this for over an hour. "Ain't never had much use for school."

Riley snorted. "That much is obvious. You've been held back twice—and you have to practically get a grade of zero to be flunked in this day and age. Is it your goal to endlessly repeat the ninth grade?"

"It's my goal to eliminate all fat white cops from the planet," the kid said, words now less casual.

Riley pointed out, with elaborate confusion on his face, "But *you're* white."

"As well as only a doughnut or two short of type two diabetes," Jack added. He moved closer to Ronnie, aka Reign, Soltis, a boy not yet old enough to drive. Because as absurd as this gangsta-glamorizing punk seemed, there was nothing funny about the things he had done. Nothing at all.

Ronnie Soltis had managed to amass a criminal record that would be the envy of most Quincy Avenue gangbangers. It dated back to his eighth birthday, beginning with theft and progressing to burglary, arson, dealing, destruction of private property (the home of a rival marijuana dealer), destruction of public property (the county library, for reasons never fully explained), aggravated menacing (various activities relating to his drug business), assaults, plural, aggravated assault (the stabbing of another young man in the eye; the boy had five years and a hundred pounds on him but lacked the killer instinct), and at least two attempted rapes. Those had been foiled only because Ronnie preferred to choose victims he felt were worthy of him—in this case, pretty, slender girls who happened to be athletic enough to outrun him. Pretty much anyone could outrun Ronnie, who spent all his spare time on video games. And now he had progressed to attempted murder, his failure due only to the restrictions of physics. But he had tried. He would keep trying.

Jack was not the first to feel an itch to knock some sense into the kid. He figured he would not be the last.

Because Ronnie Soltis's true goal was to be the baddest mother in the valley. He wanted to rule the underworld with an iron fist, to be, if not respected, then at least feared by all. And Ronnie Soltis was making good progress for someone who had been raised in the very un-underworld-like suburb of Solon, about as far from the ghetto as one could get and still be in Cuyahoga County, and despite a standard of living that meant if he had ever had to actually *live* in a ghetto, he certainly would not feel so enamored. His overwhelmed parents had long since given up, Social Services had thrown up their hands, and the cops were barely holding off a strong feeling of futility.

"I need to know about the bottle," Riley was saying, his fair skin splotching and coloring as he fought back the annoyance. His extra thirty pounds weren't helping the blood flow either. Jack took another step, reached the table.

"Don't know what you're talking about." In Ronnie-speak it came out *"dohnowutyertalkinbout."*

"The one that had gasoline in it. The one you stuffed your shirt into the top of and lit on fire."

"Not my shirt. I got my shirt on," the kid snorted, plucking at the bright orange fabric to prove his point. Jack hovered around the edge of the table, only two feet from Ronnie's chair.

"And dropped into the open window of D'Andre Junior's Cadillac. You know D'Andre, right?"

"Nevuhhurdahim."

"You and your pal Scrubs smashed D'Andre's hand last week for skimming the count. Dropped a concrete block on it."

"Nevuhhurdahim."

Jack moved, slow, nonthreatening, to stand just behind Ronnie's right shoulder. Ronnie removed his arm from where it had been hanging over the back of the chair and deposited it in his lap.

"With your record, we could have had you tried as an adult. You wouldn't have seen daylight until your thirtieth birthday. So you sent him a message that he might want to drop the charges, right?"

The kid stared at the one-way glass in front of him as if checking out his haircut, supremely unconcerned by the cops on either side of him. But his unnatural stillness told Jack that he was all too aware; his muscles tensed a little more with every inch closer Jack came. The instinctual recognition of one predator for another.

10

"His girlfriend, Laila, was going to testify against you, wasn't she? Is that why you targeted the Cadillac even though you knew D'Andre Junior wouldn't be riding in it on a Sunday morning? Hell, D'Andre would probably be struck by lightning if he ever crossed the threshold of a church. Just Laila and her two little girls would be in that car. You knew that, didn't you?"

"Dohnowutyertalkinbout."

Jack switched to the side of the kid's chair. The kid pulled in his right foot, which had been extended as far as possible under the table in the adolescent sprawl of disrespect. Classic body language of the lost.

"Burned one of the kids pretty badly. The other one got broken glass in her arm. Just two and three years old."

Ronnie said nothing, but the silence didn't have a feel of shame to it. Not the slightest flicker of remorse passed over his expression. He kept any smart comment to himself and darted another look at Jack out of the corner of his eye. Then he pulled in his other foot.

"Tough enough to get a three-year-old to sit still for stitches, but try to treat burns on a baby—she just wouldn't stop screaming, the nurses said."

The kid straightened his spine, sat up with his feet tucked underneath his chair, but this didn't signal any willingness to either face or confess any facts—simply an automatic, involuntary reaction to Jack invading the buffer zone of his personal space. A triumph of sorts, but a useless, meaningless one. Ronnie gazed up at Riley and said, "Ain't you got any sort of coffee in this shithouse?"

Jack had a fleeting vision of ending Ronnie Soltis's life right then and there, saving D'Andre's life, sparing Laila and her tiny girls any future malice. It would be so easy—or it would have been had his "murder room" not been dismantled. No, selective and well-justified murder could not be his plan anymore, not since he had the misfortune to meet up with Maggie Gardiner.

Now he had to be—what, the reformed Jack? The kinder and gentler Jack? Given Ronnie's obvious issues with anger and impulse control, his determined and hell-bent path toward self-demolition, the kindest, gentlest thing to do would be to ply young Ronnie with his favorite food and drink and some quiet conversation until the kid felt as comfortable on this planet as he ever would, pump three bullets into the back of his head, and put Ronnie Soltis out of his misery before he could cause any further destruction to everyone and everything in his orbit.

But, alas, that had been last month.

Jack couldn't stand to be in that room another moment. "Let's go, Riley. I'm sure the king's daddy's lawyer is here by now."

Riley said, "It's lunchtime, anyway."

They left without another word. As Jack held the door for his partner, he saw the look of slight disappointment cross the kid's face as his playthings left the room. But no matter. There would be plenty of others.

Ronnie Soltis stretched his legs out again, rubbed the wrist with the cuff, and waited for his attorney.

Jack shut the door and walked away.

Chapter 2

Maggie Gardiner stepped out of the marked city car, hitched her camera bag over her shoulder, and gazed up at the vast, dark structure in front of her. The offices of the city's newspaper, the *Herald*, occupied the largest building within city limits, though to judge from recent reports on the demise of the American newspaper, it would probably be shuttered and turned into luxury lakeview condos within the next decade. The thought made her slam the car's door with an unfair amount of force.

Maggie had thrown on her uniform and pulled her dark hair back, but that had been as glamorous as she felt like getting for a late-night call-out. The cool spring air pricked her bare forearms. She approached the entrance, framed by an empty flagpole and a motto engraved in stone over the doors: *"Give light and the people will find their own way."*

She stopped and thought about that. A wonderful sentiment. She could use a little light these days, because her way didn't seem clear at all.

She tugged at the glass door. Nothing.

A small plaque to the left of the door read: AFTER HOURS PLEASE PRESS BUTTON. She pressed.

Nothing.

A person entered the lobby from a rear door, a slender girl in a starched uniform. She pushed the door's bar from the inside and let Maggie in.

Maggie introduced herself and asked if there were police officers present. The girl's face took on a look of solemn concern. "Oh yes, for Mr. Davis. It's so awful what happened. I'll get someone—you should have come in the rear entrance—it's going to be a long walk from here—hang on a sec and I'll get you Kevin."

The lobby had obviously had a makeover at some point in history. The woman led Maggie to a long desk topped with granite in order to find a phone. Oversized, framed prints of front pages through the years lined the walls on both sides, announcing stories from the Torso killings during the Great Depression to Carl Stokes's election as mayor to the football team defecting to Baltimore. Leather sofas surrounded a glass coffee table, which held only a copy of the previous day's edition.

The woman dialed the phone. From the notations on her uniform she served as the nighttime security guard. She didn't look strong enough to take on a half-drowned kitten, but Maggie knew appearances could deceive. "Can you come up and escort the, um—"

"Forensic tech," Maggie supplied for her. Actually her title was forensic scientist, but she opted for something shorter and more descriptive.

"The CSI," the girl finished, and hung up. "He'll be right here. So . . . you're forensics? What are you going to do? I heard it was a suicide. It's so awful!"

"Yes, awful," Maggie agreed, debating whether to move her car wherever the girl suggested in case she had to make a number of trips back to it, or get the gist of the situation down first. The Medical Examiner's personnel handled the body, so often in cases of suicide she would take some photographs and collect a few relevant items and that was that. But she had a vague premonition that this one might get more complicated.

A door to her right opened and a tall black man in a white shirt and loosened tie interrupted the girl's questions. He gave Maggie an enthusiastic welcome, which told her he either didn't know the recently deceased Mr. Davis or didn't like him very much.

He ushered her through a long corridor with what appeared to be conference rooms lining either side, and emerged into a cavernous oval with the length and height of an indoor stadium. The ceiling soared at least one hundred feet above them, and half its fluorescent lights had been turned off. The floor area had been filled with desks, clustered in haphazard rows. Large windows lined the north side. Somewhere beyond their inky blackness roiled Lake Erie, in what must be a great view during the daylight hours. The south walls faced the less picturesque visitors' parking lot and Superior Avenue. No one was present at that hour, what was essentially the middle of the night.

Maggie hustled to keep up with Kevin as she took all this in, winding through the churning sea of reporters' desks. Their surfaces were piled with papers, books, all sorts of odds and ends from journalism awards to troll dolls to a miniature slot machine. Maggie liked this space much better than the slick lobby.

Many desks, however, were blank and abandoned.

"We're dying," Kevin noted, matter-of-factly. "We all know it. Print journalism will gasp its last breath within a few years. At least that's what we hear every single day, but there are still die-hard fans who want to *read* their news, not listen to some wildly biased talking head or have to balance a delicate and breakable piece of electronics just to find out what the weather's going to be. You read the *Herald*?"

She answered truthfully. "Every day."

"Home delivery?"

"Yep."

"Bless you. I'd kiss you on the mouth right here and now, except we had some kind of sensitivity training last year and apparently I'm not supposed to do that."

17

Maggie laughed.

"You should have come in by the rear entrance. It's a long walk from here."

"So I heard."

"That's okay, I can give you the tour. I'm Kevin Harding, by the way, Printing Supervisor. I used to be Entertainment Editor, got to do the hard-charging stories like what Princess Kate wore to the Bahamas and the new season at Playhouse Square, but now I have a real job."

"Too bad. Keeping up with the Kardashians sounds like fun."

"Yeah." But his face didn't look as if it had been.

The arena area had a second level—a ring of offices along the outer wall, more than one floor above, nearly two. Only a few were lit, including a large space at the easternmost tip of the oval. The hallway outside these offices had a clear glass railing, giving the illusion that anyone on that walkway had nothing to keep them from falling the considerable distance to the floor below.

It was a very impressive-looking interior, for a staff who functioned within the written word. Maggie loved space and thought it a perfect setting for a newspaper, and wondered if the dramatic surroundings reminded the reporters every day to respect the dramas, large and small, that affected their readers' lives.

Kevin Harding kept walking. "The body is in the offset room. Do you know how a paper is printed?"

"Vaguely. But that's probably changed in the digital age."

"As far as the actual printing is concerned, yes and no." They reached the east wall. He used his key card to exit the lofty atrium, into a space that was equally impressive in a totally different way. Overhead lights burst into illumination as they entered, as if by magic, to reveal a maze of huge and inexplicable machinery. If the atrium represented pure creativity, then this place embodied pure function. The floors were concrete, clean but stained, and so were the walls.

"The master sheet is made on a piece of flexible aluminum, using the reaction of oil and water and ultraviolet light. The point is that the ink sticks to the printed areas and the rest washes away. That's done in here." Her nose wrinkled from the smell, not offensive but definitely chemical as they passed a roomful of paper rolls, most standing on their ends but some on their sides, ready to be rotated into the printing process, and huge drums of liquid ink. The rolls only came up to her chest but were enormously round, and she guessed that they could easily kill someone. Kevin told her they weighed nearly 1900 pounds each.

They entered the next section. "Wow," Maggie said.

Kevin let her take it in. "Yeah, it's pretty impressive."

Though they had been on the ground floor, it became the second level in this room and they took a metal staircase down. The three-story-high ceiling allowed for four towers of steel machinery to function, squeezing an unbroken stream of moving newspaper between huge, horizontal rollers. The rollers were stacked vertically inside the steel-framed towers, and not all the towers were the same size. The tallest had four sets of rollers, others two or one. The paper ribbon stretched from the top of one to the bottom of the next like a spiderweb. The noise drowned out everything else and Kevin had to shout as he led her along.

"The aluminum sheets are wound around the rolls there, but they print on a rubber roll next to it, which then prints on the paper. That's why it's called offset. There's one on each side of the paper, so it prints on both sides at once. Every turn prints eight sheets of newspaper."

She could see the rolls and the paper, but there seemed to be much more than that, from the huge boxes feeding the paper in and suspended vats of what must be ink, feeding through metal tubes to a mechanism that ran parallel to the rollers, an array of scaffolding and even steps surrounding each tower. What appeared to be super heavy-duty skateboards moved around in a set of tracks that wound around the bottoms of the roller towers. Kevin told her they would carry the huge rolls of paper into place. The clacking filled her ears, and the speed with which the paper moved made her dizzy. Or perhaps the fumes from the ink and its solvents did that.

"The taller towers with more rollers are doing the color printing, the shorter ones, all black. Four colors, of course—red, blue, yellow, and black. The paper roll then feeds into the folder, where the paper is folded and cut and sent to binding."

She followed him to the other end of the roller towers. The stream of paper exited the printing process, was cut into two by a tiny rotating pizza-cutter–like blade, and folded over each side of a V-shaped wedge, only to disappear into a contraption that folded and sliced and spit out what would appear at her front door every morning. She would have thought this would cause the whole stream to flutter and snap back into the towers as if untying one end of a clothesline, but by that point the next newspaper had been folded and the paper just kept flowing. Each finished paper wound up suspended from an overhead conveyor belt, held by a clip, and moved into the next area, visible through glass windows.

"What?" Kevin asked her. "You're frowning."

"I just can't believe it picks up and carries each paper individually like that. It seems so— delicate. I thought they'd be stacked—"

"Oh, they're not done yet. Different sections have to be added and then the inserts—all those sale papers that only the real shopaholics look at. You ever wonder about those Post-it note ads that we stick over the headline on the front page?"

"I hate those."

"Everybody does. But they're great advertising. Those get stuck on as the papers are going by on the overhead conveyor."

The papers flowed into the center of a carousel that had at least a dozen small platforms radiating from it, with a human stationed at each one. They were stacking some papers, setting them on the platforms to straighten them out, and—she couldn't figure out the rest from her vantage point but assumed they were somehow piling up and binding the papers. At the far end of the building, probably half a football field away from her, people moved around a loading dock and shuffled the stacks onto trucks backed up to the open overhead doors. And from there, she thought, to a public wanting something to read with their morning cup of coffee in a glorious and time-honored tradition. "How many—"

"Twelve papers a second. Fifteen hundred feet per minute . . . twenty-five feet per second," Kevin answered, shouting over the noise. "Now, if we could only *sell* twelve per second. . . ."

She could have stood there for another hour, absorbing all the action in front of her, where the pressed wood pulp went at each step and how and why, but she hadn't come there for a tour.

"Where's . . ." She refrained from saying *the body,* and asked instead, "Where are the police officers?"

"Ah, come this way." They backtracked past the folder/cutter and stepped under the moving stream of newspaper to the other side of the long room. She followed, ducking her head much lower than it needed to be ducked—she couldn't imagine what a mess an obstruction in the paper stream would cause. And it would cause one hell of a paper cut.

On the other side of the roller towers, Kevin Harding pointed upward.

She followed the gesture.

On the highest platform of the tallest stack, a uniformed officer and two men in plainclothes peered over the railing. Two weren't looking at her, though. Instead their attention rested on a man who hung in midair between that platform and the next lower one, swinging ever so slightly from the end of a thin white rope. The other end of the rope had been attached to the railing the men stood behind.

"That's Davis," Kevin told her.

Maggie's attention was usurped from the unfortunate Mr. Davis. One of the men on the platform *was* looking at her, and she knew why.

Jack Renner.

Chapter 3

Maggie opened her camera bag, then snapped a few shots looking up at the body from different spots on the floor. Then she started up the steps. Kevin remained below, which was fine with her. The platforms didn't appear too spacious. Or maybe he wanted to keep his distance from the body of his coworker.

She had thirty feet of stairway to prepare to meet Jack, and her mind ping-ponged with every *clack* of the paper rollers. There was nothing to prepare for, of course, since they would not say anything about their past association, would act in front of other people as if their acquaintance had been casual. She would function exactly as she always functioned at a crime scene: professional, courteous, and observing more than she spoke.

Still her heart pounded with a near panic she couldn't control. This seemed a test of sorts, to see if their tenuous pact could hold up in the real world.

Maggie reached the top of the steps. Back to work. Calm. Professional.

Jack stared, but so did his partner, Riley, and the uniformed officer she didn't recognize.

"Morning," Riley said.

She took a deep breath. Normal, everything was

normal. *She* was normal. Problem was, she no longer knew what that word meant.

"I don't think it is, quite," she said. "Please tell me you haven't touched that railing."

All three men looked sheepish.

She sighed, a bit more theatrically than necessary.

Four people moving about on a platform designed for a single mechanic required coordination. The uniform, low man on the totem, shuffled to the next level. Jack and Riley switched places with her. They brushed chests while passing, inevitable at those quarters. Even as Maggie hoped the inking mechanism wouldn't grab up her hair as it shuttled along the rollers, she could feel the heat emanating from Jack's torso. She wondered at his thoughts. Did he feel amused? Awkward? Threatened?

She did not want him to feel threatened. She had seen his handiwork close-up.

But the idea of him feeling amused ticked her off.

She reached the railing. The rope, she now saw, was not a rope at all but a flat mesh strap about an inch wide. It appeared new and a little shiny, clean, tied off at the round metal bar with two simple square knots. The strap hung as straight and true as a Foucault pendulum with the fully grown male pulling down the other end, quivering only slightly with the vibration of the tower's machinery. She followed its line and caught herself before putting one hand on the railing. She couldn't blame the cops. At that height the urge to steady oneself was an instinctual and involuntary reaction before peering over to a thirty-five-foot drop with nothing but two thin bars of steel to keep you from plunging into that abyss.

As from below, she noted the jeans, pale blue collared shirt, battered running shoes, and black watch with a rubbery band. From above she could also see that his sandy-blond hair had grown thin at the top, a perfectly round skullcap. She took a few more photos.

Then she straightened, turned to the cops, and waited.

"Robert Davis," Riley said. "Forty-four, married, two kids, copy editor here for at least six years. Lives in Garfield Heights. No known health problems, at least none documented in the HR file. No EMS or cop calls on record for him or his address. ID'd by the printing supervisor, but we haven't—obviously—pulled him up or checked for a wallet yet, so we haven't made notification."

Meaning his wife and kids would have a few more hours of sleep before their world fell apart. Maggie asked, "Any history of depression or suicide attempts?"

"Who knows? The only person here to even recognize him is the printing supervisor, and he knew him only as another guy who worked here. They weren't best buddies."

Yeah, he hadn't seemed too broken up about it. "Any conflicts? He about to be fired or something?"

"Not according to the HR gal we woke up, but she might not have been told yet. Layoffs have been a scourge upon the earth in this place for years, according to the printing supervisor."

"So I heard. Why was Davis here in the middle of the night?"

"It's a newspaper," Riley said. "They write all day and print all night. Copy editors often work late checking stories before they go to print, according to the supervisor. That's maybe why his family hasn't called to see where he is—they're probably used to it."

She darted a glance at Jack. He stood as he always did, weight balanced, shoulders slightly hunched as if to downplay his height, a fiftyish, brown-haired, strong but not buff, calm, and utterly ordinary man. No one could ever guess what he had been up to for the past ten or so years. She knew only his most recent history, and wasn't sure she wanted to hear the rest. He returned her gaze—steady, neutral, noncommittal. They would play it cool, for both their sakes. She gave him the barest nod. Their deal stood.

"He couldn't confirm the clothing," Riley was saying, "but I'm guessing our poor Mr. Davis never went home last night. Of course he could have a cell phone in his pocket that's been going off for hours. Who could hear it over this racket?"

"Can't they turn it off?"

"No," Riley and Jack answered in unison. Riley said, "It would cause a huge disruption in the process and cost thousands upon thousands of dollars in late papers and lost revenue, blah blah blah. The supervisor nearly fainted when I suggested it. We didn't insist."

"Okay," Maggie said. Whether the machinery turned or not didn't affect their work. It was just loud.

"Too bad. I was really looking forward to yelling, *'Stop the presses!'*" At her blank look Riley added, "You know, like in the old movies. The really old movies? *Stop the presses?* Ah, you're too young. How are you going to get him off that? Pull him up or lower him down?"

She glanced over the edge again. The body hung only a few feet below the next platform down. If they could pull it up slightly, the body snatchers could maneuver him onto that level. Simpler than the other two alternatives.

First, though, she would need to process the railing, exercise in frustration though it may be after at least three men had been leaning on it. The fingerprint kit in her vehicle, at the other end of a long walk through the facility, would be required. She really should move her car.

The body snatchers arrived. Maggie guided them in through the loading dock, where the truck crews shuffled their morning cargo. This attracted attention from the loading staff, which had been incurious until now. Maggie could see why. The cutting and folding process did not require the high ceilings of the roller tower area, so once the paper had been guided into that machine, the building became one level. This effectively cut off the view of the upper roller towers from the loading dock area. The forklift workers and truck drivers hadn't noticed Davis's body because they couldn't see it from where they were.

The body snatchers' official term remained "ambulance crew," even though their "ambulance" was a van without lights or sirens. Their transports did not require haste, and they had not been trained in lifesaving techniques. They had, however, gained extensive experience in retrieving dead bodies from awkward and inconvenient areas, such as drainage ditches, too-small bathrooms, fire escapes, heating ducts, and once, a still-smoking chimney. They didn't even blink at the suspended Mr. Davis.

The heftier member of the team, Deion, went to the uppermost platform to pull upward on the strap. Maggie and the less-buff Tony waited on the second-highest level to pull in the victim as if they were landing a prize tuna. The Medical

Examiner's investigator, a statuesque blonde who happened to be six months' pregnant, supervised.

"Ready?" Deion called from above.

Davis faced away from them. The opposite wall had only a few windows, spaced to be visible from the roller towers. Past them the dark water swirled in what would be a gorgeous view during the day. She wondered if he had wanted one last glimpse before he went, or if the printing tower was simply the highest spot he could find in the building.

She also wondered where Printing Supervisor Kevin had been when Davis made his lonely climb to the top.

The body quivered and inched up. She and Tony reached out. Tony pulled the back of the man's shirt and she grabbed his belt, resolving to let go if he started to fall. She would not let a dead man kill her.

She became aware of Jack standing behind her. She would not let the cops assist in the recovery, both because she didn't automatically leave heavy lifting to men, and because she wanted to minimize the amount of personnel making contact with her victim. The ME investigator, obviously, should not be doing any heavy lifting in her condition.

But Robert Davis was frickin' heavy. Her shoulders strained as she pulled. Deion kept the tension on the strap as she and Tony wrestled the stiffening body toward them. They had to stop with his thighs resting on the metal pipe railing, since the strap didn't allow enough slack to go farther.

"Cutting," Deion told them, screeching to be heard over the machinery.

"Hang on to him," Tony told her.

The strap went slack, its loose end free-falling through the air in an undulating flash. She and Tony pulled with a quick ferocity, hauling Mr. Davis in before he could tip the balance of their collective weight. When his feet cleared the railing they lowered him, not too gently, onto a sheet laid out for just that purpose. Maggie straightened, sure her shoulders would be feeling the strain in a few hours.

Deion clattered down the metal steps. Jack made way for him.

"Okay?" he asked.

"Yeah," Tony told him. Then, "Dude—what's that?"

Deion looked down at his neatly pressed pants, which now bore a distinctive dark stripe from hip to hip. Obviously he had leaned against the railing Maggie had just processed with finger-print powder. He brushed at it. Then he looked at Maggie.

"Oops," she admitted. "I forgot to tell you."

The investigator hid a snicker behind one hand.

With an impatient puff of air he brushed (futilely) at the stripe. But he spoke to her kindly

31

enough to say, "That strap is still up there. Want me to get it?"

Maggie panted. "No, I will."

"You sure? I can grab—"

"*No.*"

Three men and a woman looked at her.

Breath caught, she explained, "I'll collect it. Because we have a problem."

They kept looking.

"This isn't a suicide."

Chapter 4

Riley's eyebrows disappeared into the crop of reddish hair. He pinched the bridge of his fleshy nose between his thumb and index finger, a picture-perfect expression of not-so-patient exasperation. "What do you mean, not suicide?"

"The vee," she said, crouching next to the body. She no longer had to shout to be heard; the day's paper had finished printing. Two areas over the binding mechanism hummed over the cut, collated stacks. Beyond them, the papers were trundled to the loading docks to be placed on idling trucks. Relative serenity reigned in the printing room.

"See the furrow in his neck? When someone is hung, the rope is pulled upward. The knot isn't at the back of their neck; it's more at the nape or even at the back of their head, depending on the elasticity of the rope. It forms a vee shape. When someone is strangled, the rope is pulled straight back, making more of a circle. The difference in the furrows is obvious."

The investigator, rubbing her belly, backed Maggie up. "Exactly. Homicide."

The two detectives bent over to gaze at the dead man's neck. So did the uniformed policeman, who had returned to their little group. He looked curious, but the two detectives appeared to each have a touch of indigestion.

"There's something of a vee furrow as well," Jack pointed out. "Maybe he tied the knot straight back and then over time the strap stretched out, increasing the vee."

The ME investigator dashed his hopes. "Nope, there's two distinct furrows—one strangulation, one hanging. Not a progression from one to the other." With that she closed her notebook and started down the steps to get the rest of the information from the HR girl, leaving the crime scene to the cops.

The team of Tony and Deion returned, picked up the sheet at all four corners, and maneuvered the corpse down the narrow, winding staircase. This would add another story of a retrieval in odd circumstances to their long list of tales.

"Maggie," Riley said, "it's the middle of the night. Suicide call, snap some pictures, inform the grieving widow, and go back to bed. That's how it's supposed to go."

"Sorry," she said, not meaning it and knowing he didn't, either. Riley was already running through scenarios and suspects in his head, she guessed, intrigued and disgusted and angry at this waste of life. She had never asked Jack what Riley knew or didn't know about his partner's extracurricular activities, but felt sure that the answer would be: absolutely zero.

Somewhere below them, she heard Tony and Deion bickering amiably as they negotiated the turns with their heavy and awkward cargo—such as Robert Davis had become.

Riley said, "Okay . . . Preggers Barbie said between eight p.m. and midnight as an educated guess."

Jack supplied, "Supervisor Harding said the print run starts about ten. The guy wasn't hanging here then."

Riley said, "Body discovered at one-thirty a.m. What, Harding never came back in here for three and a half hours? What kind of supervisor does that?"

"He said if there's no mechanical difficulties, there's no reason to. His job is in the next two rooms, making sure the human beings running the cutter don't fall into the blades and watching the binding and the moving out to the trucks. He spends most of his shift on the loading dock, according to him. We're going to have to establish who was in the building during those hours, who had access to this room—"

"Surveillance, videos, key card swipes," Riley mused aloud.

"Family. ME's willing to call it with the wallet." Davis's pocket had held his wallet with his press pass, driver's license, health insurance card, fifty-two dollars in cash, and a photo of black-haired boys. His face, mottled and swollen, tongue protruding, no longer truly resembled his DL photo; but from the shape of the nose and the color of the hair and the presence of the wallet itself, the investigator felt comfortable concluding that this man was, indeed, Robert Davis.

His pockets had not contained a cell phone, an odd omission in this day and age.

Riley and Jack were still adding items to their to-do list. "Office," Jack said.

"Immediately," Riley agreed. "Of course, the guy's had four hours or so."

"Yeah."

In near unison, they looked at Maggie and said her name. She raised her eyebrows.

"We'll need photos of the office, in case we find anything good in there," Riley said.

"We'll need the surveillance video downloaded," Jack said.

"Got it," she said.

Maggie sat in the security office with the skinny girl. Her name badge read, REBECCA. She might not look like a physical fortress, but she could operate the security footage with the deft hand of the digital-age generation, for which Maggie felt grateful. Retrieving video from surveillance systems could often turn into an exercise in frustration. While worlds better than the old and scratchy VHS tapes, digital video surveillance still existed in a developing stage. Many mom-

and-pop systems had sprung up and then faded, leaving purchasers with no tech support, no manual, and no real training. Maggie would often have to start pushing buttons and locating menus and might, after a great deal of trial and error, obtain the images. Sometimes this would take five minutes, sometimes several hours. Sometimes the personnel could do it for her, and she always felt like buying them a coffee for it.

Unfortunately the surveillance cameras covered only the outside exits, parking lots, loading dock, and public lobby. Apparently those who spent their careers keeping tabs on what other people were doing didn't care to be watched over themselves. But then newspapers feared attacks from outside—disgruntled subjects of unflattering stories, terrorists, fanatics—not those employed to work there. Maggie seemed to be learning, however, that it had to be exactly one of those employees who had killed Robert Davis.

No terrorist or fanatic or disgruntled subject had entered the building since the public lobby closed at five p.m. One reporter could be seen letting a man in a side door, but also escorted him out well before the eight p.m. print run. Usually most staff left by late afternoon, but Rebecca explained that many of the editors and copy editors worked late. Reporters might be there at any odd hour, finishing stories, doing research, or talking to people they couldn't get ahold of during the day.

Of course the whole printing and shipping staff worked at night—about fifty people if one included the truck drivers. Shipping and trucking usually stayed around the loading dock area, but they would use the restrooms and the vending area in the east break room.

Rebecca knew her stuff, rattling all this off to Maggie without being asked. She had only been there for three months, but found the job easy and enjoyed the constant activity in the building. "A newspaper never sleeps," she said. "But, she warned, don't let some of these guys start talking about the old days—meaning, like, fifteen years ago for some of them. They'll go on for*ever*."

There were eight employee entrances. All were monitored with cameras. Key cards were required to unlock them, as well to get through certain interior doors of the building. The admin staff, secretaries, accountants, and whatnot did not have access to the printing area, for their own safety and for the premiums on the liability insurance. Key card swipes were not recorded or stored, so there was no way to tell who opened what door and when.

Five extra doors were fire exits that did not have cameras but would set off alarms if disturbed. As so often happened with key card entrances, no swipe was required to exit, only to enter. If someone could get into an unauthorized part of the building—by accompanying someone else, by propping a door, by following a key card holder through the opening—they would have no difficulty leaving the area afterward.

The *Herald* employed 152 people, 255 if you included the truckers and the carriers.

Rebecca finished her summary and asked, "You want video of all the doors from eight p.m. until—when?"

"How about now?" Maggie asked. The killer most likely would have left before the body was discovered. But then, since the person must have been an employee of the *Herald*, they had a legitimate reason to be here and no reason to run away. They might have sidled out a door five minutes ago. They might still be in the building.

"That's a lot of video," Rebecca said. "Do you have a jump drive?"

"Yes."

"How big?"

Maggie fished a USB stick out of her camera bag. "Eight gigs."

"Mmm . . . that might not do it." Maggie handed it to her and Rebecca plugged it in. Maggie watched a sped-up video of employees moving through the east parking lot. As the sun set and the night grew dark, cars and humans were reduced to grainy blobs. The system wasn't substandard, relatively, but photography is all about light. A camera can't do much without it. Plus there had been a steady drizzle all evening, so many staff members were obscured further by raincoat hoods and umbrellas.

It might be possible to make a guess at who was who by matching up a general description with a fuzzy vehicle, but it wouldn't be enough to serve as evidence at a murder trial. The visitors' parking lot camera had a cobweb over it. The cars showed up clearly during the day, but at night, as the camera tried to focus, it chose the item closest to it, which left them with nothing but a crisscrossing of lines made white by the proximity. Occasionally the owner would stroll by on his eight legs, disproportionately huge, blindingly white, and terrifying.

She pondered how Robert Davis had gotten to the top of that roller tower since he hadn't wanted to kill himself. Either the killer was very strong, to carry a full-grown dead weight up four flights of steps, or he had enticed Robert Davis to come to the top with him. Or her. Maggie and the two detectives had scoured the walkway without finding a single indication of struggle—no torn fabric, no blood, no scrapes or scuffs that didn't appear to have been there for a decade. The body had no injuries other than the neck, at least none she could see in her quick examination.

A pinpoint of blood on one of his fingers probably came from a scratch on his throat as he tried to pull the strap away from his larynx, but Robert Davis had been a nail-biter, chomping them down too short to do much damage to himself or the strap. Unfortunately that meant he hadn't done much damage to the killer, either, and they would not be likely to find the killer's DNA on Davis's hands. His clothing showed no tears, and his battered sneakers had so many scars it would be impossible to tell if any were fresh. So she assumed, pending the ME's report, no protracted struggle. Either the killer had been very strong, or Davis had already been weakened, maybe by a blow to the head, maybe drunk or drugged.

Or he hadn't minded dying.

Security associate Rebecca interrupted Maggie's thoughts. "If it's okay that I ask, why do you need all this? I mean, I'm sorry the guy killed himself, but what is video of people coming in and going out going to tell you?"

The staff had not been told that the suicide had actually been a homicide. Jack and Riley thought that detail might best be withheld for a while. "It's just dotting i's and crossing t's. When did he get to work? Was he visibly upset when he came here? Just—details."

The slender girl pursed her lips and clicked her mouse.

Chapter 5

Jack took in the office as Riley talked. The managing editor for print was obviously the top guy in the building. His office spread twice the square feet of the others they'd passed, and was positioned at high noon in the upper oval, looking down on the reporters' bullpen. This part of the building stretched its elevation enough above the printing room to have windows open to the sky. The occupant would have a skewed view of the lake, but the windows would backlight him every morning in brilliant beams until he resembled Jesus emerging from the tomb on Easter morning. Not that Managing Editor Franklin Roth resembled that deity in the least.

Dressed in worn slacks and a wrinkled dress shirt with a stain on the pocket, gray hair awry, Franklin Roth sat behind his desk rubbing one eye and looking as if he had rolled from bed into his car. He probably had—it *was* three o'clock in the morning. The HR "girl," by contrast, a well-put-together fiftyish brunette, had brushed her hair into a quick chignon, applied a base coat of makeup, and pulled on a blazer over pressed slacks before arriving. Such were, Jack thought, the differences between men and women. Or perhaps between professions—press people always seemed to take pride in looking a little scruffy.

"How long had Robert Davis worked here?" Riley asked, after thanking them both for coming in at such a godawful hour.

"Fifteen years," HR answered, holding the dead man's personnel file. "First as a classifieds editor, then a reporter for a while, then a copy editor for Business and Classifieds and then for News."

"Any recent disruptions to his job? Was he in danger of getting fired, demoted?"

"No," she said.

Jack asked the editor for confirmation.

"No, he wasn't." Roth paused to slurp coffee out of a mug dwarfed by his large hands. His denial sounded less than definite, so the cops gave him the staring silence until he added, "Two years ago we cut one third of our newsroom staff. Layoffs and pink slips are a constant fear when you work in a business that a grade-school kid can tell you is on its last legs. The online stuff hasn't found its rhythm, and print hasn't turned a profit in years. The upcoming generations don't read anymore, and half their teachers will tell you they can't but have to be passed to the next grade anyway. There's wars going on while all the public wants to hear about is who wore the most hideous gown up the red carpet and the latest all-time best diet. Hell, who *doesn't* want to commit suicide these days?" He sipped with an air of despondence, then noticed the cops' expressions and got back on track. "But there weren't any layoffs planned, and I had no problem with Bob's work."

Riley said, "And you are—forgive me if this is blunt—the boss of this paper, right?"

"No. Yes—you could call me the functional boss. The actual boss is the publisher, Jon Tamerlane, but he's not around much."

"Trust-fund baby," the HR girl supplied, probably so Roth wouldn't have to. "This paper is only one of his concerns. He spends most of his time in the south of France, researching alternate energy sources or the next great wines or whatever."

"Okay," Riley said, "so you're the boots on the ground. Did you know Davis well?"

"Worked with him every day since he got here, about fifteen years ago."

Jack surveyed the office as Roth spoke. He had expected to see a wall of framed photographs of Roth with famous people and poster-size sheets of front pages, but the one set of shelves held only battered books, what seemed to be family photos, and various mementos from an autographed baseball to a troll doll. A single shelf reluctantly conceded to prestige: It bulged with at least twenty different plaques, awards, and ribbons, all crammed together and with engravings he could not make out from where he sat. The oversized gold medals, however, he recognized—they were Pulitzers. He counted four. He guessed those made Franklin Roth something of a living legend in journalistic circles.

"What was his beat?" Riley asked, attempting to use the lingo, which made Roth smile.

"He was a copy editor. He checked over *other* people's beats. He wrote headlines, captions, designed the font sizes, did the layout. He handled the Local section, though he had taken over Nation and State when Jerome was out or on vacation. He was good. Not the best I've ever seen, but good. As I said, I had no problem with him or his work."

"Who did?" Jack asked.

Roth hitched one ankle up to the opposite knee and poked at an ear with a finger. If he hadn't been such a large, portly, gruff-looking man, Jack would have accused him of fidgeting. "We're in the news business. Everyone gets mad at you at some point in this job, or you're not doing it right."

"Who's been mad recently?"

Another pause, but it seemed Roth only wanted to marshal his thoughts. "A copy editor decides what goes into the paper, whether it's on page one above the fold or buried in a lower corner on eight. They write your headline—which is an art in itself—and your photo captions, and say whether it screams or whispers."

This seemed to surprise Riley. "I thought you did that. I mean . . . the editor . . ."

Roth chuckled. "A long time ago when papers were smaller operations in smaller towns, yes, the editor did all that. But for many years it's been the copy editor, while my job has shifted into the business end of things and, every year, further away from the writing end." He appeared unhappy about that, but shook it off and went on. "A copy editor checks facts—within reason. With a daily there is no way a copy editor has time to double-check every name or date or number. He can hold or cut the story if he thinks a reporter has played a little fast and loose with the truth. He can even change the copy, the text, if he thinks something is too wordy or too opaque or just could be said better. That makes reporters crazy. They're writers, after all, and every writer thinks every word they write is sacred. It's okay for *them* to change it, fifty times if necessary, but for some-one *else* to change it is like your neighbor French-kissing your wife—it simply isn't right."

The HR woman, whose eyes had been glazing over, woke up and snickered at this.

"Okay," Jack said. "Did Bob Davis kiss some-one's wife?"

"Uh, yeah. Pretty regularly. Most copy editors will change text and then kick it back to the reporters to get their 'approval,' even though they don't need to. It saves face all around, and give-

46

and-take is a normal part of newspaper writing. We all tell one another how to write something better all the time. Davis felt comfortable with making changes that the reporter didn't see until it showed up on their doorstep the next morning. Mostly minor stuff. Word usage. Bob hated italics with a passion and resisted the change to 'shined' instead of 'shone.' That kind of thing."

"Any arguments? Between him and the reporters under him?"

"Mmm . . . don't say 'under him' if you talk to any of them. Reporters don't work for the copy editor. Most of them feel being a copy editor is a demotion from reporter. They have different jobs, that's all. Arguments? Every day. Writers don't like their headline, don't like how many words were cut, don't like *which* words were cut, think the caption doesn't explain the photo or feel he cropped the photo too much. That's part of normal life at a newspaper. It's the process and everyone knows it." He seemed to remember that they were talking about a suicide, and added, "Nothing worth killing yourself over. He hadn't acted depressed or anything. Not that he and I were best buddies. Nation and State keeps me pretty busy, what with the terrorists and the DC politics and our senators. I spend more of my time on that end."

"So no big blowups recently?" Riley pressed. "No reporters in screaming matches?"

Again, Roth hesitated. The HR woman shot him a conspiratorial glance. Jack knew what he said next would be a massive understatement. "He may have been getting frustrated with Correa."

The cops waited.

Roth shifted, alternating his ankle to knee pose. "Since the major corruption trials a few years ago and the county shakeup, Roger Correa has been doing the follow-up investigative pieces on the minor crooks who escaped the original fallout. The city alderman who got campaign workers to paint his house, the chick in the city manager's office who somehow steered a landscaping bid to her husband's company, that sort of thing. Correa has been working on this story in which county advertising space—spots for posters or advertisements in newsletters—has been under-bid. He says the county property guy, some idiot named Martin, got together with people at each concern—the information office, the building manager who handles those glass display cases you see when you walk into City Hall, that kind of stuff—and conspired with them to bid less and less for the spaces."

Riley blinked. Jack's mind had wandered off, wondering how one would convince a copy editor to go to the top of the roller towers. He pulled it back.

"End result, the county property office is still charging the businesses the same amount for the advertising, but paying the county less than ever for the use of the space. Profit margin doubles, and he kicks some back to the individual managers. How this money actually changes hands is the last link in the chain that Correa had been yanking on."

"Okay," Riley said.

Roth said, "Bob wanted to hold the story until Correa figured out that last detail and got it verified. Correa considered said detail unimportant—he could prove that the rents had gone way down while the advert costs hadn't, so ergo, extra money had to have been received that didn't make it into county coffers. Good enough."

"What did you think?" Jack asked.

"Eh, I was okay with Correa running with it. Let the—um—you guys figure out where the hard cash went. But I let Bob handle it. It was his decision."

"How irate did this Roger Correa get?"

"Correa wakes up irate, and the day goes downhill from there. Before he started on this story it was the mayor's secret girlfriend, but he could never get her on record, the county treasurer's assistant buying a manicurist shop with staff for a couple bucks—which he *did* get on record—a grainy photo of the stadium contractor receiving an envelope or a napkin or a sack of burgers from a city councilman. Whatever story it is, he always insists it could have had a much bigger impact if only we'd written a different headline, put it on a different page, used five photos instead of one, and most importantly, given him more inches to work with. Column inches, I mean, right?" He chuckled as if he found Roger Correa's temper a lovable foible, and maybe he did. Then he glanced at the cops and realized he'd gotten off topic.

"He'd gripe to Bob, to me, to anyone who would listen. But they didn't have any fistfights over it, not that I heard. Besides, that would hardly have made Bob kill himself. Roger, I could see, out of sheer frustration, emotional little shit that he is. But not Bob. Bob had, shall we say, an infallible sense of his own expertise."

Jack asked, "Anyone else? That he might have had a serious conflict with?"

Roth frowned as if his patience had drained along with his coffee. "He accused Bart of plagiarism about a year ago, but that proved to be in error. Russo, Cannady, and Mills thought his headlines were too stuffy, and DeRosso thinks—thought—they were too silly. Palmer thought Davis never gave his photographs enough space, but since he won a Pulitzer a few years back his sense of expertise is a bit overdeveloped. As I said, normal. Every newspaper is like that and should be. If my people don't think their stuff is worth fighting for, I don't want them here."

Jack asked, "What about friends? Anyone he

was particularly close to, palled around with? Confided in?"

"Hell, I don't know. Ask Janelle, she probably saw the most of him. She's the layout editor. Or you could ask, you know, his *wife*." Something seemed to penetrate his tired brain, the idea that perhaps the officers were asking a lot of questions about a simple suicide. He *was* a newsman. "Why so much interest?"

"We're just trying to make sense of what happened. For the family's sake," Riley answered, but his primness smacked of evasion and acted upon the newsman as blood in the water affects a shark.

Roth said, "I used to work the crime beat, you know, back when we still called it a crime beat. I've rolled up on a lot of suicides, and usually it's *Guy killed himself, too bad, so sad, end of story*. So what's with all the questions?"

"Industrial setting," Riley said with a brisk air. "Semi-public place, lots of people around. It's different."

Roth did not appear remotely convinced.

Chapter 6

After security associate Rebecca started the video backup process, she escorted Maggie to Robert Davis's office. "Office" turned out to be a bit of a misnomer, since the reporters and editors and copy editors all worked in the one huge room. Only a lucky few—the high-level editors like Franklin Roth, the affiliates editor, the sales director/circulation manager—were allotted the individual rooms along the upper level. The rank and file were slung into one churning pot of industry and ego.

Industrial-size desks faced one another with a chest-high bulletin board in between, two at a time, spanning the room in slightly imperfect rows. Each writer had a set of file cabinets to border their area and at least one flat-screen monitor. The same messiness that had surrounded manual typewriters, however, persisted. Pens, paper clips, coffee mugs, the inevitable plastic sports bottles, business cards, notebooks, CDs, bags of chips and granola bars, photos of battle scenes and kids' T-ball cards pinned side by side, flyers, press releases, novelty USB drives, and cell phone chargers covered the surfaces and sometimes spilled into open drawers. The only items missing were ashtrays and the errant bottle of Scotch. The building had been made smoke-free long ago, and anyway cigarettes were too expensive these days to leave lying around.

Robert Davis's desk had a spot at the end of one of the haphazard rows, with three monitors instead of two and an extra surface area for laying out copy. Maggie snapped a few photographs of the surfaces. She saw pictures of two brown-haired boys of about five and seven, the images caught on the fly as they rushed headlong toward a ball or a dog or a piece of cake, energy and impishness and complete joy evident in their stride. No picture of the wife, but then the desk didn't have a lot of free space.

She pulled on a pair of latex gloves. Past editions had been stacked to one side, printed stories or parts of stories and a few photos scattered across the rest. Robert Davis had liked Trident gum in wilder flavors and hadn't been too fussy about washing out his coffee mug (a free gift from Progressive insurance). He did not have a bottle of Scotch in his bottom drawer or someone else's wife's panties stuffed in his ergonomic chair. He had not left blood spattered across his keyboard, or his cell phone, or signs of a struggle.

"No note," Rebecca pointed out. Maggie remembered in time that staff still believed the death a suicide.

She moved the computer mouse. The monitor

sprang to life in glorious Technicolor—or rather, 24-bit RGB. Davis had been working on a story by L. Russo about the latest round of school rankings and a story by Missy Cannady about the Cleveland Clinic's latest specialty (Pediatric Endocrinology) coming to the Medical Mart building and the effect it might have on the project's overall profit margin. Then a couple of paragraphs, no byline noted, about the New Horizons halfway house at East 22nd and Payne Avenue.

If there was something in this worth murdering over, Maggie couldn't see it.

Rebecca left her, saying something about the day shift arriving soon, and Maggie snapped a photo of the monitor. She itched to shuffle through the papers on the desk but didn't. That would be the detectives' job, not hers. She disturbed nothing. Fortunately for her limited capability for patience, they showed up in short order. Then *they* shuffled.

Reinforcements had arrived to talk to every employee who had been in the building during the relevant time period. Everyone on the printing and loading staff had to be interviewed: What had they seen, heard, thought? Most of the truckers had already left. It was a newspaper, and nothing took precedence over getting those printed papers out to the public in time for their morning coffee. Not even murder.

Besides, most of the loading staff had entry only to the loading dock. They could not enter the printing area, unless, of course, someone let them in.

Jack sorted through the items on the desk while Riley took over the computer. He examined the same paste-up of stories Maggie had seen and reached the same conclusion: "Doesn't look like anything earth-shattering to me." He explored the rest of the computer's desktop, having Maggie snap pictures here and there—his e-mails, the approved proofs of the paper that had just been printed, various folders of photos.

Stories covered blurbs about road repair on Chester and a town hall meeting with the city's mayor. More paragraphs were devoted to the bidding war between two doctors' offices for the last Medical Mart vacancy and an alternative high school that closed because it turned out to be more of a day care for wayward teens than a place of instruction. Riley made a note of the school's name, even though it had been shut down by the state and some irate parents, not as a result of investigative journalism.

"Riveting," Riley said. "No wonder they're losing customers."

"But relevant to people's actual lives," Maggie said. In between reading over Riley's shoulder, she read over Jack's. He had discovered every reporter's beating heart: a small, spiral-bound notebook half-full of barely legible scrawls. Even though Robert Davis had become a copy editor, the habit had remained. From all the paperwork on the desk she could tell the handwriting belonged to him . . . and he had inked his name on the creased front cover.

The scrawls weren't easy to make out. Something about *sale,* and *H* (maybe *Herald,* she thought—Kevin Harding had hinted that sale and bankruptcy hovered like twin vultures over every newsroom these days), and *TM.* Roth's name had been mentioned here and there, along with Russo, Correa, and Truss. Jack frowned at the book, dwarfed by his large hand, obviously as perplexed as she felt.

Riley snickered. "That Roth guy wasn't kidding about Correa and his temper. E-mail sent yesterday: **'This story needs to be front page above fold! Barkley will wring every last cent out of city coffers as managers sit around with thumbs up asses! You have balls the size of mustard seeds!!'** Guy uses more exclamation points than my daughter. And she's in seventh grade."

"I'm not sure that's the best analogy," Maggie pointed out. "Aren't mustard seeds renowned for growing into huge trees?"

Both men glanced at her, conveying either astonishment at this profound insight or gentle pity that she, the female, just didn't get it.

"Who's Barkley?" she countered.

Riley muttered, "Maybe the guy who's skimming the advertising space. Or—here's another one from Correa with an attachment. A zoning map for Payne Avenue. Wow, exciting. And a note with it—*'Give me at least five inches, you fu'*— hmm. You know, it's kind of nice to be investigating grown-ups who leave clues in complete sentences. If I have to flick through one more set of **Wh R u, stuf to crib YK** text messages I'm going to both puke *and* sell my stock in Apple."

"Speaking of cell phones," Jack said.

"Yeah, I'd like to know where his went. Especially if it went into his killer's pocket."

Maggie said, "Call the phone company. Maybe they can track the GPS."

"We don't know which carrier he uses."

"Maybe it's company issued."

"It's not," Jack said. "We asked. The *Herald* can no longer afford perks like that."

Riley clicked through a few more e-mails. "Then you know what we have to do."

"Yep," Jack said. "It's time to wake up the wife."

Chapter 7

No one likes being woken up several hours before sunrise. No one *especially* likes being woken up to be told their spouse, their life partner, and the father of their children has been found dead. But Stephanie Davis didn't seem to mind too much.

At first she did. She turned pale with an expression of uncomprehending shock, as if the two men in her kitchen had materialized from the linoleum and begun spouting some alien language. They could not doubt that she had been woken up from slumber—the bleariness, mussed blond hair, and a slight crease in one cheek from a wrinkled pillow were unmistakable. She wore a flannel pajama set with cats on it and had never quite lost the baby weight. Jack didn't think she had driven to the *Herald* offices, murdered her husband, somehow hefted his body up four flights of steps to dangle him from a railing, and then returned home to drift into a deep and untroubled sleep—but then, she could have had help.

She could have been having an affair with one of Davis's coworkers—hardly an unusual occurrence on this planet—who then killed his rival in a fit of rage while she slumbered, unaware. In that case, though she might have been unaware of her husband's death, she would have all the answers to it.

But that didn't seem to fit, either. The death seemed a complete surprise. As is common with mothers, her first thoughts were for her children.

"What am I going to tell them?" she said. "Bob wasn't a super-involved dad—he was always at work—but of course he was their *dad* and the boys are only fourteen and seventeen. They're too young yet to lose their father. . . ."

Jack made her some tea. Riley waited patiently across the table from her. A mutt of a dog waited outside the sliding glass doors, wanting to know what was going on. He scratched at the glass but didn't bark. No sounds came from the rest of the house; teenage boys sleep like—well, like the dead.

They told her only that Robert Davis had been found hanging. If she had been behind some sort of conspiracy to murder, she should have jumped on the suicide idea.

"I can't see him killing himself." Her voice shook, and so did her hands as she lifted the steaming mug. But her eyes were dry. "Not in a million years. Bob never seemed depressed. He didn't even seem *unhappy*. Pensive, irritated, busy, stressed—but not unhappy. He loved his job. He felt a sense of—I don't know, *power,* I guess, in being able to control other people's stories."

"He enjoyed the power?"

"Every man enjoys power," she blurted, remembered her audience, and softened it. "I mean . . . of course he did. I'm not saying that he liked to throw his weight around. He cared about putting out a quality product. He felt that the entire industry is fighting for its life. He just . . . always believed he was right. About everything."

"Had he had any conflicts with anyone lately?"

As the editor had, she snorted.

Riley amended, "Anyone in particular? Lately?"

"He was a *copy editor,*" she said, as if showing patience with a particularly dense child. Obviously Stephanie Davis, like the *Herald*'s editor, knew what that meant. Robert had probably described his responsibilities to her ad nauseam.

But Riley persisted. "Any conflict feel especially pervasive? Get especially nasty?"

"Enough for him to kill himself? No, not a chance. That's just not what Bob would do." Her stunned mind searched for words. "He had stopped talking to me about work. I'd come home every day—I'm a manager at Kohl's— expecting to have him say that he had been laid off. The best that could happen would be for him to be moved over to the digital edition. That will stick around, yes, but the staff is minimal and it's not profitable. None of it is profitable anymore."

"The editor insists Bob was not going to lose his job."

She warmed her hands around her mug, speaking listlessly but with certainty. "They don't know. The *Herald* could be bought out on any given day like every other paper in the country; then some big corporation comes in and slashes jobs. It's only a matter of time." She spoke without hope, as if this painful truth had been accepted long ago.

The dog whined, trying to catch her eye through the glass. She looked at the brown mongrel as if wondering where he came from.

Riley tried to guide her back on topic. "So he didn't mention conflicts or fights or maybe even a special project with anyone at the paper?"

"No. Like I said, he didn't talk about it anymore. Sometimes I'd get a hint from his phone calls, but only that."

"Phone calls?" Riley would have made a good shrink, Jack thought. He had the repeating back the last few words technique down pat.

She crossed her arms over her chest, holding the flannel to herself, rubbing her arms in an unconscious and self-soothing gesture. "Lots of phone calls. That's part of working at a paper. Decisions, last-minute problems, reporters calling at all hours to complain about how he treated their story. Mills called every week. Correa, especially."

"Roger Correa?"

"Roger." She smiled. "Fireplug of a guy with the

energy of a fleet of fire trucks. Spouts off with the force of ten hoses, to continue the analogy."

Riley chuckled. "Are you a writer, too?"

She said, too casually, "I tried. Bob said—well, it's a tough business. Anyway, I kind of liked Roger. I couldn't help it."

Jack asked, "You met him?"

She gave a *pftt* of sound. "Bob worked there a long time. Dinners, company events, the awards ceremonies—I met everyone at some point."

"Okay. But Roger and Bob didn't get along?"

She gave a decisive shake of her head. "I doubt Roger gets along with anybody. Bob said Roger lived in some black-and-white fantasy world where reporters were white knights protecting the less fortunate. He thought all the good citizens of the city should unite and buy the paper to keep it going." She chuckled. "Bob said that Roger went to bed every night and dreamt he was Humphrey Bogart in *Deadline—U.S.A.*"

"What's that?" Riley asked.

Again that pitying look. "You'd better rent the DVD if you're going to hang around reporters," Stephanie Davis advised. "It's their Bible, raison d'être, and call to arms all in one."

Outside, the dog gave up, turned his back to them with an air of dismissal, and lay down, nose across its front paws.

Some memory sparked to life in Stephanie's head. "He argued with someone a few times last week. Always around seven o'clock or so, after dinner. I didn't think it was Roger—when it's him he says, *'Look, Roger—'* a lot. But Bob was angry, that controlled kind of angry he'd get when his voice would get quieter instead of louder. Something about Wilson. . . ."

"He was talking to someone named Wilson?"

She frowned. "No, I think they were talking about someone *named* Wilson. I overheard bits and pieces and I wasn't even paying attention. I figured it for more *Herald* drama, and I've got my own problems with work and the boys and running this house by myself, more or less. Bob thought everything he didn't want to do was women's work."

"Do you know anyone named Wilson? First or last?"

"No."

"Any idea what they were arguing about? Even an impression?"

She said no, but then added, "Bob said, 'You don't know what you're talking about,' more than once. It seemed like he said *no,* and *that's not true,* and that sort of thing. I figured one of the reporters had been chasing some wild rumor he wanted Bob to print and Bob wouldn't do it. They're all trying to do investigative pieces these days, working on their own, since the paper can't afford to pay actual investigative staff now. They figure if they break some huge scandal, win a Pulitzer, they'll get the immunity idol and finally have job security. Nice theory." She sipped tea that must have grown cold, her shock wearing off. "When can I plan the funeral for, what day? When will we have his . . . his body . . . back?"

Riley gave Jack a glance. This part could get tricky. Then he informed Stephanie Davis that there were some questions to be answered about her husband's death. Mainly that they believed it to be a deliberate act by someone other than her husband.

If she had been surprised at the death, the idea of murder stunned her. "You mean he was *killed?*"

Riley tried once more while her mind still reeled. "Can you think of anyone who might have wanted your husband dead?"

She pinched the bridge of her nose and then, eyes still shut, waved her hand around with quick, chopping motions. "Wait, wait. You mean to tell me Bob was *murdered?* Someone *murdered* him?"

"We have reason to believe that, yes, ma'am."

She stared at him, eyes wide, one hand covering her mouth in horror. All she said was, "I hope he wasn't afraid."

Riley pressed. "Can you think of anyone who wanted your husband dead?"

In a tiny voice she said, "Me."

Chapter 8

Maggie rubbed one eye and noted that her coffee cup had again, mysteriously, gone dry. Were mice sneaking up and drinking from it while she stared at her computer screen? She hit *Pause* on the progress line and went for a refill, blinking as she left the dimmed video analysis room for the harsh fluorescent light of the lab.

The crime lab, indeed, most of the building, rested under an early-morning calm before the bulk of the staff, cops, and, in other parts of the Justice Center, judges, lawyers, defendants, and reluctant jurors made their way in for a day's work. Maggie's boss, Denny, remained on leave following the birth of his third child. For reasons of seniority he had left Maggie in charge, a position she neither wanted nor cared for.

It had been a relatively quiet few weeks with only an occasional drive-by shooting (shooting, not hitting) and one grow-house bust, but now that trend faltered. Josh had called in sick with a migraine, and Amy had gone straight to a smash-and-grab in Tower City. Maggie would be watching black-and-white images move around the screen until the ME's office called with a time for the autopsy. She looked forward to the interruption. This kind of TV watching was not fun.

Carol, the DNA analyst, came in armed for the day with a newspaper, homemade granola, two pairs of reading glasses in case she misplaced ne, fresh pictures of grandchildren, and enough snacks to stock a Super Bowl party. And more coffee.

"You look beat," she said. Carol had long since appointed herself den mother of the forensics department, and had been especially solicitous to Maggie of late.

"I'm tired because I had a call-out." She filled in her coworker and finished by asking to see that day's edition of the *Herald*. She hadn't been home to get her own. Together they pored over the pages, trying to find something that might explain a man's murder. Maggie read articles about the relationship of the city treasurer to a construction firm, the shortage of qualified applicants for math teachers in northern Ohio, and a lively debate over whether restaurants should have with-kids and without-kids sections just as they used to have smoking and nonsmoking.

"That's an idea whose time has come," Carol said. "My husband keeps suggesting that we dine in strip clubs, because at least there won't be any kids. I'm almost ready to take him up on it."

Maggie refolded the paper. Maybe Robert Davis's murder had nothing to do with the paper and everything to do with Robert Davis. Or maybe it had to do with a story that had not yet been printed.

Maybe anything, she said to herself, and went back to the video analysis room.

The small space did not live up to its grand title. It had originally been a supply closet, and later was chosen for the video equipment because it lacked windows. They kept the lights low since Josh insisted it made the videos easier to see, though Maggie thought its only effect was to make it easier to fall asleep.

The *Herald*'s surveillance system gave her a grid of twelve camera angles, eight entrances, two parking lots, the loading dock, and the inside of the public lobby. The resolution was not bad— not NASA quality, but in keeping with modern technology. But most of the cameras were outdoors and exposed to the elements, which left dust, grime, and water spots to obscure the lenses. These did not affect the frames much during the day, but at night they aggravated the lack of light. Of course, the spider remained the star of the show over the visitors' parking lot.

The video was not multiplexed, when the recorded images flicked rapidly from camera to camera resulting in a series of separated stills rather than a movie, so that made things easier in a way. Nothing would be missed because the video had rotated to some other camera. The cameras were motion-activated, which reduced, somewhat, the sheer amount of video to look at because the camera went dark during the periods when nothing moved. Unfortunately during the day something was always moving in a busy, well-populated structure, and at night even a passing gnat would activate the lens.

Carol wandered in carrying a coffee mug and a timer to look over Maggie's shoulder. The timer would remind her when to return to the DNA lab for the next step in the STR—short tandem repeats method of analysis—process. "What are you looking for?"

"I haven't the slightest idea."

"Might make it tough to know it when you see it, then."

"We don't know if someone broke in to kill Robert Davis, or came in to work and got into a fight with Davis, or they don't work there and Davis let them in, or if they were there the whole time and were still there when we showed up."

"Mmm," Carol murmured into her coffee cup. "Usually you have choice words for detectives who give you such open-ended tasks."

"Yeah, I know. It probably isn't a good use of my time. But I keep hoping I'll see Davis let someone in. Or maybe see a person running away like the hounds of hell are chasing him some time between ten and one-thirty."

"But you can only see the outside of the doors. You can't even see who let somebody in when somebody lets somebody in."

The cameras were mounted over the center of the exterior doors, aimed straight down. They showed about five feet of the outside sidewalk, but nothing of the inside. "I know. And so far no one *has* been let in at all. People walk up, flash their key card at the proximity reader, and enter. Everyone in that building was allowed to be in that building."

"What about the loading dock? That looks wide open."

"Supposedly that entire corner of the building is secured by keyed doors, so that loading staff can only access that area. But reporters and admin people go into it all the time to use the vending machines and get fresh coffee, so it wouldn't be hard to find someone propping a door. Someone on the dock could follow a reporter back in. But the dock area isn't opened at all until halfway through the print run, when a supply of the papers is done and ready to go on the trucks."

"So the truckers and loaders are cleared."

"It would have required pretty dicey timing for one of them to have done it, yeah."

"Another triumph for the blue-collar set."

"You could say that."

"No one bolting from the place because he just killed someone?"

"Nope. Besides, this person was tough enough to manually strangle a grown, healthy man, then heft him over a railing to make it look like a suicide. They might have had to lug his body up four flights of steps beforehand, unless they somehow convinced him to make the climb as well, come with me and never mind about the length of rope sticking out of my pocket. None of that sounds like the bolting type. I'll bet this person left Robert Davis dangling and then walked casually back to his workspace, chatted with coworkers, maybe had a smoke and a bag of chips before heading off to his car as if it were the end of one more completely ordinary day."

"You think this was premeditated?"

"I don't know. It could be two people—that would certainly make getting his body up those steps much easier. But who *plans* to strangle someone? It's not an easy or sure way to kill."

"But it's quiet," Carol pointed out.

"Wouldn't have mattered with those presses running. You could fire an UZI in there and no one in the next room would hear it."

"Maybe it wasn't planned, then. He used a strap because it happened to be there."

"But it wasn't," Maggie argued. "The editor said they didn't use strap like that for anything in the building. String, yes, not ropes or mesh straps. Of course it could have been hanging around—"

"Badump-bump."

"No pun intended! Hanging around for some other reason, a quick fix, a gag gift, something left over from a story—who knows what when you've got a building full of people who deal with every topic under the sun. But it seemed clean to me, almost pristine, as if it had just been cut off a roll at the hardware store that afternoon."

"So we're back to, who *plans* to strangle someone?"

"Unless they brought the strap in for some other reason."

"Which puts us back to *un*premeditated," Carol said, then glanced at the phone display as it rang. "ME's office."

"Good. I was about to go blind." Maggie answered the call, picking up her coffee cup. It had again gone dry.

Chapter 9

"That was weird," Riley said as he turned a corner onto Euclid and waited for three CSU students to amble through the crosswalk, each one carrying books under one arm with a cell phone glued to the opposite ear. "Think they'd get off the phone if I hit them?"

"Maybe," Jack said. "But then they'd just switch to texting."

"I can see my wife saying she wanted me dead—just like Stephanie Davis did. She's not angry, she don't want him to feel bad or hurt or anything, and of course she's sad for her babies. But yeah, frankly, my life would be a hell of a lot better if he simply disappeared from the face of the earth. That's why my wife *divorced* me. She didn't sit there every day doing my laundry and fixing me a hot dog and gazing across the table listening to my war stories while thinking, *Gee, it would be nice if you stopped breathing.* You ever been married?"

He had, but it would be best not to get into that. "No."

"Smart man. You buy it?"

"The wife?"

"Yeah, her 'I didn't love him and am just waiting for you to leave so I can break out the champagne, but I didn't kill him and don't know who did.' That."

They passed under the chandelier over the street in front of Playhouse Square. "I don't see why she would tell us that if she *had* killed him. She would have sobbed and moaned and insisted her life had ended with his."

"She wants out of the marriage, bet it's another man. Lover killed the husband, but she doesn't know it, so she's honest. Noodle Shop for lunch?"

"It's nine-thirty."

Riley, solemn, said: "Planning. It's the key to time management."

"If you say so. She didn't seem dumb to me. She would have figured out her lover's hand in this pretty quick."

"We caught her off guard."

"Yes, but people are unhappy for all sorts of reasons."

Riley crossed East Ninth, giving Jack a sidelong glance that said he guessed there might be a lot behind that statement. Riley wasn't dumb, something that made Jack worry with a low-level gnawing rumble that never quite went away.

But Riley said only, "If the wife doesn't pan out, then we're back to his job. What the hell was going on at that paper?"

"You know what I think?"

"Noodle Shop is good?"

"No, I—sure, Noodles is fine—I think we should talk to this Roger Correa guy."

Robert Davis had been stripped of his clothing, washed clean, and now lay flat on a steel table that drained into a sink along the wall. The lights were operating-room bright and the staff fitted out with plastic aprons, Tyvek sleeve guards, and double layers of latex gloves. Maggie stood far enough away to avoid contact with his bodily fluids as the deiner, or assistant, finished dousing the man with a soft rubber hose.

The pathologist assigned his case was a man of medium height and age, a pale complexion, sandy-blond hair, and a not terribly friendly personality. But Robert Davis no longer needed friendliness. Efficiency would be more to his liking at this stage.

The doctor began with an external examination, noting every fact about the condition of the body—an appendectomy scar, bitten nails, a bruise on his right ankle, a mole that might have needed a check for basal cell carcinoma in another half a year or so, and of course, the deep furrows in the neck. Davis had no other signs of injury. He had not fought with his attacker. He had been caught off guard as the strap came around his neck from behind, pulled and scratched at it, probably bruised his ankle while kicking his feet around. But he had not fought a prolonged battle.

Maggie left the autopsy room and went to the amphitheater, where a forensic tech had spread out Davis's clothing. There Maggie "taped" the items, using clear packaging tape to pick up any stray hairs, fibers, or other trace evidence that the killer might have left as he pulled Davis's body close to get the maximum pressure out of the strap. The ME's office didn't work with hairs or fibers anymore, so they let her have it. She made her collections from the outside of the shirt and pants and shoes, skipping the undershirt and underwear, especially since the latter had been filled during the death throes and now smelled very bad. The forensic tech would photograph them—quickly—and then bind them up in a red bag for disposal. If Davis had soiled his shorts with vital evidence it would be lost, but the ME's office had a limit to their willingness to store fermenting biohazards. Besides, the odds of that were slim.

She and the tech examined the strap, and Maggie's impressions of it did not change. It nearly glowed in fresh white perfection, except for a few smears around the knot of such a faint color that Maggie could not guess if they were blood, dirt, or printer's ink. The forensic tech collected "touch" DNA for her, scrubbing the twists of the nylon with two moistened cotton swabs.

Touch DNA was always a crapshoot—there

might be a sufficient amount of skin cells present to get a profile, or there might not. What they thought looked like a stain might be a smudge of dirt from the kid at the hardware store. Any residue on the noose might be from the victim's own fingers as he fought to free himself, and they couldn't be sure what section of the strap had been used for the murder as opposed to the hanging.

The killer might have used the center of the strap to strangle Davis, putting the most pressure on the skin of his hands, after which tying the knots for the noose and around the railing would have been relatively stress-free once the victim was dead or unconscious. But they couldn't swab or test every inch, so the tech started with the two knot areas—obviously the killer had to have touched those. If those swabs didn't pan out, they could put the strap under some UV light and try to pick up bodily residues on the rest of the length. She thanked the forensic tech, wished her luck on the upcoming delivery, and went back to the autopsy room.

She had timed it well. By this time the pathologist had removed and sectioned the internal organs, and the deiner had cut and pulled the scalp. He now used a bone saw to make a neat incision around the top of the skull, so it could be removed to reveal the brain—like popping the lid off a roaster to reveal the turkey. Maggie asked the pathologist if there had been anything interesting in the rest of the body, and he answered with his usual loquacity, "No."

Then he reconsidered. "He had some kidney stones brewing. He would have been in agony sometime next month, probably. And a small ulcer in his duodenum. Not very big. He probably thought it was acid reflux."

"He was stressed," Maggie concluded.

"Everybody's stressed," the pathologist said, and moved to the exposed skull.

The deiner pointed to a spot on the inside of the scalp and muttered something. The pathologist murmured agreement.

"What?" Maggie asked.

"A bruise. Some sort of blunt trauma to the top of the head, just below the crest." He fluffed the hair at the back of his own head in illustration, apparently forgetting that his gloved fingers were covered in someone else's blood.

"The killer clocked him in the head?"

The doctor winced at her phrasing. "Or he fell during the struggle. Or got injured before the strangling for other reasons entirely. It didn't swell much because the heart stopped beating soon after. That's why I didn't find a lump on the outside."

"Is it enough to—"

"No."

"No, what?"

"Don't ask." He pried off the skull cap with a

metal wedge. "Don't ask if it was enough of an injury to knock him unconscious. There's no way for me to tell from a hematoma exactly what would be sufficient to knock someone out. Can't do it."

Maggie said nothing.

He found a slight corresponding bruise to the brain, but still refused to say whether it would have rendered Robert Davis unconscious. Maggie had been to a lot of autopsies, however, and she didn't think much of it, either. It would have hurt, certainly, but to knock out a strong, healthy man like Davis? Not likely.

She waited as the brain was sliced into sections, which appeared to be the consistency and roughly the shape of a huge, fresh mushroom. The pathologist moved on to the larynx, a stiff, whitish tube of about six inches. It crunched when he cut into it. He examined the blood vessels and the broken hyoid bone. He prodded at it for so long that Maggie lost her customary patience. "What do you see?"

"Guy strangled to death." He continued to poke. "What I can't be one hundred percent sure of is, did he actually die when the guy strangled him, or did he just pass out and then die when the guy hung him? The hanging didn't break his neck, so asphyxia is the cause of death. But did he die once or twice? That is the question."

"It's kind of surprising his neck didn't break

after being tossed off a platform. He's a big guy."

"Eh, some people are flexible." He added a few slivers of the tissue to the formalin-filled quart container, then tossed the dissected larynx into the red biohazard bag nestled between the dead man's legs. "Either way, it's still homicide."

Maggie's phone rang.

"Communications called," Carol began. She had unofficially taken over dispatching duties while Denny was home with the new baby. "They got a guy shot in an alley. Amy's at a sexual assault, and Josh is still home with cold compresses. I bet he's hung over. Don't you bet he's hung over?"

"Nah, migraines run in his family."

"That boy gives *me* a migraine."

Maggie hung up, collected her tapings, thanked the pathologist, and left. Ten blocks away she could still smell wisps of death.

Chapter 10

The door to Roger Correa's bungalow opened to reveal a young woman dressed in black. Black hair, black skintight sleeveless leather vest over a sleeveless black T-shirt that didn't seem warm enough for this cool spring morning, tight black jeans, scuffed black Nikes, black hematite cross around her neck, and enough black eyeliner to have cleared out an entire shelf at Walgreens. Riley goggled. "I thought the Goth look was so last millennium."

The girl didn't bat an eye. "What's Goth?"

"Roger Correa?" Jack asked. "Does he live here?"

She considered this new speaker. Though skinny to the point of scrawny, she gave the distinct impression that they would not be budging over the threshold unless she decided, out of her own generosity, to let them in. "Yeah."

Jack enunciated with marked patience: "Could we speak with him, please?"

Shoving herself off the doorjamb, she turned and walked back into the house, leaving them to come with her or wait as they pleased. She shouted "Roger!" loudly enough to wake the neighbors, and they followed the back of the sleeveless leather vest. It had been decorated with everything from sequins to studs to feathers, all in, of course, black.

"That had better damn well be his daughter," Riley hissed to his partner. Riley's two girls were entering the teenage years and he had grown very sensitive to topics such as May-December romances, predatory old goats, and sugar daddies.

Jack sincerely doubted the girl was Roger Correa's daughter.

He had expected to find Correa asleep. He didn't know what hours a reporter usually worked but assumed they were flexible. But the man was awake, dressed, voluble, and already surrounded by his troops.

They had assembled in his living room, which no longer resembled any sort of home-like space but a staging area for journalistic battle. Card tables, end tables, and the dining table held stacks of papers, newspapers, printouts, laptops, tablets, and smartphones. The walls had been covered with bulletin boards, decorated with e-mails, flyers, photos, clippings, and hand-lettered index cards. Each had a banner at the top declaring its focus in bold strokes with a Sharpie marker: *East 22nd, CM's ads, TM, ProLabs*.

In addition to the not-Goth girl, the room contained another four people: a tall young man with black skin and a headset who barely glanced up as they walked in, his fingers flying over a keyboard so fast the individual taps combined into one solid drone; a white guy with glasses and a buzz cut who frowned at his phone as if reading a Dear John text from his girlfriend; a boy of indeterminate race, age, or socioeconomic status who, while surrounded by impressive industriousness, had enough self-assurance to lie back on some pillows next to the unused fireplace and stare at the ceiling, listening to something through earbuds; and a dark-skinned girl wearing a plain T-shirt and cardigan sweater that somehow managed to look as if it had been purchased directly off a Paris runway. None of them fit Stephanie Davis's description of Roger Correa, who appeared that moment from the hallway.

Though not particularly tall, he didn't quite fit the description, either. In his forties with dark hair and a perfectly trimmed goatee, the muscles underneath his worn jeans and dress shirt hinted at a restless power. He held a coffee cup in one hand, and at his side stood a German shepherd approximately the size of a small pony, calm but watchful. Correa seemed surprised but not concerned at finding two detectives inside his war room.

"Roger Correa?" Riley asked.

"Yeah?"

Riley flashed a badge. "Is there somewhere we could talk?"

This got all the kids' attentions. Their eyes swiveled to where the cops stood in perfect unison. Correa remained sanguine.

"Sure. Come into the kitchen."

They followed him, picking through the room's occupants—half of whom preferred the floor to the chairs as a place to sit—as if they were large and possibly dangerous birds it might be better not to disturb. Not-Goth girl, however, came with them, unwilling to let her boss or mentor or hero or whatever Correa was to her be hassled by The Man.

The kitchen appeared more normal—table, refrigerator, sink with dirty dishes. The German shepherd took up a sentry position in the corner, next to his food bowl.

"Tea?" Correa offered.

Jack declined, but Riley accepted. Riley had had a seminar once that taught always to accept a witness's or suspect's hospitality if offered. It put them at ease and created a bond. But Jack couldn't stomach tea, not even for the good of the investigation.

As Correa puttered, Riley asked when he had left the *Herald* offices the previous day, and Correa said about five, maybe five-thirty. He had not returned. Riley explained that they needed to ask Correa some questions about Robert Davis, which seemed to perplex Correa. He had more questions than they did until Riley admitted that Davis had been found dead. Correa did not seem as shocked, of course, as Stephanie Davis, but he seemed plenty surprised. As before, Riley and

Jack did not mention homicide, letting Correa think of suicide first.

As with Stephanie Davis, Correa said, "Can't see it. Davis thinks too much of himself. He loved being the one who said what got in and what got out, what he felt important enough for the best placement and what he put at the back of Section D. He had, shall we say, a healthy self-esteem."

"No arguments or conflicts with anyone lately?"

The man didn't chuckle, he actually laughed out loud. "*Conflicts?* Every day. That's life at a newspaper. It always was, but now that we're all fighting to exist *and* keep our jobs *and* still do a halfway decent job of bringing the truth to the citizens of this fair city, there's conflict out the wazoo."

The German shepherd apparently decided that first, the situation did not give him cause for concern, and second, no one seemed likely to fill his bowl in the next few minutes. He lay down, snout along two crossed paws. From his chair Jack could see part of the living room, where the dark girl continued to type with the same lightning speed as the black kid, and the one on the pillows continued to stare at the ceiling. "If you don't mind my asking, what are you doing here? Do these people work for the paper?"

Correa set Riley's tea in front of him and sank his form onto a kitchen chair's loose cushion. Holding his cup, he propped his feet on a cardboard box from Office Depot and rubbed his face with the free hand. "Let me explain the—Chaz, I'm okay, really, these guys are not going to waterboard me."

Not-Goth girl gave both cops a sharp look to say she would be monitoring their behavior, but returned to the living room.

Correa started again. "Let me explain the state of independent journalism in America today. Newspapers existed to 'comfort the afflicted and afflict the comfortable,' as Mary Jones said, and survived on advertising. Ads and classifieds paid the bills. Profit margins weren't huge, but were acceptable, back when not every human being felt they had a God-given right to live like Donald Trump. Along comes the Internet. No one needs classified ads anymore, and advertisers can use websites and review sites that are free and live forever in cyberspace, not thrown out with the recycling that evening. Advertising revenues plummet. At the same time, because since the eighties or so papers are owned by big corporations, modest profit margins are no longer acceptable. They have to be *big* profit margins, and maintained no matter how revenues fall. Hell, in 2008, Gannett slashed ten percent of its workforce when they were still making eighteen percent! McClatchy slashed a third when they were making twenty-one. So costs must be cut, which to corporations means they cut staff and product—not, of course, their bonuses. You know what is first to get the ax? Investigative reporting. It's the least cost-effective type of content in any newspaper—any news outlet, period. Editors and producers can pump months of salary, overtime, and expenses into a topic and then have it not pan out. They may not get a usable story—wasted money, in their eyes. Corporations hate to waste money that could be going into shareholder dividends instead."

He had obviously been preaching this gospel for quite some time, and to anyone who would listen. Jack and Riley listened.

"They increase the fluff—what the Kardashians are wearing to the Oscars, what Princess Kate feeds her royal baby—not only because that's what Americans, who now have the attention span of the average gnat, want to read, but because it's *cheap.* That's why you see a lot of guest pieces, or consultants—especially on broadcast news—people who are there purely to pump the agenda they're paid to pump whether it's via a remote head shot with a microphone or a press release that we reprint verbatim. It's ready-made content, it looks good, and it's free. But is it real news? Hell no."

Riley nodded. "That explains a lot."

Jack couldn't tell if he meant it or just wanted to play Correa a bit, because, in truth, it *did* explain a lot.

"So the paper pays me to clean up this spoon-fed stuff and make it look real, and write fluff, and maybe sometimes go out and see what's actually happening as long as I don't turn in any overtime or expenses. But to do my job, my *real* job, which is to look past what the people in power tell us they're doing, with taxpayer money and resources and goodwill, to what they're actually doing, *that* isn't in the budget."

The German shepherd sat up, yawned, and wandered out to the living room.

"And that's what these kids here are working on?"

"Right. Citizen journalism. They come in before school and their jobs and their dates and coordinate, research, write up their notes. They work on their lunch hours, after work, in the middle of the night when they can't sleep. Their families call it a hobby or an obsession or a calling, depending on their level of indulgence. And they do it for no other reason than the good of the people. I can't pay them a penny. I can't put them on my byline, because the paper refuses to admit they exist. I can't even keep them in coffee— they have a kitty to support that. And I'm afraid, gentlemen, that you're looking at the future of journalism."

They heard the front door open and close. "Melanie," Correa told them. "She's a doctor at Metro."

Jack peeked into the living room. Not-Goth girl peeked back, but the richly dressed female had disappeared. He made an attempt to steer the conversation back to the murder. "So, Robert Davis. Did he know about your unofficial staff?"

"Sure. I don't make it a secret that I have help with my stories, that I *need* help with my stories because the paper gives me nothing. Corporate didn't want to hear the details, but they were fine with the work. You know why?"

"Because it's free."

"Yep. As long as the readers aren't told that most of their real news is coming from unpaid volunteers with no training or accountability, everybody is happy."

"So, Robert Davis—"

"A copy editor," Correa sneered. "He couldn't make it as a reporter so he stays in the office. Look, a copy editor can do a great job, a vital job. They can put everything together, they can make it look great, they can make the layout make sense, they can give you a headline that both describes the story and pulls readers right into it. Or they can be a corporate hack who kills anything that might make the corporation's subsidiaries lose business. Robert Davis was that kind of copy editor."

The dog wandered back in again, carrying a leash in its mouth. It presented said leash to its owner. Roger took it, looped the strap over a cabinet knob, and told the animal, "Ten minutes. Maybe fifteen."

The dog returned to the living room.

"What kind of subsidiaries?"

"The *Herald* is owned by The Phoenix Group. They also own MegaTheaters, Division Outdoor Advertising, and Smith-Gifford, which is basically a headhunter firm for lobbyists. So MegaTheaters gets cheaper advertising for their cinemas in our entertainment section, Smith-Gifford's politicians get gentler treatment in our news section, and our story about price fixing by Division Outdoor got trimmed to a blurb and buried at the back of B. And that's how things are done in this age of maximum profits and minimum public responsibility." The front legs of his chair hit the floor with a thump when he stood up to pace, as if only physical activity could soothe his agitation. And made himself another cup of tea while at it.

"So," Riley said again. "Robert Davis. Did you see him yesterday?"

Correa retraced his movements for them, a confusing trail through the *Herald* building and surrounding city, but it summed up as encountering Davis only once since the previous morn. Correa had figured out how the county property manager had translated the overbilling for the ad space into cash in his own pocket—by creating a phony repair firm and having the finance unit write checks to same. The checks went into an account created by the manager, and he split his withdrawals with the various building managers. It wasn't enough to retire to Aruba with, but it was enough for an extra car or an extra apartment or a set of braces for one or two of the kids. Davis refused to run the story because Correa had only a shredded bank statement, pulled out of the manager's garbage and painstakingly pieced back together by one of his protégés.

"*Only* a bank statement," Correa scoffed. "You know what I'd call the phony company's bank statement? I'd call that *proof.* Wouldn't you call that proof?"

"Yeah, I would." Riley must have felt that a good eruption of righteous indignation would prompt more spontaneous statements, the kind that were admissible even when rights hadn't yet been read. He egged the reporter on. "But Davis didn't think so?"

"He gave me some song and dance about needing documentation linking the manager to the phony business, which I've got, but in bits and pieces. I was going to get it together today, leave him no excuse not to run it in tomorrow's edition. More tea?"

"No, thanks. Why do you think he dragged his feet?"

"Because he walks tall but has a spine of over-cooked rotini. Because he enjoys making guys

90

like me jump through hoops, because pretending that he's upholding some kind of standard means he doesn't have to face the fact that he just likes making guys like me jump through hoops. But mostly because he's buddy-buddy with the city manager's office and happy to let them spoon-feed us content that's easier and cheaper than paying guys like me to go out and get the whole story. The city manager's office is still sensitive about any scandals, since they exist only because the county voted to get rid of the old council system because of *their* thirty or forty or fifty years of scandals. They're usually grateful for our help, of course—thank you for letting us know this guy has been robbing us blind, but we'd rather keep this little matter in-house, you know. Except the whole point of a newspaper is to let things *out* of the house."

"Davis didn't see it that way?"

"Davis aspired to be a corporate flunky, because corporate flunkies keep their jobs when pains in the ass like me get pink slips. Which isn't stupid, I guess. Davis wasn't stupid." He ran a hand through his hair, which made it both stand up and stick out at odd angles. Then something occurred to him, just as it had to the editor. "Why all the questions? I mean, tragic and all, but some guy offs himself and you guys spend all morning doing a psychological autopsy? Since when?"

"We check out every death," Riley said. "But in

this case, we're not so sure Davis did this to himself."

Roger Correa had no poker face. His eyes bulged, he leaned forward, he sucked in breath. "You mean someone wrapped a rope around Davis's neck and then tossed him off a printing tower platform? Seriously? Wow"—he sat back, a look of near ecstasy illuminating his face— "what a *story*. Murder in the print room. Copy editor becomes a subject of his own paper. . . . It would be a better story if it were a reporter. Hell, it would be a better story if it were *me*."

Chapter 11

"Can you think of who might have wanted to kill him?" Jack interrupted, annoyed by Correa's hope that a coworker's murder could increase circulation.

The reporter thought on this for perhaps a second or two. "No. Who might be *angry,* everybody, me especially, who might *dislike* him, everybody, who might want his job, about five people, but kill? No one at the paper hated him *that* much. Arguing with copy editors is like the FOP asking for a raise at contract time. It's just expected. Have you talked to his wife? Spouses don't need much of a motive."

"Speaking from experience?" Riley asked.

"I've been a reporter for twenty-five years."

"What if someone didn't want a story printed?"

"They still wouldn't kill a copy editor. It'd be like—well, like killing one of you guys because you arrested a criminal. The bad guy kills you, the arrest still stands, he's still going to go to trial. If he kills the prosecutor or the judge, someone else will take over the case. Kill the copy editor, the paper still hits the streets."

Riley asked a few more questions but didn't get anything new. Correa had disliked Davis, but he couldn't think of a single person who might want to kill him or what they might think they ad accomplished by doing so. As he spoke he rolled his head back and forth, then stuck each arm out and pulled it to the opposite side. Evidently Correa had, at last, tired of talking and wanted to limber up for that day's battle. He stood. "Anything else I can tell you guys? I do have to get to the paper. It'll be chaos today. No one likes to gossip more than newspapermen, which I guess makes sense. News is just gossip you can't be sued for."

Riley asked for the names of the people involved in the county advertising scam and wrote them down. "Can you tell us what else you're working on?"

"Yeah, sure—um . . . hmm." He considered them, then shrugged off the hesitation. "Sorry, newsman's habit—you never want anyone else to steal your scoops. But then I remember that there isn't a rival paper to sell the scoop to, not in this city. Not for the past, oh, forty years. Besides, you guys don't look like blabbermouths."

"Tight-lipped Louie, that's what they call me," Riley said.

"Don't believe him," Jack said. Riley gave him an odd look, not because he'd been contradicted, but because Jack so rarely made any comment that even remotely resembled a joke.

No matter, because Correa had already led them back into what had been the living room to gesture at the various bulletin boards. The black kid still typed without ceasing, the not-Goth girl watched a video on her phone, the buzz cut pulled one wire out of a tangled mass and plugged it into the black kid's second laptop, and the German shepherd had curled up against the boy on the pillows. Both appeared to be fast asleep, but then the dog opened one eye, regarded them, and shut it again. Apparently it had decided not to hold Correa to the fifteen-minute promise.

Correa waved a hand at one of the boards. "The CM ad scam you already know about. East Twenty-second is a building that's been sold to a company called New Horizons. Supposedly they're running a halfway house. Problem is no one has ever heard of New Horizons, they have no track record, and their CEO is an ex-GE account executive who flunked Sociology 101. So why is a big-money man involved in a social program? Maybe he's having a midlife crisis and wants to make the world a better place. Maybe he's trying to impress a girl, which, let's face it, is the reason for most of the stupid things men do. Or maybe he thinks he can somehow turn a profit by giving ex-cons a place to shoot hoops that doesn't have barbed wire marking the boundaries. He wouldn't be the first. Anyway . . ."

He moved on to the next board. "ProLabs. Similar situation. The state and the county gave them a huge tax incentive to put their headquarters in lovable, livable Cleveland. Maybe they'll cure cancer. Maybe they'll be the final cherry on the sundae to make Cleveland the medical research capital of the world and we can tell Johns Hopkins to kiss our behinds. But so far they've been there for a year and have created exactly two jobs, and everybody's still getting sick, so I think the taxpayers are due for an update. No one in the city seems to care that so far they've gotten zero return on a massive investment."

"Why not?"

"That's the question. Maybe a slow start was explained and expected. Maybe the deputy mayor's daughter is married to the ProLabs CFO. Maybe someone at ProLabs has a picture of the city manager with a goat. Nobody knows, so someone needs to find out. And that someone is going to be Billy." He nodded at the guy next to the German shepherd, who didn't look as if he were going to find out anything for at least several more hours, and would smell of dog hair when he did.

Riley nodded. "And TM?" He glanced at the last board.

Correa's already flushed face darkened even further. He spoke with a voice usually reserved for child molesters. "TransMedia. The conglomerate that has swallowed or strangled most of the major dailies in this country and half of the minor ones. And the *Herald* is next on their list."

"You're going to be bought?"

"According to downstairs—that means the business offices, which are actually upstairs in our building—no. They say TM made an offer and the *Herald* isn't interested. But they're lying."

"How do you know?"

"The publisher had lunch with TM execs three times in the past month. He makes at least two phone calls to their numbers a *day*—I know because the . . . never mind," he added before giving up the name of whomever he had spying for him.

"Jon Tamerlane?" Jack asked. "I thought he was never around."

"He's not, works mostly out of New York or the Isle of Nice or whatever, but he still owns the paper. He may not know an adjective from apple pie, but I'll bet he can read a balance sheet upside down and backward. TransMedia has to show him the courtesy of pretending he has some idea of what the *Herald* does, what the *Herald* is. It's like shaking hands with your girlfriend's father, when you both know his opinion really doesn't matter. But then the dealing can be passed on to the next level. In this case, our advertising director met with their advertising rajah in Atlantic City last Thursday."

"How do you—"

"That's what happens when your entire staff is trained in one skill—finding stuff out. Because we have contacts and informants and access to something magic called Google. Yeah, something's up, and obviously all us schlubs will be kept in the dark like mushrooms until the boot comes down. We'll walk in one day and find out half of us will be laid off, and the other half will be required to write whatever the TM stockholders tell them to write. And that, gentlemen," Correa finished, "is The State of Journalism in America today."

He showed them to the door.

Jack and his partner climbed into the battered Crown Vic. "I thought writers preferred writing to talking," Riley said. "Information overload, big-time."

"I think my ears are bleeding."

"Mine too." Riley shook his head. "Let's go get noodles."

Jack didn't argue.

Chapter 12

The alley in question turned out to be off East 55th, around the corner from a magnet school full of economically poor but college-bound achievers and a body repair shop that had been shut down three times for chopping. Around the other corner sat a Dunkin' Donuts. The smell reminded Maggie that she needed lunch, particularly since she hadn't had breakfast.

"Hi, Maggie," a uniformed patrol officer greeted her.

"I have to have a doughnut."

White teeth glistened in his black face. "I hear you."

"I mean, I *have* to have a doughnut. Like, right now."

"Don't worry. If they run out, they'll make more." She followed him into the alley as he filled her in, her mind on the crime, stomach still thinking about doughnuts. "A parent dropping off their kid at the school noticed the feet sticking out. Cash taken from the wallet, but ID and cards still here. He's a major frequent flier, so probably a drug buy gone bad, falling out with a compatriot, what have you. His car's parked up the street, unscathed. His parents' car, actually. He's not old enough to drive yet."

"Wow," she said, stomach forgotten. "Short life."

"Thug life usually is. Detectives are canvassing, they should be back soon."

The alley smelled of oil, urine, and rotting food, but did not have much clutter—coffee cans outside doorways to be used as ashtrays, the Dumpster, two empty beer bottles that had been there a while, and one scrawny cat with a calm, freezing cold gaze from her perch on a fire escape.

"Funny thing is," the cop went on, "today is garbage day. If they had tossed the body in the Dumpster, the forklift would dump him, body goes to the landfill with the rest of the trash, maybe no one notices it at all. Kid becomes a missing person, not a murder."

They had reached the corpse.

"But if it was one guy, probably couldn't lift him," the cop went on. "He'd have needed help from another guy, maybe two. This kid didn't miss too many meals."

Maggie snapped photos in quick succession.

The dead boy wore a burgundy sweatshirt over a black T-shirt, neither of which was tucked into the leather belt around the baggy blue jeans. Scuffed-up tennis shoes, wallet lying on the damp concrete next to the right hip. He had fallen on his face, the brown hair at the back of his head now a mass of dried red clots. His brain had ceased to function before he could even put a hand to his wound; his fingers, nails bitten to the quick, were clean and empty, fingers lying loose, palms up. Black lines had snaked underneath his skin as his blood died and decayed. Two rings, both gold, still glittered against the pale skin.

"ME investigator is on the way," the cop told her.

"I know, I talked to her before I left; she was just finishing something up, which gives me time for a doughnut." Maggie made a few notes on her clipboard, sketching the walls, the Dumpster, the body, adding an arrow pointing north to orient her drawing. The cop crouched to reexamine the victim's head.

"Looks like a small caliber," he mused. "Maybe a twenty-two."

Maggie's pen stilled over her notes. Jack's choice of caliber, but, as he and other officers had pointed out to her, a popular choice for many people on either side of the law. Cheap, in these days of expensive ammunition, and the guns used to fire them could also be gotten at a good price. Small and easy to conceal. It meant nothing.

"What's his name?" She detected a slight quaver in her voice, but the officer didn't seem to notice.

He consulted his notepad to make sure he had it right. "Ronald Soltis, aka Reign, but the detective said no one called him that except himself. Spoiled rich boy with delusions of life in gangsta's paradise."

Coincidence, Maggie thought. Just a coincidence that Jack had been all too aware of Ronald Soltis.

But she no longer wanted a doughnut.

Maggie got back to the Justice Center in time to make an afternoon meeting in the homicide unit. Her presence was not always required or requested, but since the detectives hadn't made it to the autopsy, Patty Wildwood asked her if she would sit in. That suited Maggie, who wanted a chance to talk to Jack.

Though she had no idea what she would say. *Did you kill Ronald Soltis?* Did she even want to know?

She transported her steaming cup of coffee—her only source of nourishment in the past eighteen hours—into the conference room/ storage area that the detectives used when they needed to spread out. She moved a few reams of copy paper off a folding chair and sat down next to Jack, surprising him. He and Riley were finishing off cartons of Asian dishes and the smell did not calm the butterflies in her stomach.

"Hello," he said, as if she were a skunk in the neighbor's yard. Nothing to worry about, but then it could change direction at any moment. So best be ready to run.

To make things worse, her ex-husband walked in. Rick Gardiner and Maggie were on amiable terms, not friends but not enemies. Still she couldn't help but tense up in his presence. Speaking of skunks . . .

Patty Wildwood and her partner, Tim, arrived and sat. Patty dropped a file folder on the table and said, "Okay. What do we got on this *Herald* thing? We're sure it's a murder?"

Maggie repeated what the pathologist had told her.

"So it's probably a man," Rick said.

"It doesn't take that much to strangle someone," Patty's partner, Tim, said. "Not from behind."

"But to carry them up four flights of steps?"

"He could have already been up there," Riley said. "It almost had to be someone who worked at the paper, so it wouldn't have been hard to get the guy up there. *C'mon, I want to show you something. What? Just come on.* He'd have gone. If it's somebody he knew, somebody he'd been working with for years—no matter how much he bitched, if the person insisted, he'd have gone. Anyone would."

"But then they had to pitch him over a railing," Rick pointed out. "Right?"

Maggie said, "Not necessarily. The strangling came first, so he was either dead or unconscious when the killer tied the noose around his neck. All they'd have to do is snake the other end under the bottom rung to the outside of the railing. Then they could just roll or push the body under the bottom rung and off the platform and the strap would be on the outside just as if he had jumped over the top."

"And it was some kind of strap, not a rope?" Patty confirmed.

Maggie nodded. "Nylon."

"He was a big guy? And it didn't break?"

"An inch-wide nylon strap can usually hold up to a thousand pounds."

"Any chance of tracing that to its source?"

"Honestly? I doubt it. It's regular old Nylon 6 fiber; you can buy it for sixty cents a yard from any number of manufacturers."

"But why use that instead of a rope?" Riley mused aloud.

"Because they had that, and didn't have a rope," Patty mused back.

"Because it's easier on the hands," Rick said. "The flatter surface wouldn't cut into the skin like a rope would if you wrapped it around your palms once or twice."

"Why strangle at all?" Riley asked. "You could have emptied a clip in that room without anyone hearing it, so being quiet wasn't a factor. Why not shove him off the platform?"

Maggie said, "The railing is in the way, and the fall might not be fatal. It's impossible to calculate the distance necessary to kill someone."

"Because it's not the fall, it's the sudden stop at the end?"

"People can fall eight feet and die, and others can fall a hundred and eight feet and live. It's not a certain way to kill someone."

"And somebody wanted to make damn sure this guy was dead," Riley finished. "Besides, strangling's so . . ."

"Personal?" Patty suggested.

Maggie agreed. "It's personal, but it could also be a logical choice. The most common methods for murder are gunshot, stabbing, beating, and strangling. Everything else runs far, far behind those categories. If he—or she—didn't have a gun or a knife—"

"Or a baseball bat," Riley put in.

"That leaves strangling. It's less messy and even easier than stabbing or beating, once you've got that ligature around the neck," Maggie said. "The killer only had to compress the carotid arteries and Davis could have been out in under fifteen seconds—but a lot of victims who are strangled survive. The hanging solved that problem since it guaranteed the victim would never regain consciousness. Quick and certain."

"Fifteen seconds is a long time with a full-grown guy like Davis thrashing around," Riley said.

Maggie told them about the bruise on Davis's head.

"Okay, forget that. No cameras and nobody saw or heard anything?" one of the other detectives asked.

Riley confirmed it.

"Outside cameras?"

Maggie said, "Nothing that stands out, no disturbances, no fights, no one running away. Of course, I have no idea whom to look for."

"Anything on the body?"

"Dirt smudges on the clothes, probably from the platform. Various fibers, a few dog hairs. A few wood grains, like sawdust."

Riley leaned forward to look around Jack. "Dog? What kind of dog?"

"Don't know yet. I haven't had a chance to mount them."

He looked at Jack.

"Why?" Patty asked.

"Possible suspect has a German shepherd."

"I doubt it's a German shepherd. They're kind of short for that . . . though it's possible. Some breeds, like Labradors, always have short hair. Poodles always have long. Most other ones can have either, so it *could* be a short-haired German shepherd that also has double dominant black alleles—"

"Never mind," Riley said.

Jack added, "The victim had a dog, too."

Patty asked about the possible suspect and they described Roger Correa, which took some time. Maggie sat and thought about Ronald Soltis instead. Then they described Stephanie Davis, the editor, and the printing supervisor, which took much less time.

"Okay," Patty said. "I guess we'll all keep canvassing until something breaks. Tim and I will help, too. Rick, you and Will are on the Soltis thing."

Rick said of his partner, "He's at the autopsy now."

"Maggie? You were at the body—what can you tell us?"

Other than your most likely suspect is sitting right next to me? she thought. "Shot in the back of the head, small caliber, been there at least a day. Cash robbed, but nothing else. No signs of a struggle."

"Just wham, bam, thank you, ma'am?"

"Yes."

"Drugs 'r' bad," Patty summarized. "Well, he had people lined around the block with reasons to take him out, beginning with D'Andre Junior. The street crimes guys will be your best buddies for this one, Rick."

"I know it."

Patty had a way of managing without managing, necessary when working in a pit of egos such as a detective unit. "Okay. Anybody need anything else?"

"Winning lotto numbers?" Riley suggested.

"A team in the playoffs?" another detective said.

He and Riley discussed sports as everyone else stood to leave. Maggie saw a window of opportunity and ducked her head toward Jack, speaking as quietly as she could. "I have to talk to you."

"Not here," he hissed, then stood up and walked away in one hasty motion.

Nonplussed, she gathered up her notes and left the table. But not before she noticed her ex-husband watching them with narrowed eyes.

Chapter 13

The wind whipped around her, prodding and pushing, reminding her with every step that the world could be a cruel and unforgiving place. Trees whispered as she passed, and each shadow at the corner of her vision had to be stared at until it resolved into something benign—a dog, a kid shooting hoops in their driveway, a husband taking out the trash. Or those two boys huddled near the corner of a house, conversing, smoking, watching her. Not benign, perhaps, but they let her pass.

Jack's house sat four blocks from the bus stop. Not all the streetlights worked, but a pleasant spring night in a working-class neighborhood seemed safe enough. Except that a woman alone is never safe enough, and Maggie knew that only too well. She fingered the pepper spray in her pocket and stopped in front of his address.

A simple bungalow with a million siblings throughout the Cleveland area. It had white siding, a detached garage, and probably six rooms total, not including the basement. For the fiftieth time she questioned her decision to pay him a visit. What if he didn't live alone? What if this wasn't even his house? He probably gave a fake address to the police department.

He had faked everything else, including his name.

She had hoped she could just walk away from Jack. They would go back to being model employees, each doing their jobs and studiously avoiding the other. Instead she obsessed in her mind, tried desperately to sort through the jumble in her head, walked around in a daze and unable to clear her thoughts for more than a few seconds at a time. Her coworker Carol, her boss Denny noticed, but felt it normal after what had happened. She had seen things no human ought to.

She had said nothing to her brother; eventually, however, he would call, maybe stop by on a layover and would know from her first word that something had gone badly wrong. She could not tell him, of course. Alex must never know, and at the same time she had never been able to keep anything from him. Texting, words without inflection, had saved her so far, but at some point he would want a real-time chat. Maggie worried more about facing her brother than facing the entire criminal justice system. It didn't know her like he did.

How much less complicated her life would be if she had never met Jack Renner.

But now she stood in front of his home, and waiting on the sidewalk all night didn't seem like much of a plan. She walked up the driveway, climbed the three steps to the storm door on the side of the house, and knocked.

She heard activity. His large figure loomed behind the frosted glass and the door opened.

"What the hell are you doing here?" Jack demanded.

She swallowed. "We have to talk."

"About what? And—" He pushed the storm door open, nearly hitting her. "Get in here before anyone sees you."

He reached out a hand as if to hustle her in but drew it back, letting her brush past him without even the slightest physical contact. She entered a kitchen stocked with the barest essentials— coffeemaker, dish drainer, a ragged towel, an old Formica-topped table with a couple of chairs. A scent she couldn't identify lingered, probably from his dinner. Fairly clean for a bachelor. Even with the subject at hand gnawing at her insides, she found herself fascinated by how Jack lived. Did he watch reality shows? Did he cook for himself or live on takeout? Did he have girl-friends? Family? What *was* he—a human being with one warped area of himself, or a killing machine 100% focused on ridding the world of crime one criminal at a time?

Eggs, she realized. Perhaps he had made an omelet.

He had turned around, blocking her from going into the rest of the house, waiting for an explanation. He wore old jeans and a navy sweatshirt and athletic socks, but seemed no less intimidating than he did in his detective getup of dress shirt and suit coat. And definitely not pleased at her presence.

"Ronald Soltis," she said, and watched for his reaction.

He didn't give one. "What about him?"

She waited. He raised one eyebrow at her.

"You and Riley were assigned to his case. I saw that in RMS."

Still he said nothing. He seemed almost amused, which ticked her off.

"Well?"

"Do you want to know if I killed him, Maggie?"

"Yes."

"Then ask me," he said with no amusement at all.

She forced herself to speak. "Did you kill him?"

"No."

They stared at each other. A white cat wandered into the room.

"Anything else?" Jack asked.

She was afraid to say that she didn't believe him, because part of her did. She just wasn't sure. She couldn't be sure of *anything* where Jack was concerned. He had killed quite a number of Cleveland's worst, until she had made the connection between the vigilante-like murders. Her existence had put a stop to his "work." No wonder she felt terrified to approach his house, to be anywhere around him.

Yet sticking her head under the covers could not be an option. Not for her. "I thought we had a deal. If we're going to do this—"

"Do *what?* We're not going to *do* anything. We're not partners, Maggie. We're not friends."

With a frown she said, "I know that."

He ignored her scowl and spoke more calmly. "Look, we intersected at one point, and that point is in the past. I'm sorry you're all discombobulated because you've always been the good girl, thought following the rules would pay off. But it doesn't. I can't help you deal with that. Right now all we need to *do* is maintain absolutely zero connection between me, you, and what happened. That means you don't show up at my *house.*"

She kept her voice as level and matter-of-fact as his. "What choice did I have? You said no phones, so I can't call you. I don't even have your number."

"And we'll keep it that way. Cell phone records live forever. And Riley's girlfriend lives out this way—what happens if he just happens to drive by and sees your car in my drive?"

"I don't have a car."

"How'd you get here?"

"Bus."

"You walked here in the pitch-dark? Are you *crazy?* Jeez, Maggie, don't you see enough of what this city can do . . . ?" He ran a hand through his hair, so exasperated that she almost smiled.

In a way this demonstration of normality calmed her, and she said, "I thought we needed to get some things straight."

Either Jack felt tired—unsurprising since they'd both been up all night—or willing to take some pity on her, because he gestured toward one of the kitchen chairs. "Sit down, Maggie. Want a drink? All I have is bourbon."

She couldn't stand the stuff, but that didn't matter right now. "Sure."

She sat on the hard kitchen chair. The cat tensed at her feet, readied itself, and jumped into her lap.

Jack set a shot glass in front of her and put down one for himself, taking the other chair as he opened a bottle of Four Roses. "That's Greta."

Maggie petted the animal, stroking the top of its head, and sipped from the glass. She grimaced.

"Not a bourbon lover?"

"Not much, no."

"You must have gone to the same seminar Riley did."

She didn't ask what he meant. They sat and listened to the cat purr.

"So, what is our deal, Maggie? You don't tell your coworkers about my murders, and I don't tell them about yours. In return you give me six months to get my affairs in order and clear out. In return for *that*, I stop killing people. Is that an accurate summary?"

She sipped. "Yes."

"Okay, then. My end of the bargain's holding up. I didn't kill Ronald Soltis. I'm glad someone did, but it wasn't me. And by the way, I was with you at the *Herald* offices all last night, or did that escape your notice?"

"He'd been there for at least two days."

"Good for him." He drained his glass, poured another.

"He was shot in the back of the head with a twenty-two, Jack. What was I supposed to think?"

"You should think—first of all, I don't care what you think, because you're already in this up to your neck. You want to keep that very clear in your mind."

"I wouldn't be here if it wasn't," she said in her most withering tone.

"Just making sure. But you *should* think that twenty-twos are a very popular caliber and Ronnie had amassed a lot of enemies in his short life, and that that's what happens when stupid kids who think they're tough try to throw around their weight in the territories of people who really are. That's what you should think."

"Wouldn't he have had a posse? Some muscle to go with him? All thugs do."

"Posses can be bought off. That *honor among thieves* thing has always been an urban myth. Every single one would sell every single other one out for a dime bag."

The cat snuggled deeper into her stomach. She believed him, but was that only because she wanted to, because she so desperately wanted to wash her hands of all Jack's crimes? If Ronald Soltis had died because she hadn't turned Jack in, then that spattered his blood over her face. No amount of rationalizing could bury that shining fact.

Jack had lied every day to everyone around him and done such a good job. He lied to people who listened to lies all day long. Her abilities and intelligence and experience, so effective against inanimate evidence such as blood and fibers, were those of a rank amateur against someone like Jack.

"All right," she said, and bit back *I'm sorry*. She would not apologize for doubting him where any sensible person would. Any sensible person who hadn't flung themselves into a web of the deepest deceit possible. "There's something else. I need your fingerprints."

"Hell no!"

"Jack. They wouldn't let me back into the crime scene. Josh and Amy processed and collected all the prints. They ran the prints through our AFIS. *All* of them. The only hits were your— victim's. Of course they didn't hit on you because personnel prints aren't in my database."

"They wouldn't anyway."

"But—"

116

"The prints turned in with my application packet aren't mine. Long story."

"Okay," she said, letting her voice express her deep and abiding disapproval at someone who dared to mess with her fingerprint database. "The catch is, Rick wants to send them to the FBI. Unsolved serial killer case, that's not unreasonable."

As luck would have it—or wouldn't—investigation of the series of murders had been assigned to Rick Gardiner and his partner. Not ideal, but that didn't worry her much. Rick lived in a perpetual state of too much occupation with his own thoughts to be able to guess at hers. Better he investigate than a detective like Patty Wildwood, who might actually pick up on non-verbal clues.

"You can't let him do that," Jack said.

"I figured as much. But I can't pull yours out of all the prints left at the scene if I don't know which ones are yours. The only way I can eliminate your prints is if I identify them first."

He digested this. "I see your point. I got into the scene with the first responders, so my prints can be explained—"

"—but not if they don't match what's in your file."

"Take a new set. Just for elimination purposes."

"How am I going to explain that?"

"I realized I wasn't wearing gloves at the scene,

117

came to you and confessed to contaminating the evidence."

Maggie sat, working out different scenarios in her mind. It felt sketchy, but it could work. She could always ask a few other people who had been at the scene for their prints as well in order to disguise the process. She could say that inking a new set in her office would save a headache trying to get HR to release them. The biggest factor in their favor was that no one at the department, no one, would ever suspect that the killer had been a cop. They would not be looking for suspicious activity within their own walls; therefore, they wouldn't see it. It almost scared her, how easily she could see it working.

The cat purred.

"She doesn't usually like anyone except me," Jack said. "And she only makes an exception for me because I feed her."

"They know a cat person when they find one."

They regarded each other.

"Don't come here again," Jack warned.

"Don't kill anyone."

He burst out with a snort of laughter, quickly stifled, and Maggie smiled. But only for a split second. Then Jack stood and grabbed his jacket from the back of a different chair, his abrupt movement startling the cat. "Come on. I'll drive you home."

"I thought we shouldn't be seen together."

"Yeah, but you getting mugged two blocks from my house wouldn't help our case any, either."

She set the cat on the floor as gently as possible, but still the feline stalked off with an aggrieved air. Maggie brushed hair off her dark jeans. "Don't wait too long to get this place on the market. Sellers aren't having an easy time of it."

His face darkened, and that slight air of comradeship that had drifted up between them evaporated. "It's a rental."

"Didn't mean to nag."

"Come on." He shut the door behind them with a bang and led her to his car. They rode most of the way in silence.

Around East 30th Jack's phone rang. Maggie could hear Riley's excited voice from the passenger side.

"You won't believe this," Riley said. "We got another one."

"Another what?"

"Another *Herald* employee."

Maggie's phone trilled as well.

Chapter 14

Jerry Wilton had been Director of Advertising for barely two years, responsible for maintaining a cash flow that dried up a little more every day in this new digital paradigm. He had to cajole, promise, and deal to the best of his ability in order to bring paying customers to the pages of the *Herald*. He was also responsible for monitoring, verifying, and, the corporation hoped, increasing the numbers of papers bought on a daily basis.

Had been, that is, until someone strung him up from a weightlifting frame in his own living room. Now he hung perfectly still, facing the side of the room with the eighty-inch flat-screen and the Bose speakers and the kitchen with the gleaming espresso machine and stainless-steel pots hanging over the island. Some fault in the floor's level kept him from watching his own blood as it spread across the floor because it traveled in the other direction, behind him. If he had been able to peek straight downward, if the strap around his throat gave just enough for that, he would have been able to see his internal organs slipping onto the polished hardwood after his killer sawed his midsection open with one slightly jagged cut. The knife lay on the floor next to the offal. The pricey apartment now smelled like an autopsy suite in full swing.

Maggie stared, taking this in.

Jack took a step forward.

"Don't," she ordered. "There's not much I can do about the first two cops on the scene, but I could still get some usable shoeprints."

"How long's *that* going to take?" Riley muttered.

"It's worth it," she promised.

The living room had been sparsely furnished in order to leave Wilton plenty of room to work out—nothing other than a leather couch, coffee table, end table, and workout equipment.

Fifteen minutes later she had covered the beautiful hardwood with enough black powder to keep the crime-scene cleanup people cursing for an hour, photographed and lifted several prints, and spread disposable drop cloths so that she and the detectives could walk their bootied feet around the body without tracking the stuff through the rest of the apartment. Only then could they approach the dead man.

Jerry Wilton had light brown skin, close-cropped hair, and a figure that came from spending a lot of time using the chin-up bar from which he now hung. He was tall—his toes barely cleared the floor, the noose hiked up to within six inches of the bar. The strap had been looped over it and then tied off on the base.

He was dressed in sweats and a T-shirt as if he

had indeed been working with the bar when the killer called, so he might not have been expecting a visitor, or if he had it was someone Jerry Wilton knew well enough not to care what he looked like when they arrived. There were no signs of a break-in, indicating he had opened the door without any fuss, but neither were there any signs of shared snacks or drinks. None of the neighbors reported hearing an argument. The killer could have had a key, but after a quick check of the rest of the apartment, Maggie doubted that anyone else lived there. No women's items, no makeup or panties around, and all the male clothing seemed the same size. The bed had been made, sort of, and the bathroom was tolerably clean. The medicine cabinet held a store aisle's worth of vitamins and supplements, but no prescription or illegal drugs.

Wilton had an appreciation for imported beer and Jack Daniel's whiskey, but not to excess—there were no piles of empties to be found. The kitchen appeared neat at first, but then Maggie noticed a smear of butter on the island and toast crumbs on the counter, and the few dishes in the sink had dried and crusted. She found Wilton's—or maybe the cleaning lady's—secret: a large drawer stuffed with junk mail, bills, receipts, menus, and a few greeting cards from someone named Natasha who wrote with a looping feminine script and who *really* wanted the two of them to get back together. The garbage smelled of takeout that needed to be taken out. Bachelors, Maggie thought.

As at his workplace, Wilton's apartment had a view of the lake—so close that he hadn't bothered with blinds on his windows. His only possible voyeurs would be seagulls or someone with a boat and one hell of a telephoto lens.

Jerry Wilton had apparently used the guest room as an office. There they found *Herald* circulation reports, advertising revenue statements, a laptop, and all manner of memos, printed e-mails, meeting agendas, and notes scribbled on Post-its, bar tabs, and the occasional paper towel. The organization Jerry Wilton applied to his physical shape didn't extend to his paperwork, and the room drowned in it. Maggie wondered if any item there could explain his death, and if so, how she would be able to tell.

She returned to the body.

"Whaddya think, Maggie?" Riley asked. Jack was back to pretending he barely knew her. He had even dropped her a block from the Justice Center so it would appear that she had walked from her loft as usual. Not that she blamed him. She felt every bit as invested in keeping their secret as he did.

"Same as before. Strangled—there's one furrow—and then hung. Tossed the strap over the top bar, looped once around the frame here and gave it a heave-ho."

"Not as easy as tossing off the printer platform."

"I don't know," she said. "Give me a lever—then he took the guy's own knife from that block in the kitchen and tried a little disembowelment."

"What's the point?" Jack asked. "Why cut up someone who's already dead?"

Riley added, "Especially if you're trying to make it look like a suicide. We'd hardly buy the guy gutting himself when he's swinging from a rope."

"Because we already knew he isn't," Maggie said. "He tried that with Robert Davis, but we knew it wasn't suicide but homicide. We would know this wasn't suicide, either. He added the slashing just to make it clear that he knows we know."

"You're making my head swim," Riley said.

Jack said, "He's playing with us."

Maggie said, "Yeah."

Chapter 15

Maggie taped the clothing—just the back, obviously the front was a lost cause, soaked in still-damp blood—where it hung. Technically this was not kosher, since the Medical Examiner's investigator hadn't arrived yet, but she wanted the most pristine sample possible before the clothing came into contact with body snatchers and their sheets and bags. Since she didn't move the body, it couldn't really be considered molestation of same. And she doubted they would care anyway. Much.

Under the thin T-shirt, Jerry Wilton's body felt like a slab of marble.

"Who found him?" she asked.

"Buddy who lives on another floor came over to watch the game. He knocks, the door swings open. These places were built to look fancy, but some things are cheaper than they appear, and the door never fit the jamb quite right. You have to pull it to get it to latch. Apparently the killer didn't know that, or didn't care."

Maggie looked around at the fashionably sparse apartment. "No signs of a struggle, but he's got this open area here, space cleared to work out in. He could have thrashed around by the weights here and not been able to reach anything to kick over. Or the killer put everything back. The weights are willy-nilly, but they might have been like that anyway. Or"—she stretched upward, standing on her toes to reach the back of Wilton's head with her gloved fingers—"someone used one of those weights to clock him in the skull."

"That makes the strangling part go so much more smoothly," Riley said.

"It does indeed. But I can't be sure. We'll have to wait for the pathologist."

"What about the strap?"

"Looks the same as with Davis. White nylon, and clean."

"He really wants us to know it's him. The same guy."

Maggie said, "And he doesn't care about appearing premeditated. Maybe, *maybe,* he was carrying a strap around the *Herald* offices for some other reason and got into a fight with Davis. But he wouldn't still be toting it around afterward, and he certainly wouldn't have brought it here except for the express purpose of doing exactly what he did."

"Boats," Riley said.

"What?"

"I was thinking, who uses rope for anything anymore? Especially clean white nylon like that. Tying up boats, that's the only place you still use rope."

"True. But you can still get it in any hardware store."

Jack had been poking through the papers in Wilton's home office and walked in holding some clippings and an index card. The clippings were the *Herald* stories on the alternative high school, written by L. Russo. "A guy with no kids interested in education? And this—" Jack held out the index card. Right after *oil change* and *M Bday,* it read: *TM mtg GL 9:30.*

"Fascinating," Riley said. "What the hell does it mean?"

"It means the *Herald*'s circulation manager was talking to someone from TM. TransMedia."

"Who's TransMedia?" Maggie asked.

Riley said, "The hated enemy, according to Correa. But hardly a secret. He had the TM exec's social schedule committed to memory."

Jack studied the index card as if it were the Rosetta Stone. "Well, there are secrets and then there are secrets."

"That's profound, partner."

"Come look at this."

They followed him into the home office.

He sat at a wide, flat desk and put on a pair of reading glasses that made him look more like a professor to Maggie than a cop . . . or a killer. She wondered if that had been the Jack his victims had seen . . . until they didn't. He had already separated pages into two piles. He tapped one with a finger.

"These all seem to be circulation reports printed

off the *Herald*'s system—same dates in the upper left corner, same number in the bottom right that I'm guessing is the asset tag for his printer. February fourth—311,605. February fourth Dig—I'm guessing that means online hits or views or whatever—296,462. February fifth—that's a Sunday—431,465. Digital 354,002."

"Who says newspapers are dying?" Riley said.

"Out of 3.8 million people in the area? Those aren't great numbers."

Riley argued, "That's people. You have to go by *families*. A house only gets one paper."

"Yeah, true—anyway, my point is, then we have this stack. No dates of the printouts in the corner. No asset numbers in the other corner. Different font. Paper looks like the paper in that printer in the corner over there, but then copy paper is copy paper is copy paper."

"Mr. Sherlock Holmes here," Riley said.

She watched over his shoulder.

"These also seem to be circulation numbers. We find February fourth—788,528. Digital, February fourth—902,549. February fifth—1,599,610. Digital—"

"He was cooking the books," Maggie said.

"Looks that way."

"And then the killer found out."

Jack said, "Or the killer didn't want anyone else to find out."

"But then he left the papers here, for us to find."

Riley said, "Or the *killer* was cooking the books, and *Wilton* found out. That's a powerful motive."

Maggie said, "Still, then he leaves the evidence here."

Jack said, "Didn't Correa say this guy met with his TransMedia counterpart in Atlantic City?"

"Yeah," Riley said. "Maybe we should ask him which set of numbers Wilton gave him."

"But we still don't know *when* Wilton found out what. And where does Davis fit in? He was a copy editor. What would he have to do with circulation reports?"

The three considered this in silence.

Jack pulled over yet another series of papers. "Then there's this. Stock reports for the *Herald* mixed in with stock reports for TransMedia. No cooking there—these are printed off Hoovers.com. No comparison, either. TM is trading at thirty-three dollars a share. Herald Enterprises is four dollars and thirteen cents."

Riley said, "But if TM bought it—"

"Stock would soar. Or at least vastly improve."

"Maybe Wilton was looking to make a killing and retire to Aruba."

"Dunno. If you buy stock in your own company, is that insider trading?"

"You're asking me? To me, stock is stuff that moos and gets ground up into hamburger."

Maggie read the framed certificates on the

wall. "He knew numbers. CPA, MBA from OSU—not surprising that he would be paying attention to the stock prices."

Riley snapped his fingers. "Davis's widow said he'd been talking about someone named Wilson. Could she have heard Wil*ton* instead?"

Jack said, "Yeah, but if Davis and Wilton were working at cross-purposes, why are they both dead?"

"Cell phone," Riley said.

"Can't find it," Jack told him. "Not even the charger for it. Three old models in the drawer over there."

Riley looked at Maggie.

"It's not in his pocket," she said.

"Home phone?"

"Doesn't have one," Jack told him.

"Kids these days. Maybe it's in his car."

"Nobody leaves their phone in their car," Maggie said. "And he didn't have keys in his pocket, either. They weren't in the kitchen. There's a basketful of them stuck in one of the drawers, but from the dust I'd say they were old spares."

Riley dispatched the patrol officer to ask the buddy from the other floor what Wilton drove and where it might be right then. Then he rubbed his head, a set of fingers on each temple, and walked around in a small circle. "So this guy kills people, then takes their phones. He leaves everything else—Davis's layouts, Wilton's laptop. We've got to see what's on that laptop."

"No," Maggie said.

"We can't wait for EI," he whined, referring to the electronics investigators who handled the complex tasks of cracking computers, cell phones, tablets, GPSs, and all the other gizmos that had become so necessary to everyday life. "They'll take days. A week, probably."

"If you so much as turn it on, you might trigger an erasure. This is a young guy, probably tech savvy, maybe with something to hide. He might have thought ahead to an SEC investigation. He could have set a booby trap."

Riley sighed.

"And on top of that, Zoe would yell at you. You don't want that."

"All right. At least I got to hear you say 'booby.'"

She gave him the expected look of exasperation.

Jack said, "The cell phone thing is weird, but if the motive is some sort of shady business dealings, then why leave it here for us to find? This could all still come down to somebody French-kissing somebody else's wife, and the business end of it is irrelevant to the murders."

Riley said, "The difference in the circulation reports is definitely interesting. Something is up at that paper—we need to figure out who was trying to fool whom. And who found out about it."

"That's profound," Jack said, "partner."

"Obviously the cell phones are important to this guy. We need to get the search warrants in motion so we can see what he's seeing. I'll go write them. You want to stay here and poke around some more?"

Jack surveyed the room, the heaps of paperwork he hadn't yet touched. Then they both looked at Maggie.

"Sure," she said.

Chapter 16

The body snatchers came and removed the corpse of Jerry Wilton, and a patrol officer remained stationed at the door. No one disturbed Jack and Maggie as they sorted through Wilton's home. They checked Wilton's Lexus but found it locked and undisturbed. The victim had kept his car even neater than his home, and no cell phone rested on the seat. They couldn't do any more without a key, so Maggie and Jack had returned to the quiet apartment.

They did not use the silence for further tête-à-têtes. Maggie supposed they had already addressed any issue they could and said anything they could say about this deeply weird situation. She did not believe that Jack had not killed Ronald Soltis—he had no reason to tell her the truth and every reason not to—but she didn't quite believe that he had. Aside from the similar MO, she had no proof of his involvement. She mentally shelved the topic until more evidence appeared. For two hours they barely spoke, other than to make comments such as: "I'm putting these here."

Jerry Wilton had not only been monitoring the *Herald*'s circulation, but—reasonably—that of other newspapers as well. He had a semiannual report from the NAA, Newspaper Association of

America, showing how dailies in other major cities were faring. Most of them seemed much more robust than the *Herald*.

"Jack."

"Mmm?"

"This circulation report comes out every six months. This one is dated over four months ago."

"So? He probably sends the figures to the NAA or whatever, so he could send whatever he wanted."

"But at the bottom it says that all numbers are independently verified by outside auditors. A firm called Media Audit Incorporated."

He got it. "So if Wilton had been cooking up the circulation data, he'd only have another month and a half, say, to keep it up before the next report comes out. But are figures automatically audited, or only when requested? That could buy him a few more months."

"I don't know."

"One way or another, he couldn't have kept it up for long."

They sat cross-legged on the floor, facing each other, stacks of paper between them. Problem was, they had very little idea what any of it meant.

Some papers mentioned TransMedia. Wilton had circled some of the circulation data and written *TM* next to the circles. He had also taken interest in the vagaries of their stock prices.

Maggie said, "We don't know if Wilton was

the one cooking books, or he's the one who discovered it."

"Or whom he told either way."

"And the only people we can ask might be coconspirators."

"Who will know that this is no longer a routine investigation of a suicide. The guts on the floor in there kind of made that clear."

"On the other hand, coconspirators now have a motive to talk—if they think they might be next."

"Unless they're the ones doing the killing," he pointed out.

They moved to the *Herald* offices, where the printing crew toiled through the run. Rebecca, the security guard, let them in with a weary air as if she had been expecting them. It turned out she had—Managing Editor Franklin Roth had beat them to the place and waited in his office to assist. The older man looked as if he hadn't slept in a week and had aged at least five years since the previous evening. But he was still an ex-crime beat reporter. "What the hell is going on?" he asked without preamble.

"Someone is killing your employees," Jack told him. "We need to find out who and why."

Roth asked a number of questions as he guided them to Wilton's office, again betraying the who-what-where-when pattern of reporters everywhere.

He got little for his troubles, however. Jack would only tell him that both Davis and Wilton had been murdered by person or persons unknown. He did not describe Wilton's gory tableau. Maggie said nothing.

Roth pulled out a set of keys as they walked. Apparently the main doors of the building had gone to the more modern proximity-sensor key cards, but the upper offices that ringed the perimeter of the atrium-like space still opened the old-fashioned way. Maggie thought the clear Plexiglas barrier and railing quite fashionable until she stopped and tried to look down on the reporters' bullpen. The barrier only reached to the upper thigh, and the clear acrylic railing wobbled when she put her hands on it. She jumped back in alarm.

"Yeah," Roth said as he paused in front of Wilton's office. "Stylish design. Absolutely useless in keeping people from plunging twenty or thirty feet. Luckily OSHA inspectors are more concerned about people falling into the printing press than falling over the railing."

Maggie stayed to the center of the walkway but couldn't resist a cautious peek over. The reporters' desks appeared even more chaotic when viewed from above.

"I don't get it," Roth said, more to himself than to them. "Davis was a copy editor. Wilton was a numbers man, frankly, a bean counter. A downstairs man. They probably never even met each other."

"Downstairs?" Maggie asked. Clearly the rank-and-file reporters were downstairs, where the higher-ups with private offices could gaze down at their hive of activity like senators at the Colosseum.

"The business and writing sides of a newspaper were always kept separate. Publishers and advertising execs were one side—we call that downstairs, I forget what paper that originated with. Then the reporters and editors were the other half—upstairs. There used to be a Chinese wall in between the two floors, so that editors and writers could report what needed to be reported without worrying about ticking off an advertiser. But those days are long over and publishers and editors are essentially the same thing. Now I edit this paper while caring very *much* what the advertisers think. I have to. Or there isn't going to be a paper at all."

Roth had opened a door bearing a number instead of Wilton's name—183. Maggie took one glance and knew this could not be the domain of the more than passably tidy Wilton. His home office might not have been perfectly organized, but it didn't look the way this did, as if a maelstrom had passed through.

"I think someone beat us to it," she said.

Chapter 17

Riley was off trying to locate members of Jerry Wilton's family while Jack knocked on the door of *Herald* reporter L. Russo. Not only had Wilton's home office contained clippings of Russo's articles, but his office at the paper had as well. Either a shut-down alternative high school had been very important to Jerry Wilton, or L. Russo had.

Ten minutes later, Jack had his answer.

L. Russo turned out to be Laurine ("Lori, please") Russo, a brown-eyed, blond-haired beauty who lived in Little Italy, only a few doors from the Algebra Tea House. Her equally beautiful husband had not been at all pleased to find Jack standing on his doorstep at eleven p.m. He had stood in the kitchen doorway, arms crossed, for a good five or ten minutes until he felt confident that Jack's visit stemmed from legitimate police business. Then he straightened and asked his wife, "You want me to pause it?"

"No, thanks, sweetie, I've seen this one before."

He gave Jack one last dark look with dark eyes, and retreated up the hall. From photos on the wall Jack assumed they had two matching children, young enough to be fast asleep at the late hour. Lori herself was wrapped in a fuzzy robe and seemed shocked, but not distraught, at the news of Wilton's death. Apparently he had been liked but, after all, merely a coworker.

Jack told her the articles she had written about the closure of the alternative high school had been found in the victim's home. He didn't add that they had also been found in his office at the *Herald*. But her face cleared. "Oh, that's easy. His cousin went there."

"Who would that be?"

The words spilled easily. "His aunt Mirabell's grandson Damon. Mirabell is such a doll—I talked to her, too, for the story. Apparently her daughter moved to Arizona for a job but left Damon with Mirabell so he could finish up junior year. Why is it that people can have a bunch of great kids, but there's always one that's just an asshole from birth?" She glanced up at the photos of her own kids, perhaps thinking that if she stopped at two, it might improve her odds. "Anyway, the second his mom was out of town, the kid never goes to school, starts with the petty crimes, gets kicked out of school, and has to go to the alternative, quote unquote, school. You know, there didn't used to be so many options. It's so hard for parents to decide now. When we were kids"—she waved her hand, including herself and Jack in the same group—"a school was a school. Private schools were a little more stringent, but pretty much everyone learned the same stuff.

Then somewhere along the line some genius comes up with the idea that kids should only have to learn what and when they damn well wanted. We started jumping through hoops to keep them all on the same level, encourage every single one to go to college and be a doctor or a lawyer, which they can't handle so they drop out and deal drugs. Used to be—hey, you want some coffee? It's already made."

"Yes, thank you." Caffeine could only be a good idea.

She jumped up to putter at the counter and then warned, "It's decaf."

Jack swallowed, reminded himself of Riley's seminar. "Okay."

She tapped a large pet bowl out of her way to open a cabinet and take out two mugs.

"You have a dog?" Jack asked.

"Yeah."

"What kind?"

She gave him a curious look, but said, "I couldn't tell you—just a mutt we rescued from the pound when the kids were little."

He listened to the silent house. No scratching, whimpering, or barking. Not much of a watchdog. "Where is it?"

"She sleeps in the kids' room. Very protective. Anyway . . ." She got back to the topic of schooling as she poured. "Used to be when a kid couldn't do the work, they flunked, they got D minuses, they figured out school wasn't for them and they learned a trade, became a mechanic or a plumber. They'd probably end up making more than the doctor anyway." She returned to the table with two cups. "My kids are in elementary now and I second-guess where we've got them every day. Now we have charter schools and magnet schools and alternative schools, and they'll all tell you they're great and their kids are brilliant. They'll tell you things like sixty percent of the kids are on the honor roll. What they don't tell you is that all you have to do to get on the honor roll is show up. I've been writing about education for years—double duty, I guess, for selfish reasons—I wanted a good basis in the facts to make decisions about my own kids. But it's fascinating, it really is . . . anyway, I was doing a survey of types of high schools. I had to make an appointment to visit this school—Green Market High School, it was called. I couldn't just pop in, but okay, not unreasonable, security in schools is high these days, especially considering that most of these students used to be drug dealers. I saw sparkling classrooms with obedient children raising their hands and answering intelligent questions. But once in a while one of the kids would glance at me." She gave a tiny shudder. "The looks on those kids' faces—"

"Violent?" Jack asked.

"Withering. Like, *you're just as much of an idiot*

as every other adult in our lives, lady, so what exactly the hell do you think you're *going to do?*"

"What did you do?"

"I met up with a few of them outside school, befriended them . . . okay, I bribed them with cigarettes . . . and through thorough and skillful questioning"—she made a face—"discovered that they couldn't name a Founding Father, describe the difference between an atom and a molecule, or knew that Iowa was a state. They spent most of their time in the building on their phones, surfing the web, or drawing, which was actually the only thing I liked about the place. Those kids could benefit from a little art therapy."

She seemed to realize that she'd been talking for a while, coughed, and paused. But Jack didn't mind. At least it made a break from The State of Journalism in America Today.

Lori described how she had located a few parents who gave a crap whether their kids learned anything or not, and got a reluctant state board involved. Jack asked a few more questions, but it seemed clear that either Lori Russo was a very good liar, or Jerry Wilton's interest in her work had been purely due to his family connection.

Jack had closed his largely empty notebook and put it in his pocket when she said, "But I'm so glad to talk to you."

"Really? Why?"

"Have you gotten anywhere with our murdering vigilante?"

Jack could not have been more surprised. Of course the paper had covered the story, and nothing captured the public imagination like a murder room. But the attention didn't worry him—the paper couldn't know anything the police didn't, and since he hadn't been killing pretty girls, interest should fade quickly. "The investigation is ongoing, of course."

She leaned forward over her coffee cup, the long hair snaking over her shoulders. "Any suspects?"

"I can't talk about an open—"

"You know about the others, right?"

Jack felt a little less unsurprised. "Yes, we are examining prior deaths—"

"I've been helping Isaac Mills with the story, and we looked up unsolved homicides for the past five years. There are a lot—no offense, I mean the usual gang bangers, plenty of witnesses but no one saw anything, they just solve the case in their own way. Like the Mafia. But, see, most of them were shot where they fell. Because of the murder room, we looked at ones where the body had obviously been moved."

"Uh-huh."

"There was a Marcus Day, a Brian Johnson—can you get me some details on that murder room? Public goes nuts over weird stuff like that. If I could get in there with a camera—we have to take most of our own photos these days—get the details—anyway, I started looking in other cities."

"Oh," Jack said. "Did you?"

"There were at least five in Chicago? Shots to the back of the head, twenty-two caliber, body moved. And there are four in Atlanta that I think are the same pattern. Isaac doesn't agree, but I say . . . I mean, these were all scumbags who washed out of court a couple of times . . . do you ever think that maybe it's a lawyer?"

"Huh," Jack said. *Yeah, let's go with that.* "You think?"

"Or a judge. Or—no offense again—a cop?"

Jack smiled but tried not to make it mocking. Nothing would spur a reporter to action like laughing at their theory. "None taken."

"I think there were a few in Phoenix as well."

Jack tried not to choke on his last swig of the awful coffee. "So you think he's moved on?"

Unhappily, she said, "That seems to be his pattern—maybe the murders begin to attract too much scrutiny so he leaves town, starts again somewhere else. And they definitely attracted attention here—he left a witness this time. So I'm sure he got the hell out of here."

Yeah, let's go with that.

Jack thanked her for her time, got back into his car, and drove away, hoping that in the future Lori Russo would stick to the education beat.

Chapter 18

Maggie drank the coffee even though it had long stopped working its magic on her corpuscles. She had managed a few hours of sleep after leaving the *Herald*'s offices, but they did not come near making up for the previous night and day. When she yawned for the third time in as many minutes she received a sharp poke in the ribs. "Hey!"

"Cut that out," Zoe told her, before returning her hand to her mouse. "You're making me sleepy."

"I deserve to be sleepy. My head hit the pillow for about three hours last night, total." It hadn't spent much of that time in a REM cycle; instead her mind kept going over Ronald Soltis's death in an alley, with no evidence and no witnesses and no gang taking credit for it. As if, like Day and Johnson and the others, some unknown force had arrived, taken his life, and melted back into the city's society without leaving a trace for her to find. An uncomfortably familiar death.

"More than me," Zoe said, not that the young woman showed it. Her ponytail bobbed as she cocked her head at the screen, and even in the dim light of the darkened room her eyes showed no signs of redness or drooping. The resilience of youth.

"Hot date?"

"Sure. With a troll and a wizard. Online tournament of the War of the Roses."

"I thought the War of the Roses was fought by human beings."

"Different war."

"So you work on computers all day and then go home and play on computers all night?"

"Why do you think I'm fifty pounds overweight?"

A regrettable but accurate statement, so Maggie said nothing. Wilton's computer sat in front of them, connected to Zoe's equipment and from there to Zoe's computer, the web of wires and thin cables making it look as if the victim's laptop had been placed on some sort of electronic life support.

Zoe went on, shifting her frame. "So this case gets to jump the line just because the guy who owned this laptop got his guts splattered across the floor?"

"Yep."

"I got no problem with that." She slurped something out of the bottom of a tall plastic cup and rattled the ice cubes. "Please tell me this thing wasn't in the room or anywhere within splashing distance."

"Different room entirely."

"Yay," Zoe said with intense relief. "Okay, what do we got? E-mail?"

"The lifeblood of modern communications."

Zoe chuckled, and after a few clicks they were looking at Jerry Wilton's inbox.

Maggie scanned the message list, ignoring the spam and the advertisements. Zoe started clicking again.

Messages from the lovelorn Natasha, inviting Wilton to a wine tasting and a football game. He had not replied.

"Poor Natasha," Zoe sighed. "That's just how I am with Jeff."

There were also messages from a Suzanne, with similar invitations, carefully worded to be friendly but not overtly romantic. Suzanne either knew the value of subtlety, or she was simply a friend or the significant other of a mutual friend. Wilton replied to her, and very nicely, too, but nothing about their messages mentioned the *Herald*, stocks, or circulation figures.

Then they hit on one that asked simply, **"How much do you want me to buy?"**

Wilton had promptly written back to that person: **"4000 this week."**

The e-mail address was "prettyshania" at a free e-mail site.

"Well, well," Zoe said. "Let's see what else pretty little Shania has been up to." She searched the e-mail program for messages with that address, and a long list appeared. They began to read through them in reverse chronological order.

Wilton had instructed Shania to buy shares in

amounts ranging from two hundred to nine thousand. Sometimes she prompted him for that week's assignment, but most of the time he e-mailed her first and she wrote back simply "okay" or "got it." Maggie made a list for herself of the dates and amounts in the e-mails, but nowhere did he explain shares of *what*. "They must have met in person as well," Zoe said.

"Actually talking to someone face-to-face. The one thing that doesn't leave a record."

Shania would occasionally ask about "the account," as in, "the account doesn't have enough for that." Wilton would then promise to take care of it, and apparently he did because no follow-up appeared.

"Look at this one," Zoe said.

Shania had asked her common question— "How much should I buy?"—but then skipped a line and added: "Don't forget about Tom's B-day."

Wilton had not responded, so they didn't learn any more about Tom and his impending birthday, but still the comment changed the tone. Then they got as far back as the Christmas season, and Shania used the missives to ask where he would go on Christmas Eve, that dinner was at five-thirty, and had he gotten Sophie a present because she hadn't. She didn't, as she put it, "feel the need."

"This isn't just a business relationship," Zoe concluded.

"They know each other. But they're not

boyfriend-girlfriend," Maggie mused. Neither of them had ever written words like *love,* or commented on any activities other than buying or selling, or referred to seeing each other outside cyberspace—other than the holidays. "It sounds like they're—"

"Relatives," Zoe finished. "Let's find out who Shania is."

She wheeled herself a few feet away to her own computer, a massive thing with two monitors, high-resolution graphics, and a fan that made it sound like the space shuttle taking off.

"Do you have spy techware, like super . . . powered . . . NSA stuff?" Maggie asked. She didn't know the technical terms.

"Yeah, it's mega-secret. I could have you killed just for seeing me use it. It's called Google."

She put Shania's e-mail address into the search box and hit *Enter.*

Several hits popped up. Zoe clicked on the first one.

Maggie stared. "Shania's on Facebook?"

"Isn't everyone? Social girl. She's also on LinkedIn, Twitter, Instagram, blah blah blah. Old school. Let's see—is she a gamer?"

A figure appeared in the doorway to interrupt this quest. "Maggie."

"Mmm?"

It was Carol, who told her, "IA called. You missed your—"

"Damn! My meeting with them. I totally forgot—"

"Don't worry, I told them you were working a homicide from last night and that homicides take precedence—I didn't actually say that, but they should know it. She said just to come in tomorrow, same time. Didn't sound like a big deal."

"It shouldn't. We've been over it four times already."

"Exactly! I think your ex-husband is just using this as an excuse to see you."

"I doubt that. I don't think he wants to hang with me any more than I want to be around him."

Carol leaned against the doorjamb, patting her pockets in succession to locate her cigarettes. She couldn't smoke indoors, of course, but it seemed to reassure her to know the cancer sticks were available. "Don't kid yourself. You ignore it, but he still looks at you like—well, like there's a connection there."

"He's a man. When they sell a car and later see the new owner driving it, a guy will always say, 'There's my car.'"

"What a romantic analogy."

"It's nothing personal. It was a serial killer and I saw him, so of course they're going to go over it again and again," Maggie explained with a sangfroid she absolutely did not feel. "Thanks for running interference."

"Well, homicides *do* take precedence, so IA can wait." Carol paused, then added, "The shrink, however—you really should talk to her."

"I'm going to, really. I just haven't had time."

"Make time. You need to talk to *somebody*."

"I talk to you."

"No, you don't." Gently. "Not really."

As she left, Maggie turned to see what Zoe had found, worrying that Rick might track her down and go into one of his epic rants. Then she reminded herself that she didn't have to care. They weren't married anymore.

"Got her," Zoe interrupted them.

Shania turned out to be a pretty girl with dark skin, long hair, and a job in the PR department for the Cleveland Indians. Her profile picture showed her in a team jersey holding a GO TRIBE sign. Her last name was Paulson and her page had been stuffed with photos of friends, a boyfriend, check-ins from the city's hot spots, and no mention of Jerry Wilton, stock trading, or the Cleveland *Herald*.

"Can you get her address?" Maggie asked.

"From Facebook? Of course not. Let's try something else that's super secret and incredibly high-tech."

"The white pages?"

"You got it."

She meant the online telephone directory, of

course. Maggie wasn't sure the paper books were even produced anymore. They would die along with newspapers.

"Nope, must be unlisted. But you know her name and where she works. Can't be that hard to show up at her door and ask her who the hell Jerry Wilton is to her, and by the way did you know that he's dead?"

Maggie assured her, "Not me, missy. I'm a lab tech. I don't show up on people's doorsteps. We have detectives for that."

Chapter 19

The detectives did, indeed, show up on Shania Paulson's doorstep. But they needn't have bothered. She wasn't home anyway.

Through neighbors they located her mother's home and went there. But Shania Paulson's mother, two sisters, and a cousin didn't need to be informed of Jerry Wilton's death. They already knew. The weeping lady who answered the door made that clear. Shania wasn't there, and they shouldn't disturb her mother, whose name was Mirabell and who had just learned that her handsome, successful nephew had been murdered. He had been more like a son to her, since Wilton's parents had passed some time before.

They asked to speak to Mirabell. The weeping lady wasn't going to allow it until, after further questioning, Riley let it slip that they had been the detectives at the scene of Wilton's murder. Then she ushered them right into a living room crowded with heavy furniture, Mirabell herself, and four sympathetic church ladies, all of whom peppered the detectives until Jack felt like bolting for the door. They wanted to know everything, how and when and why and by whom Jerry had been found, who had done it, and did they think he had suffered? The men stuck to the "that's still under investigation" dodge, but Riley did assure Wilton's aunt Mirabell that he believed the death had been quick and that Jerry had probably been gone before he even knew it. Jack guessed that when Aunt Mirabell learned the truth about the strangling, hanging, and disembowelment, she would be looking to shatter Riley's kneecaps for glossing over those details, but his partner would have to cross that bridge on his own when he stumbled onto it.

Jack didn't ask about the ne'er-do-well grandson and his educational progress.

"So Shania is Jerry's cousin?" Riley asked.

Mirabell, a short but wiry woman, confirmed this. "Why are you asking about Shania?"

"We'd like to talk to her."

The mother of the woman in question stiffened in concern. "Why? Shania's all right, I called her this morning to tell her about Jerry."

"Have you spoken to her since?"

"No."

"Do you know where she is right now?"

"No . . . you don't think whoever killed him might be after—"

"No, no," Riley said, though Jack wasn't so sure. Cousin Shania might be in very great danger indeed. "We just want to ask her about some e-mails she and Jerry had sent back and forth."

"Oh. Yes, they spoke all the time. Those two always got along, since they were tiny. My son, not as much. He and Jerry—what about the e-mails? What's Shania got to do with Jerry getting killed?"

"Probably nothing, but we have to check out every lead. Can you put us in touch with her?"

Mirabell didn't like the situation and really didn't like Riley's smooth evasions, but a mother's concern trumped all and she gave them Shania Paulson's phone number, boss's name, likely hangouts, and closest friends. She'd have given this information to the FBI and the 101st Airborne as well if she could have, but settled for dispatching the church ladies to their respective phone trees with the express purpose of tracking down her youngest daughter before she got herself murdered, too.

Riley and Jack left before Mirabell could demand to accompany them on a tour of Shania's favorite haunts. They went to Shania Paulson's workplace, spoke with her boss, contacted her friends, put a BOLO out on her car. They even got the super to open up her apartment, hoping *not* to find her disemboweled body on its floor, and didn't. All to no avail. Shania Paulson was nowhere to be found.

"Do you know whom you're looking for?" Rebecca asked Maggie. They sat in Rebecca's surveillance room, gazing at the rapidly changing television screens as each one fast-forwarded through the previous day's comings and goings. Staff moved in and out of the building, carried briefcases and tote bags and backpacks, smoked cigarettes, and argued with people on cell phones. No one seemed suspicious or even in much of a hurry.

"No," Maggie told her.

Rebecca rubbed her eyes, no doubt mentally groaning.

"Someone killed Jerry Wilton and then came here and ransacked his office, and it had to be between the time Wilton went home from work and when we got here and found the office. There shouldn't be that much activity in the second half of the day, right?"

"It's a newspaper. There's always activity, but yeah, the bulk of the employees would have gone home by then. But reporters come and go anytime, and the whole printing and shipping crew would just be getting here. They can only get into the east side of the building."

"Except this person now had Jerry Wilton's key card. So they could go anywhere."

"Um, yeah."

They watched people come and go.

"There's Roger," Rebecca said.

Maggie had asked about him earlier, having heard a description of the man's personality from Riley. Rebecca pointed at a good-looking guy briskly approaching camera 2 with a girl who seemed to be dressed entirely in black. "Who's that with him?"

"Probably a groupie. They think Roger is Bob Woodward and Charles Dickens rolled into one."

"You know Roger Correa?"

"*Everyone* knows Roger," Rebecca said.

The editor, Franklin Roth, had left about six, came back about eight, and left again shortly after. But he would not have needed Wilton's keys; as she had seen, his own gave him access to Wilton's office.

A dark and slender girl came rushing up to camera 5 about eight-thirty. Maggie squinted at the grainy image. "Do you know who that is?"

Rebecca peered. "No."

"I think that might be Jerry Wilton's cousin Shania."

Rebecca didn't evidence much curiosity in Wilton's cousin. "I don't think so. I'm pretty sure that girl works in advertising."

"So she's an employee of the *Herald*?"

"I *think* so. I can't be sure, but there's a girl who looks just like that in advertising. I don't know what her name is."

Maggie made a note of the times and had Rebecca print a still of the young woman.

When the time stamp closed on 9:05 p.m., things got a little more interesting. Someone bolted out of the door under camera 6 and ran into the dark parking lot. A few seconds later, a light-colored sedan peeled out of a space and exited onto the street.

"Who was that?" Maggie asked.

"No idea."

They worked for another hour, painstakingly noting the pale raincoat of the fleeing figure and trying to match it to the outerwear of employees coming in. The figure seemed to have long hair, or at least some sort of ponytail at the nape of their neck, unless it was some appendage on the coat and not hair at all. They wore long pants and light-colored shoes, probably athletic shoes, and carried something tucked under one arm—a purse, a folder, a portfolio, a book? It wasn't much to go on, but they eventually narrowed the possible incoming to three: a man in a trench coat who worked in accounting, a woman Rebecca knew, who worked there somewhere but did not know which department, and a young man who wore sneakers but had entered with a coat over his arm, so they could not be sure it fit their running person. Rebecca and Maggie had cursed out loud at the poor resolution of the average video surveillance system approximately sixty-seven times between the two of them, but this remained the best that they could do. Maggie collected printed stills and they sat down to go through the employee ID photos to try to find a match. Maggie's butt hurt and her stomach rumbled.

They found the guy in accounting easily

enough. The woman turned out to be a secretary for the assistant director of marketing. The young man remained unidentified as there were at least three employees who looked too similar to the grainy image to distinguish. Rebecca also found and printed the ID photo of the young black woman from the advertising department, but Maggie still could not feel certain that it had been her entering the building and not Shania Paulson.

"And there are no doors without cameras, right?" she asked.

"Just fire doors. But they'll set off the alarms if they're opened."

Maggie considered this. "Are you sure?"

The fourth of the five fire exits they visited seemed all right until Maggie followed the wiring from the push bar to a power supply box to the fire alarm—and there the conduit had a slight gap before it entered the red box. Without a flashlight and a step stool she couldn't be sure the wires remained intact, but it made her suspicious. The door advertised the fact that it served as a fire escape only and an alarm would sound if opened, and dust sat on the top of the push bar. But the spiders that live at the lake's shore didn't occupy the top corners as they had in the first three fire doors, and the floor had some faint marks like dirty footprints. The spring rains would have caused anyone using it to track in mud. One such print was cut in half right at the threshold, which could only happen if the door had been open at the time. On top of that the bolt seemed to be permanently retracted. There was nothing latching the door closed.

Maggie asked when they had last had a fire drill, and Rebecca thought it had been several years.

Maggie grasped either side of the ALARM WILL SOUND plate on the push bar, so as not to disturb any fingerprints, and pushed.

Rebecca said, *"Hey!"*

Her voice echoed in the concrete walkway, but only her voice. No alarm sounded.

Maggie held the door open. Rebecca gazed at it. "Crap."

"Crap," Maggie echoed, but for different reasons.

Maggie got her fingerprint kit from the car and dusted the door from top to bottom, including the area where the wires had been cut, but industrial, painted steel doors that aren't cleaned regularly are not good surfaces, and all she found were smudges on the inside and water spots and general grime on the outside. She seemed to have gotten more powder on herself than the door since the wind off the lake hadn't helped matters. Rebecca watched in silence, waiting (upwind) for the electricians to come and fix the wiring.

That particular door opened into a small nook

of the employee parking lot, nestled in between the range of both the employee lot and the visitor lot cameras and easily accessible by both employees and visitors. No one had assigned parking spaces except the publisher and lead editors, so there was no way to tell who would be likely to be parking nearby, and Maggie had already spent enough hours staring at less-than-clear *Herald* surveillance video to relish the idea of more.

Two men had been leaving through one of the employee entrances, then caught sight of their activity and detoured over to ask what was going on. Maggie said nothing. This was Rebecca's territory; she could tell them as much or as little as she saw fit.

One, lanky and morose, thought the recent murders were the work of terrorists bent on jihad, but the other—who turned out to be Roger Correa—said it would more likely be the work of ex-city council members rather than Middle Easterners. The former had received much more bad press from the *Herald* in recent years than the latter.

"So now Jerry," he said, watching Maggie pack up her fingerprinting equipment, which consisted of a jar of powder, a brush, a roll of tape, and some white fingerprint cards carried in a plastic fishing tackle box. "What's up with that? What did he look like?"

She stood, looked at him, and ignored the question.

"Cops got any suspects?"

She refrained from saying, "A building full of them."

He figured out that direct questions weren't direct enough. "Who're you?"

Maggie identified herself.

"Forensic tech, huh? You know what? I could use your help with something. Want to do a . . . what d'ya call 'em, ride-along? See a real-life investigative journalist in action?"

The lanky guy scoffed aloud and walked away. Rebecca hid a subtle eye-roll.

"Come on," Correa continued. "I'll spring for food."

Maggie's stomach growled, loudly and insistently. She hadn't eaten in, oh, about eighteen hours.

Roger Correa grinned. "I'll take that as a yes."

Chapter 20

"I'm sorry about this," he told her two hours later.

Maggie was halfway through a bacon cheeseburger and wishing she'd grabbed more ketchup for the fries. "Why?"

"This is not exactly the exciting chase sequence I had in mind." They'd been parked in front of a closed barber shop on East Twenty-second watching a five-story building across the street that had less than inspiring architecture and standard glass entrance doors. Correa told her they were waiting for the CEO of the recently formed New Horizons to either leave his office or receive visitors there. "This is the more tedious side of investigative journalism."

"You want to talk tedious? Yesterday I spent four hours watching black-and-white motion control-activated video surveillance."

When he smiled, which he did often, the corners of his eyes crinkled and his cheeks hinted at dimples beneath the facial hair. "Discover anything?"

"Nope." She had not lost sight of the fact that Roger Correa worked in that building full of suspects. "Did you say you needed my help with something here?"

"Yeah, if we get the opportunity." He leaned toward her and she tensed, but then he reached over the seat back to retrieve a good-size camera with a long lens from the rear floor. He set it on her lap.

"I'm going to be your cameraman?"

"My long-distance night stuff always comes out fuzzy, and I've been watching you walk around the building with that big Nikon. The paper can't afford to send anyone with me. Hell, they can't afford to pay *me* to be here. They're not going to spring for a photographer. I do all my own these days."

"So you're doing pro bono overtime?"

"That's it exactly. Investigative journalism was the first thing to be cut when the corporations took over."

"So you said." Correa had spent the better part of the previous two hours bringing Maggie up to speed on The State of Journalism in America Today, giving her ears a break only long enough to walk to Michael Symon's burger shop. Maggie had watched the double glass doors in his absence and wondered why she had come along on what might be a snipe hunt. But she had the evening free, and someone who might be a suspect but definitely was a window into the victims' world wanted to talk to her. It seemed like a good idea on all fronts. Plus it kept her from thinking about Ronald Soltis.

"Newspapers, as we know them, really haven't been around that long, mostly just since the end of the Civil War when printers discovered the cash cow known as advertising."

Maggie slurped Diet Coke.

He paused in his lecture to tell her: "Artificial sweetener will kill you, you know."

"I've heard that, too."

"But reporters more or less simply repeated what they were told—which is the way it has to be, most of the time, because no one has the time or the resources to double-check *everything*—and especially with the world wars, it was in a way a matter of patriotism. When we have a common enemy you're not going to make a big deal about a county commissioner taking a bribe because it's important that we all stick together. And that attitude has its place. But in 1971 that attitude changed forever. You know why?"

"Nixon reestablished diplomatic ties with China?"

"No! No—that was important, yes, but—the *New York Times* published the Pentagon Papers. You know what those were?"

Maggie scoffed, audibly. "Of course. Daniel Ellsberg's copies of the Vietnam Task Force Study."

"Yes, everyone remembers that as a scandal and a turning point in public perceptions about Vietnam and the beginning of Nixon's end via

Watergate; it was something that nowadays would be taken for granted. Nowadays any paper that's not crazy about the current administration wouldn't hesitate to publish them, of course they would, but at the time it was a sea change in how the press related to the government. For the first time the media said, we're not trying to be sensationalistic and this isn't all about selling papers, but this is important, and the people need to know it. Period. They had stopped accepting White House press releases as fact, and that cat never really went back into that bag. They weren't trumpeting it like the propaganda that passes for broadcast news today. But they steadily published. The government went to the Supreme Court to get the *Times* to stop, the Supreme Court said stop, and the *Times* stopped. But then the *Washington Post* started publishing them, until the Supreme Court said they had to stop. The *Post* stopped. Fifteen other papers began to publish them. Walter Cronkite interviewed Ellsberg on CBS News. No matter what the administration did, it couldn't *be* stopped."

He paused, the wonder of that glorious and gloriously *responsible* behavior still causing him awe, even so many years later. "We covered that in history class and I got off the bus that day and told my mother I wanted to be a newspaper reporter. I went to the principal and talked him into starting a school newsletter. The cafeteria and the bus loading zone safety rules were my first beat." He shot her an embarrassed smile, as if he shouldn't take as much pleasure in those memories as he did. "Enough about me. What about you? What made you decide to work with dead bodies?"

"They're much more cooperative than live ones."

He laughed. "That, I believe."

She wiped her fingers on a napkin and consolidated her trash into the takeout bag, wondering how much of herself she could share with this man. Ancient history, fine. More recent stuff, not so much. "My dad and I used to watch every cop show we could find. Alex would be out playing ball or in the garage starting a band and I'd be in the living room watching *Starsky & Hutch*, reruns of *Dragnet*, the old *Ellery Queen* show. I loved the idea of solving mysteries, of finding out the answer to the puzzle."

"But you didn't become a cop?"

"Live people—not cooperative. I guess I prefer my mysteries in the abstract sense." That had been true of most areas of her life, perhaps—all her experiences were once-removed, other people's actions, other people's tragedies. Until Jack Renner had come along and sucked her away from the abstract into the very, very concrete.

"Who's Alex?"

"My brother."

Correa reached over and brushed away a lock of hair that had fallen over her shoulder. "You're smiling. You two are close?"

"Yeah, very. Our parents passed away—car accident—a few years ago, so it's just the two of us. The two of us and his wife and two kids, who get dragged all over the country with his cover band."

"Older or younger?"

"Older."

"Ah," he said, continuing to work on his fries. "There's nothing like older brothers to keep you humble. When I told mine I wanted to be a reporter, he beat me up. He said that way I had something to report on. So I reported to mom and dad and he beat me up again. Oh, don't look like that—he didn't hurt me. Just kid stuff. Thus I had been taught everything I needed to know about journalism. You lose your job if you tell the truth, and lose your soul if you don't."

"And now here I am, having come full circle. News as an *entity,* has gone back to being the utterly biased, paid-for-by-sponsor pack of screed it started out as in the seventeen hundreds because it can't turn a profit any other way. And without that profit, no one can afford to create enough new content to fill an entire newspaper. Or an entire twenty-four-hour-a-day news channel—that's why I say not just news*papers,* but news itself, has changed. For instance, a lot of the people you see on broadcast news are not reporters. They will show a video segment that looks exactly like a regular old news broadcast, with some pretty person with a perky smile standing on a sidewalk with a microphone telling you about something that happened. She ends with, 'This is Miss Perfect Teeth in Washington, DC.' But Miss Perfect Teeth never tells the viewing audience who she works for. You *assume* she works for the network, but she actually works for a PR firm or a lobbyist or a candidate. These segments—they're called video news releases—look just as good and sometimes better than the real thing. The TV channel has twenty-four hours to fill up, this is available, and it's free. Newspapers get the same thing in printed press releases. The editors got to get the paper into the rollers, and the release is there, and it's free. So they give it to the copy editor. Why the hell not?"

"But it's not news."

"No, indeed. What *is* news anymore? We have a whole generation of people who don't remember that broadcast news used to mean someone came on and told you what happened. It wasn't four people sitting around bickering like kids on a playground about their *opinion* of what happened. Then they bring on 'experts' and 'consultants' who get a few minutes to push whatever agenda they're plugging that week. They look good, sound professional, and play into the political leanings of the target audience. But when they're done all the audience has gotten is a slightly classier version of *The Jerry Springer Show*, which apparently keeps them entertained enough that they don't complain. But what they *don't* get is useful information."

Roger Correa might be permanently nailed to a soapbox, but Maggie still found this information both fascinating and convincing. Not to mention convincingly scary. "That's awful."

"It is. Everyone keeps saying that it will all sort out and we'll settle into some balanced system of digital and print media paid for with advertising, except that's not panning out because too much of the Internet is free. Even hugely popular sites like the Drudge Report or HuffPost largely repeat content they get elsewhere and barely break even money-wise. Or maybe some system of public funding like PBS, libraries, and schools, which is not as much of a conflict of interests as it first appears. Something. Anything. But I've been watching and waiting for this 'settling' to occur and as of yet, it ain't happening." He rested one temple on the seat back, gazing at her with flashing but discouraged eyes. "So before the *Herald* disappears entirely, tell me your best story, forensic scientist. I'm a reporter. I love stories."

"I'd have to think on that a while. Most crimes are pretty mundane."

"Okay. Wildest thing you've ever seen, then?"

Still she hemmed. "It's pretty gross."

"Come on! I've seen some things, too, you know. Tell me."

"Bugs crawling around under the skin."

He froze, a piece of fried potato halfway to his lips.

"I see insect activity on the skin all the time, of course, but these were quite large, third larval stage probably and moving under the skin, and—"

He dropped the rest of his fries in his paper bag and crumpled it up.

"Sorry," she said. "You *asked*. Speaking of my mad forensic skills, what am I going to be photographing?"

He cleared his throat, pushing the image of squirming Diptera away. "The CEO of New Horizons, a guy named Barkley. Justin Barkley. He's going to be exiting his office any minute now because he has a dinner date with the esteemed councilman from district number twelve."

"And that's . . . bad news? Good news?"

"Well, that all depends on how much money changes hands, doesn't it?"

"I thought reporters kept their scoops secret," Maggie said.

Correa gave a dry chuckle. "From whom? There's no rival paper left to compete against. Broadcast doesn't care what I do because a city manager advisory council meeting doesn't make for sexy TV, and the digital side just wants an update on filming the latest *Avengers* movie in Public Square."

Maggie sat up as a man appeared in the glass doors. He stepped out, letting the door swing shut behind him, and walked to a white Lexus. She snapped photos as best she could in the low light as he drove away.

"That's it?" she asked. "That's what we waited two hours for?"

Roger opened his door and swung out into the damp night. "Yes and no. Come on."

Chapter 21

Jack and his partner visited most of Shania Paulson's usual places to be, but the woman stubbornly refused to materialize. Now he drove to the last one as Riley used his cell phone to argue with two different cell phone carriers. He and Jack were betting on one of three possibilities. One, Shania had murdered her cousin after a falling-out over their investment scheme and then for some reason decided to gut him like a fish and go on the run. This would hardly be outside the realm of their experiences. Family members had been gutting one another on a regular basis since the beginning of time. This would be a tidy solution for the cops, though not so tidy for either Shania or her cousin, and would do nothing to explain the death of Robert Davis.

Two, someone else had killed Jerry Wilton, either with or without Shania's help, and had subsequently killed her. This would create added complications and work for the cops, and wouldn't do much for Shania, either.

Three, someone else killed Jerry Wilton and Shania knew or suspected who that someone else might be, and had made herself scarce before that someone could take her out as well.

This scenario created complications for all three parties: the killer; the cops who had to track Shania down; and the girl herself, who had to stay alive.

Jack rubbed one temple. He hated this stage of detective work, running down leads that went every which way without knowing what might be a complete waste of your time, while evidence sat elsewhere, being destroyed before you could get to it. Maybe that's why he liked his personal way of doing things—waiting until other agencies had compiled a long list of the person's offenses, double-checking a few things himself, and then inviting the target in for a quiet chat, followed by three bullets to the brain. Over and done, with a minimum of fuss.

Maybe he was just lazy.

Riley hung up. "Have I told you lately how much I hate Sprint?"

"Not for at least ten minutes or so."

"They can't get us Davis's call history or text messages until they run the subpoena past their legal department, and of course they're attorneys who work attorney hours and don't come in until the stroke of nine tomorrow. I finally got them to look at the GPS and they said it's not working, must be turned off. No joke, it's turned off, it's probably at the bottom of the lake. Where are we going?"

"Shania's ex-boyfriend's."

"Another one? This girl changes guys like my older girl changes her shade of nail polish."

"You've got to kiss a lot of toads to find one prince."

Riley looked at him as if he had begun speaking in Latin. "Whatever. He lives here?"

Jack pulled the car into the skinny drive leading to a skinny white clapboard house on Madison Avenue near West 65th. "According to DMV and Shania's mother."

"So I asked them," Riley continued, "where the phone had been, just give me the *past* GPS coordinates, and the punk techno-nerd on the phone laughs like I asked him to beam me up. 'They don't store that information,' he said. 'Would crash the system if they tried to store everybody's info like that. Individual apps might, but that would be on the guy's phone, and of course we don't have the phone.' So then I try Verizon about Wilton's phone, because the court came through on that one, too, but they can't do much either because it's an iPhone and they need the code. Privacy, she said. Nice chick, but she said they'd have to get the owner to tell them the code and give them permission to use it. I said the owner is hanging in his living room staring down at his guts all over the floor. I think I made the poor girl cry."

"You're a bad man, Riley."

"I don't mean to be. Anyway, I need to fax them

a copy of the subpoena and they will tell me what they can, but it may not be much. iPhones have security on them that even the NSA can't crack, I guess. We'll have to call the North Koreans if we want to know who Wilton has been talking to."

They got out of the car. Colored lights from the television set danced across the inside of the curtains, and a man lumbered to the door when they knocked. He did not seem happy to see them. But then most people weren't.

"We're looking for Shania Paulson," Riley said.

"You and everybody else. Her mama's called here twice today trying to track that girl down."

"When did you last see her?"

He appeared to ponder this. "Saw her at work. Her work—the Indians game home opener. She was handing out keychains on the concourse level. We talked a bit."

"So you're still friendly?"

His face, which had been as intimidating as the rest of him, softened. "Hard not to be friendly with Shania."

"Do you know her cousin, Jerry Wilton?"

The caution came back. The man was weighing his words before every answer. The house behind him made no noise, the television on mute. A pug waddled out from the hallway, stared at them, huffed, and waddled back into the darkened area. "Met him."

"You heard he's dead."

"Yeah, her mama made that clear, too."

"He and Shania had some business together. You know what that was about?"

"Business? What, like drugs? You think just because Shania is black—"

Riley held up his hand. "Nothing to do with drugs. I mean actual business, like investing."

The man's eyebrows crept up his forehead. "Shania? Invest? I can't see that . . . she's a smart girl, yeah, but Suze Orman she ain't."

Riley asked a few more questions, then finished by pointing out that Jerry Wilton had been brutally murdered and everyone—the cops, the family, and probably the ghost of Jerry Wilton—was concerned for Shania's safety. He left out the part about her being the prime suspect in the same murder, and mentioned only the need to locate the woman.

The ex-boyfriend listened gravely, nodded, and promised to convince Shania to call them, should she reach out to him in any way.

Jack and Riley thanked him for his time, said good night, began to walk back to their car, and then darted around the back of the house and waited for Shania Paulson to come out. Riley took up a spot at the corner of the yard, hidden by a large oak tree. Jack waited in the shadows of the detached garage and thought of excuses to give the homeowner, should he decide to take out the garbage and wonder why two men were standing in his backyard.

The night drifted cool and damp over Jack's face. A rapid transit train rumbled through the valley behind them. Voices carried from the community garden nearby, teens hanging out where they probably shouldn't be after dark. Tree branches gave rushed whispers to the wind above his head, and birds clucked and twittered. Birds never slept, Jack had long decided. No matter what hour of the day or night you were up, some species would be out there making noise.

Whoever had sliced up Jerry Wilton was a dangerous person. He—or she—had killed at least two people so far and had gotten away with it, but more than that, had *enjoyed* it. He had great fun making it clear to the police that Davis had not been a suicide, or a fluke. He had perhaps a business-related motive for the murders, or perhaps it had been a personality conflict, but either way, once committed to the action, he couldn't resist putting his own personal flair on the tableau. He was, in short, the kind of killer that Jack hunted.

Hunt*ed,* present tense. Because no matter what he told Maggie Gardiner, he had no intention of abandoning his work. He would tone it down for a while to keep them both out of jail, but eventually he would get back to it. He saw no point in stopping. His soul was already damned, if that were an issue, and the world not yet safe for everyone, which *is* the issue. To stop trying to help the innocent would be weak. It would be *wrong*.

As he mentally reaffirmed his own commitments, Shania Paulson exited the rear door of the house, backpack strung around both shoulders, long hair pulled through the back of an Indians cap. Tall and lean, she wore jeans, running shoes, and a dark blue T-shirt with long sleeves and a low scoop neck. Even in the dim light, Jack could see why she didn't lack for male attention.

The man of the house appeared behind her, telling her that she ought to stay.

"If they tracked me here, he could, too," she told him, trotting down the steps and onto the grass. She stopped cold when she caught sight of Jack.

He held out his badge and had gotten out the first two letters of the word *police* when she bolted, running across the backyard, exactly between himself and Riley. Tufts of grass flew up from her heels as she sped away.

Animal instinct took over, and Jack's body leapt into motion before his brain caught up. He forgot the damp air and the chattering of the birds, and forgot that he could barely see and there were no streetlights where she led. The night reduced to moving and breathing. They were the gazelle and the pursuing cheetah.

Except this gazelle was damn fast and knew the territory.

The backyard exited into another backyard; the girl ran through the houses and across the street. She plunged between benches and a group of teens marking the entrance to the EcoVillage community garden. He could hear himself and Riley shouting things like, "Police! Shania! We're here to help you! You may be in danger!" in between puffs of exertion. She either didn't hear them, didn't believe them, or didn't care.

She reached the ironwork gate for the community garden and pulled herself up and over without visible exertion or pause. Jack did the same, with, he felt sure, visible exertion and great pause lest he impale himself on the narrowed tips of the fence posts. When his feet met the ground with a bone-jarring thud he hoped there wouldn't be a corresponding fence on the other side of the park. If so, he needed to catch Shania Paulson before she reached it.

The red trim of her jacket flashed in front of him, about twenty feet away. He left Riley to do his own cursing and climbing, and pounded after her. He shouted a few more things, but they had no more effect than his first attempts.

She led him through the winding sidewalks and the neatly staked and labeled vegetables, past a small potting shed. His lungs were protesting. He could hear the shouts of the teens as they egged

Riley on over the fence. His stocky partner probably represented the most entertainment they'd had all week.

There was, indeed, a corresponding fence on the other side of the park, but not as tall as the entrance, Jack saw with relief. Shania Paulson already straddled the top.

"Stop!" he called, stretching for any part of her he could grab. "We're trying to save your life!"

"Let me go!" she shouted, real panic in her voice, and his fingers just brushed the sole of her shoe as she flipped over the top of the fence.

He tried to vault it as she had, but swinging his frame, with its hundred extra pounds, required a different mass times velocity equation. The chain-link wobbled under him and he tumbled, rather than jumped, over the top. His arm slipped, and the wire peaks of the fence top nearly took out his left eye. He landed awkwardly and his knee would complain about it later. In fact, it said the hell with it and started complaining immediately.

He straightened and realized where Shania Paulson was heading.

Up a narrow sidewalk and over an elevated path sat the rapid transit station. He could hear the next Red Line train clattering up the tracks.

He shouted her name at her disappearing form. Still no effect.

She slowed to squeeze past three men moving in the opposite direction. Jack heard her voice but couldn't make out the words. He stepped onto the elevated walkway, no more than twenty feet long, with a ten-foot-high chain-link on both sides. The concrete gave him great traction and he might have gained a yard on her . . . at least until he figured out the gist of what she had said to the three men.

They formed a barrier at the other end of the walkway. Two were black and one was white and all three were big, dressed in sweats, hands in their pockets, shoulder-to-shoulder. The same grim look on each face. Behind them, Shania pulled open the glass door of the station and dashed past the attendant on duty. He didn't even have time to protest that she didn't have a bus pass or even $2.25 in exact change.

Jack put on an extra burst of speed and shouted that he was a cop.

The men didn't move. Instead, as he drew close enough to invade their personal space, they brought up arms and fists and he ran into a human brick wall.

Next thing he knew he was sitting on the sidewalk, hand scraped, and a considerable amount of wind expelled from his lungs.

The direct approach hadn't worked.

With stinging fingers, he pulled out his badge and shouted, "Cop! I'm a cop!"

The men reconsidered. One backed up, one looked as if that just made things more fun, the third considered the whole matter anew while Jack realized that not only one Red Line train had just pulled into the station, but two. He hauled himself up with a fistful of chain-link and got back into motion, protesting knee and all. The men let him brush by with only a shoulder bump. Rescuing a damsel in distress from a pursuing male was one thing. Getting hung up with the cops seemed like another thing entirely.

Jack also sped past the attendant. The guy shouted but didn't leave his booth.

Jack had to make a choice about which platform Shania would have chosen—heading east or heading west? She'd have probably picked the first to arrive, and since they were both now standing still he couldn't tell which one that was. He dashed down the first set of steps, hoping she'd be panicked enough to take the first exit open to her. Heading east, back to the city.

The train began to move just as he hit the last step. He checked each car for Shania as it passed, though by the last car the train became a blur of color and glass.

With it out of the way he looked over to the other platform, just in time to see Shania Paulson stumble into one of the train cars there and cling to a pole.

He'd never get up the steps and over to the other side before the train left. Already the doors had shut. And he wasn't about to jump down onto the rails—he'd probably touch the wrong one, and even if he didn't electrocute himself he still wouldn't be able to get into the car.

He caught her eye as the train began to move. She stared at him with fear, weariness—and just a little bit of triumph.

The train rumbled away, heading into the western suburbs.

The tiled steps behind him vibrated as Riley nearly fell down them. He slowed to a near stop when he saw Jack, alone, on an empty platform. He swiped one hand across his face and gasped for air. It must not have felt sufficient because he leaned over, hands on knees, sucking in oxygen to the depths of his lungs. Jack did the same, though with less body language.

Then Riley straightened, threw his head back, and asked, "Are we sure she doesn't *play* for the Indians?"

Chapter 22

Maggie followed Roger Correa across the parking lot in front of the building at East 22nd, feeling more uncertain with every step. "Mr. Correa—"

"Roger, for heaven's sake. We just spent two hours knee-to-knee."

"Not really, no, but fine. Roger. If you are planning to break into this CEO's office or something like that, then you can—"

"No one's breaking into anything. Think I'd bring along a member of the police department for a caper like that? Nah." He splashed through a small puddle in the asphalt and held the door for her. "We're only going to go where we're invited."

She peered into the square, empty lobby of the place before stepping through the second set of doors. Her shoes squeaked on the linoleum. Two weak overhead lights let her see the place. Two vinyl chairs, framed posters of happy teens under the New Horizons logo, and a receptionist's desk that didn't have so much as a paper clip on its blotter. "Who's inviting us?"

"A friend of mine." He continued up a barely lit hallway to a stairwell. It turned out to be even more dimly lit than the lobby, so much so that

Correa reached back and took her hand. It smelled like an apartment building long past its prime, a combination of boiled cabbage, stale beer, and uncleaned toilets. A shaggy-looking man appeared on the first landing, and Maggie's unease festered and grew.

The shaggy-looking man, however, brushed by them without a word. Roger Correa let go of her fingers and led her up to the second-floor hallway. There they found an office, one equipped with more than sufficient lighting, and a lone female behind a desk.

"Evening, Angie," Roger said.

Angie appeared to be about Maggie's age, with curly brown hair and a few acne scars. She had thin arms and fluttery hands and seemed unsurprised, yet not happy, to see Correa.

"Angie, Maggie, Maggie, Angie. Maggie's helping me out with photography tonight."

Maggie nodded at the woman, who returned the gesture while the furrow between her eyes deepened. "I could lose my job, you know."

"Don't worry. Maggie here is accustomed to confidentiality."

Angie turned watery blue eyes toward her, apparently waiting for verification. Maggie nodded again, even though she felt she was already keeping too many things in confidence for comfort. Jack and his history, in fact, had greatly strained her confidentiality limit. But she couldn't tell Angie that, and certainly not Roger Correa.

"Do you have the statements?" he asked.

"Yeah." The woman opened a desk drawer and rummaged around. Her office didn't have much in the way of décor, just another New Horizons poster and a bulletin board skewered with push-pins. They held receipts, memos, lists of names, and a blue "First Place" ribbon. It did not specify First Place in what. A glass paperweight in the shape of a cat and a framed photograph of Angie with a young boy sat on the desk, the only personal items in a sea of folders and invoices.

She handed Correa a sheet of paper.

He scanned it. "Seriously? How is he getting away with this? The prison system feeds people for two ninety-seven a day."

"The county administrator asked him that at a meeting last week."

"What'd he say?"

"That this isn't a prison."

"What is it?" Maggie asked, tired of listening to a conversation she couldn't understand.

"We are sitting in a halfway house called New Horizons. It's a residence for the recently released, such as the gentleman we passed in the stairwell. Residents are provided with a small room, private bath, basic cable, and three squares a day. There are monitors here to keep a lid on any drug or alcohol use, do bed checks, arbitrate disputes, and provide a spot of counseling and job hunt assistance. The aim is to ease the ex-cons' reentry into society and reduce recidivism."

Maggie said, "Sounds like a worthy program."

"It is," Angie hastened to assure her. "It is a worthy program."

"Except it doesn't work," Roger said. "Here, take a photo of this invoice, would you?"

"It could," Angie argued. "It *should*."

"But has it?"

She sighed, fingering a wrinkle in her brow that threatened to become permanent as Maggie snapped a picture of the paper. "Gene got arrested for disorderly and went back in for at least sixty days. Mohammad was found riding around in a stolen car but managed to explain it away as a misunderstanding. Marjorie is pregnant . . . again. Kelly failed his last two drug tests and Mr. Barkley had to call the prosecutors to try to get the warrant postponed. He has to keep him here. Our numbers go any lower and R and C will revoke our contract."

"That's the Ohio Department of Rehabilitation and Correction," Correa explained to Maggie.

"Thanks," she said. "I still don't know what we're doing here."

"New Horizons currently houses five male inmates—or clients, as Angie here prefers—and two females. Guess what their operating budget is, contracted and paid for by the state of Ohio and Cuyahoga County?" He waited for Maggie to guess, but when she frowned at him he continued without an answer. "Two point five million."

She looked around. "I'm guessing it didn't go into furnishings."

Angie pulled out a small case and started up an e-cigarette. "It sure doesn't go into my salary, I can tell you that."

"They charge the Ohio R and C fifteen dollars per inmate, sorry, client for food, let's start with that. The prison system feeds inmates for twenty percent of that. CEO Barkley got a letter from R and C last month asking why so much. He said it was because New Horizons purchases organic items from local farmers in order to support small businesses and assist in purging the effects of the drugs these people have been on. He quoted some New Agey type book on the subject and claimed it was having wonderful effects on the inm—clients. Is it having a wonderful effect, Angie?"

She puffed. "They eat mac and cheese four times a week."

"CEO Barkley does, however, pay six figures to a lobbyist to drum up more clients and contracts and well-meaning donors. For six figures, you would think he'd work very hard for this establishment. How many times have you seen said lobbyist on these premises, Angie?"

"Twice," she said, with the weary air of

someone who has been over all this, and more than once. "In three years."

"He did do one good job for his friend Barkley, though. He introduced him to the one bad apple in the county exec's advisory board, guy named Elliott. Barkley bought the guy a junket to Las Vegas, and when the topic of New Horizons came up on the board's agenda, Elliott vouched for them all the way. It kept the questions to a minimum for a good year or two—until someone at R and C noticed New Horizons's abysmal rate of return on investment."

"Huh," Maggie said. "Okay, that's all very interesting. But—"

"How do I know all this?" Correa went on. "I know all this because Angie has been letting me sneak peeks at her CEO's correspondence for the past six months. Because Angie"—he beamed at the woman behind the desk, while she just looked unhappy—"doesn't like liars any more than I do."

"What I meant to ask was, why are we sitting here? Why hasn't R and C or the county or both opened an investigation or revoked their contract?"

"That's the beauty of county corruption. It's all about defining terms. Overpriced food is used because it's supposedly organic. A coconspirator is a consultant. A contractor paid four times usual rate just ran into errors made by the builder. Everything can be explained. It's all for a good cause. That's the added aura of social programs. No one wants to be the meanie who questions too much. If the people running it say it's necessary to health and well-being, that's accepted as true even when there is absolutely no evidence to support it."

"I can't lose my job," Angie said, interrupting his philosophical digressions with a focus on practicality. "My kid has to have a special tutor. And my asshole landlord is talking about raising the rent again."

"So what are you going to do?" Maggie asked Correa.

"Publish, of course. Lay it out in an article so clearly that the county board can't ignore it, so R and C has what they need to act, so Barkley will go to jail along with his consultant and—dare I hope—board member Elliott. A real sociologist will be brought in to run this place with Angie's assistance, and maybe the less fortunate children who come to this program might actually be helped by it. Win-win for everybody. Here, take a picture of this, too. It's the plane ticket they bought for Elliott."

Angie put away her e-cig, stowing it in its little box. "Anything else? My kid's waiting for me, and my mom's waiting to get rid of my kid for the night."

Correa rose and shook her hand. "Thank you, Angela, for doing what's right. You've earned the gratitude of the city, even though they will never know it."

"Yeah, yeah," she said.

Correa and Maggie exited out the front doors. She looked around with a nightmare vision of CEO Barkley returning to get something he left in his office and stumbling onto their nefarious purpose. "You've been working on this for six months?"

"It's a time-consuming process. That's why the first axes to fall at any paper cut out investigative reporting."

"Why haven't you published already? It seems like you have plenty."

He moved closer to her, his arm brushing hers. "It's probably like a criminal trial. The prosecutor thinks he has a slam dunk, until the defense attorney gets ahold of it. I think I've got proof incontrovertible, until a copy editor or editor gets ahold of it. They worry about staying on good terms with the county exec's office and advertisers."

"Was Robert Davis holding you back?"

He stepped over a water-filled hole in the pavement. "Are you interrogating me, Maggie?"

"Yes."

He laughed. "Okay, fair enough. Yes, Bob did stand in my way. A lot. But that was his job and he did seem to care about doing it, I'll say that for him. But it wasn't just him, it was also Roth and the publisher and the state guy—"

"State guy?"

"Leroy Dunston, he covers state news. He felt I encroached on his territory too much since a lot of county funding comes from the state, so he should be reporting on its use. Problem is, the state doesn't have enough manpower to pay attention to what the counties are doing, most of the time, and neither does Dunston."

"How *will* you get this story into print?"

"Persistence"—he grinned—"is the key to success in every endeavor, from artistry to love. My mother used to say that."

"I'd say there can be a thin line between persistence and stalking."

He found that funny. "The subjects of my stories would say, 'Between persistence and harassment.' No one said journalism was easy. And now you're thinking that I'm one step closer to Davis dangling from the end of a rope."

"Strap, actually."

"What?"

She explained that the rope used was actually a flat mesh strap. Since Printing Supervisor Harding had been there, she assumed that detail would have been spread throughout the *Herald* office.

"That's right, I heard that," Correa said. "Ironic, really."

"Why?" She handed him back his camera.

"A strapline is what we call a secondary heading, a subheading under the headline."

"Why is that ironic?"

"Because it's something a copy editor would write." The pathos of this seemed to touch him and his face slid into sadness. "Poor guy." They reached the car and he jerked open the passenger door for her.

Maggie asked, "What happens if the county closes this place and Angie is out of a job?"

"Then she's screwed. But she knew that was a possible future for her the moment she started talking to me." He stopped, turning to look at her. "That's the kind of bravery they don't give you medals for. No one will ever hear her name. I do what I do for those kind of people. And I appreciate"—he reached out and stroked the edge of her jaw—"all the help I can get."

She stepped back. If he thought this was some kind of date, he had another thought coming. But she didn't step too far. As most intensely driven men do, Correa had his own kind of magnetism.

He didn't seem shot down by this not-so-subtle rejection, just got in the car and drove her back to the *Herald* parking lot.

Chapter 23

The next morning Maggie arrived at the lab early, having woken long before her alarm would have gone off. Enough with fuzzy video cameras and oral testimony by too-often-deceptive humans. She needed to get back to her roots: trace evidence, bloodstains, and gunshot residue.

She also needed to call her brother, who had left two messages asking her to do exactly that, but told herself it would be best to wait a few hours. Musicians were not early risers.

She started with Ronald Soltis. The officer at the scene hadn't asked why she taped the back of the victim's clothes, when she didn't usually tape gunshot victims. Guns didn't require the killer to get up close and personal as in bludgeoning or stabbings. Her coworkers might get curious if they happened to notice.

She found a lot of fibers on the back of Soltis's jacket and a few hairs, including a long blond one. A gangster always has to have his moll. She wondered what the current term would be for the girlfriend of a "gangsta" but figured she probably didn't want to know. He had some brown cotton, crumbles of vegetation that could be marijuana or just debris from autumn leaves, and four dog hairs from something large and dark brown. The dark blue trilobal fibers gave her a bad moment, since they were similar to the upholstery in Jack's car, but she reminded herself that dark blue interiors were common. The polarizing microscope told her that the fibers on Soltis were nylon, and most car interiors were polyester.

To be sure, she pulled out her mounted slides from the previous vigilante cases, and the shade of blue appeared markedly different. Even better, she did not find Greta's white fur. Maggie let out a breath she hadn't known she was holding and got another cup of coffee to celebrate. After three sips the doubt began to creep back in. Jack knew what she had found during her investigation of the vigilante murders that had led her to him. He would be careful not to leave those clues again. Absence of proof was not proof of absence. Not in his case.

On the tape from the upper half of Soltis's jacket back she picked up some particles of gunpowder, tiny disks with holes in them. The holes were there to increase the surface area—the surface would have burned, so the more surface area, the faster the burn and the more power behind the bullet as it exited the gun. A common type, known as perforated disk gunpowder. It told her nothing about who might have pulled the trigger.

So her Ronald Soltis investigation came out a

wash. She found nothing to implicate Jack, and nothing to point her in the direction of any other killer. Unless Ronnie's killer had long blond hair. Sometimes molls got angry.

She turned to more pressing matters, the *Herald* murder victims. The trace evidence on Robert Davis's shirt hadn't told her much, but now that she had Jerry Wilton's tapings to compare, she might find items in common. *That* would be interesting. To strangle an able-bodied adult male, one would have to get a good amount of leverage on the strap ends, pull tight, and not let up. The victim, if not unconscious, would be struggling and kicking and trying to pull the strap away from his throat and, if he could think fast enough, striking at the person behind him. Either way it took a lot of up-close and personal work, and the front of the killer should be pressed against the back of the victim. So she paid special attention to the shirt *backs*.

Robert Davis, as she had told the detectives earlier, had a number of fibers, hairs, and some dog fur. Most of the hair seemed to be his, but some errant strands were a sandy brown dyed blond, a dark brown nearly black hair, and two others of an auburn shade. Fibers were red cotton, pink polyester, blue nylon, light blue Dacron, white cotton, brown cotton, green cotton. Nothing exciting.

She examined a flake that looked like a piece

of popcorn husk, a number of shards of apparent wood, sawdust or maybe paper dust—no surprise there. She also found a few miniscule orbs that looked like tiny footballs or maybe Sugar Smacks, back when they were called Sugar Smacks, before the marketing execs caught on to the idea that sugar plus children produced a not-good image in buyers' minds.

Interesting. Unfortunately, all of it told her nothing.

She put away the tapings and mounted slides she'd made from them and pulled out the sheets from Jerry Wilton's clothing. Following the same theory, she examined the tapings from the back of his shirt. If the killer had to insist on evisceration, he had done her a favor by hanging the body first instead of letting it rest or roll around in the offal. That would have soaked the shirt, possibly washed off some of the trace evidence, and made it more difficult to pick up with tape. Not to mention messier. If he had taken the knife to the back it would have really screwed her up—duh, she reminded herself, of course slicing a person open from the back would not have the same effect. The spine and ribs would be in the way.

"What are you up to?" Carol appeared at her elbow, startling her.

"Pondering the various route options for disembowelment."

"You worry me when you say things like that."

Carol rested against the workbench, worrying a heart-shaped pendant around her neck that her daughter had given her. Though Maggie was technically acting supervisor, Carol had taken over the bulk of Denny's duties in his absence, dispatching the "youngsters" Josh and Amy, approving overtime and turning in hours worked to payroll, distributing processing requests, organizing subpoenas, and making sure the coffee cabinet remained stocked. She was babying Maggie, but with the *Herald* murders on her plate Maggie was more than willing to be babied.

"Your appointment with Dr. Michaels is this morning."

Except about that.

"I'm kind of bu—"

"You can't cancel it again, Maggie. It's mandatory. Man-da-tor-y. As in, you have to go or they stop giving you paychecks."

Maggie had to laugh. "They can't do that!"

"You really want to find out? Exactly what are you so busy with, anyway?"

"Hairs and fibers," Maggie elaborated as she adjusted the microscope settings. "Lots of synthetic fibers. Young man, liked to work out, so that's not surprising. What are you doing?"

"Supply orders."

"Any word on when Denny will be back?"

"I think he'd love to be back now, except his wife would probably slit his throat if he tried to leave. Not that I blame her. The first few months, your whole life revolves around getting sleep whenever and wherever you can."

"How's the baby doing?"

"Not sleeping like one, that's for sure. But gaining weight, so they're happy."

"Huh."

"What? Babies are supposed to gain weight."

"No, this taping. Wilton has cottons—red, blue, green, but the blue looks like the same shade as the fibers on Davis."

"Yeah, blue cotton is so unusual."

"Sarcasm is not becoming in a woman of your stature," Maggie told her. "I know, if it's denim, then it's useless, but still . . . and hey, those little orbs."

"You're getting into the paranormal, now?"

Maggie switched the microscope to a higher magnification, though peering at tape on a sheet of acetate did not make for an ideal image. If she really wanted to get a look at something, she would have to dissolve the tape adhesive and mount the item on a glass slide. "Pollen."

"Gesundheit."

"No, plant pollen. Ooo—a dog hair, too."

"It's nice to see you enjoying your work." Carol shoved off the desk. "I have to get back to the fingerprint searches. Congratulations on narrowing your search to someone with a flower and a dog."

"Wilton lived in an apartment. He had neither flowers nor dogs."

"Then you'll have to narrow it down to the specific flower and the specific dog."

"Dogs I can probably do. Flowers—not so much. Hardly anyone's looked at pollen since television went to color. It's a very dying art." Maggie leaned back and rubbed her eyebrow. "Sort of like print journalism."

"Sometimes," Carol admitted, "I have trouble following your brain down the paths it takes."

"That makes two of us," Maggie said.

Chapter 24

Stephanie Davis didn't seem as stunned to find cops on her doorstep as she had been the first time, but she did seem curious. "Did you find who killed him?" she asked upon opening the door.

They admitted that no, they hadn't, and that they would like to look through anything Bob had brought home from the *Herald* offices, if she wouldn't mind (and even if she would, though they saw no reason to go there unless necessary). Oh, and Maggie here would like to collect some fur from your dog.

Stephanie Davis had no objection. She seemed glad of the company.

"Want something to eat? Just like the past hundreds of years, all people do is bring me food. I guess it's all they can do, really, so they do it even though there's a limit to how much even teenage boys can eat, and I'm on a chronic diet. It's not like I'm going to have hordes of out-of-town relatives descending. Neither of us had large families." She led them through the kitchen. It did indeed smell of cold rigatoni and potato salad. "The boys are in school. It sounds weird, sending them to school, but when they were home we all just sat around looking at each other and that wasn't doing them any good, either. Or me."

Her face scrunched and it seemed, at the mention of her sons, that she would burst into sobs. She even turned toward the wall that held their class pictures, framed eight-by-ten glossies.

Age-wise, Ronald Soltis would have been right in between them, Maggie thought. She wondered how his mother was dealing with her grief.

Stephanie Davis fought back her tears and waved them into a small spare bedroom.

It held an old roll-top desk, unlocked and opened with some neat stacks of paper on it and pens sticking out of its cubbies, a twin bed, and a sewing machine in its own cabinet. "This is what he'd use as a desk."

"This is all the stuff he brought home from work?" Riley clarified. "Anything else? Filing cabinet? Briefcase?"

"He was a copy editor." Once again, she explained. "The biggest part of his job was approving other people's stories and doing the layout. He couldn't really do that at home. When he was a reporter, yeah, he'd bring work home all the time, but as a copy editor . . . sometimes he'd bring stories to read, but then he'd take them back. That was about it."

Riley sat down at the desk, using the one chair, and Jack stood beside him. Stephanie Davis turned to Maggie. "You wanted to see my dog?"

She led the forensic scientist out the back slider. The day was damp but clear and the dog trundled over, delighted to have visitors. "This is Killer. Bob thought that was a funny name, since he's so *not*."

Maggie petted Killer, which only made him more excited. He used the entire lower half of his body to wag his tail. She took out a disposable comb and ran it through his fur a couple times. The strands quickly accumulated.

"He sheds like a bitch—no pun intended," Stephanie confirmed. She sat on the edge of the deck, tilting her face toward the spotty sunlight.

Maggie perched on the step. Killer liked being combed so she gave him a few more passes. "We're sorry to disturb you."

"That's all right. I needed a break. There's an overwhelming amount of his crap to clean out." Slight pause. "Sorry, that sounds terrible. But seriously! He thought cleaning out a closet was beneath him, and yet he never wanted me to ever get rid of a shirt or a magazine or his bowling trophy from grade school, so it just accumulated. I'm going to have so much more room here now."

"I understand," Maggie said, though she didn't, really. She had been thrilled to rid her life of Rick's junk and have a space that was all her own—but they had been divorcing.

Stephanie fingered the necklace she wore, two boy-shaped charms with blue and red stones. "Like that room in there, I'm going to empty that out and then the boys can each have their own room. It will cut the squabbles down, I think, and they're well past the age where they need a little privacy. And money! I can live so much more economically without him turning the thermostat up or down and wanting to eat out all the time and not caring how much we pay in loan interest every month."

She was flat-out babbling, but Maggie let her. Obviously Stephanie Davis needed someone to talk to. A confessional mood might lead her to confess something interesting.

"I'm losing an income, yes, a substantial income. But there's insurance, and I can sell that ridiculously expensive car he just bought. And his golf club collection. That's going to take some work. There's a lot of money in those stupid clubs and I don't know what's worth what."

"Uh-huh."

"Maybe it's shock, making me talk like this. Do you think it's shock?"

"It could be," Maggie said. "Everyone grieves in their own way."

"Honestly, I don't think I could be described as grieving in any way, shape, or form. But it's kind of you to say so." She regarded Killer as he licked her fingers.

Maggie took the opportunity. "You told the detectives your husband had been talking to someone about someone named Wilson. He had a coworker named Wilton. Could that have been the name he mentioned?" She didn't mention Jerry Wilton's murder, unsure if anyone had told Stephanie about it. From the absent look on the woman's face, no one had.

"I guess it could have been. I really thought it was Wilson, though."

In her soothing voice, recently practiced on Denny's new baby, Maggie assured her, "Okay. Just checking."

Stephanie had not veered from her main train of thought, her relationship with her late husband. "I blame my religion, really, that I got married. If I hadn't been raised to have morals—but if I wanted to sleep with a guy, I had to marry him. So I married him only because I wanted to sleep with him. If not for that upbringing I could have just slept with him, moved on, and maybe found someone I was actually compatible with."

"You weren't happy?" Maggie stated the obvious, for lack of any other comment to make.

"Never, really. He was. He thought everything was fine. No matter what I said, he'd just brush it off. So I figured I had—literally—made my bed and would lie in it. I'm lazy, maybe, and I couldn't face a divorce. I can't be the bad guy, and he definitely would have made me the bad guy. I'm sorry for him, too, not just myself. How horrible to have a spouse, someone you think you love, who is actually hoping you'll leave the house and never come back. How terrible is that?" She rubbed her hands together as if she wished she had a cigarette or a drink or something to occupy them. "But just the idea now that I can have my life back, I can sleep when I'm tired and eat when I'm hungry and get the boys through these last few years before adulthood without him poisoning their minds with stereotypes and prejudices and—I feel like I won the lottery. I should be wearing black and crying myself to sleep and walking around in a daze, and instead I'm stuffing all his clothes into garbage bags and singing with the radio as I'm doing it. I know I'm probably talking myself into a jail cell here," she added, "going on and on about how much better my life is going to be without him."

"No," Maggie told her, though she was not at all sure about that.

"But I can't help it! I'm so sorry for my boys, of course—every time I think about them I want to start screaming. Bob wasn't much of a father, they were old enough to notice how many football games and band concerts he missed, never had time for heart-to-hearts about girls or grades—but he was still the only one they'll ever have. But all I can think about is myself. And myself wants to run singing through a meadow. Maybe turn cartwheels, except I'd probably throw out my back. Isn't that awful?"

"Maybe it's human," Maggie said.

"When I go to bed now, I can go to *sleep*. Do you know he had to have sex *every single night?* After twenty years, still, every single night! I looked forward to my periods, they were the only breaks I got. So I work all day, make dinner, clean up, do the laundry, pack lunches, pay bills, make sure the garbage is out, and then I finally crawl into bed at the end of the day—and I have one more chore to do before I will be permitted to close my eyes. Sure, I could have refused, but the pouting and drama—you know what men are like, it's easier just to give them what they want so that they'll shut up and go away. I know I didn't handle it right, should have had a lot more communication. Bob wasn't a bad guy at all . . . in many ways he was a perfectly good guy. So I didn't help anything, I didn't, certainly not with the sex. Which was lousy, but again, I do admit that that's my own fault as much as his. I could have given him some pointers, told him what to do. But you know, it's like a diet, if you aren't going to have the discipline to stick with it, then you might as well not start. You know what I'm saying? I mean, his idea of foreplay was—"

Jack opened up the slider and said that they were done, sparing Maggie the titillation of learning what Robert Davis's idea of foreplay had been.

Both Killer and Stephanie Davis seemed disappointed to lose their guests so soon. Stephanie apologized for "bending Maggie's ear," offered them more food, and forced a banana bread on them before she would let them out of the house. Maggie took it. They had a toaster at the lab and Carol loved fruit breads.

They drove away, Maggie in the backseat of the department-issue unmarked vehicle. "Learn anything?" Riley asked her. "Looked like you two were bonding."

"Stephanie would bond with a coat on a hanger at this point, poor woman, and prefers strangers with no vested interest in her husband's memory."

"She's glad he's dead, isn't she?"

"And not afraid to say so. But you guys don't suspect her—because she's female? Because her husband outweighed her by about one hundred percent? Because she's a mother?"

Riley said, "Because she was dead asleep when we came to tell her the news, and she doesn't strike me as sufficiently sociopathic to pull that off."

Jack said, "Because someone would have noticed her around the *Herald* offices. Besides, she wasn't married to Jerry Wilton, and he's dead, too."

"Okay," Maggie said. "As long as you have a good reason."

Riley asked Maggie if the new widow had told her anything interesting.

"Davis recently bought a, quote, ridiculously expensive car, unquote. How about you? Find something good?"

"Nada. Clippings and printouts of stories, nothing that looks like a motive. And the car is a Chrysler 300. Not cheap, no, but it's hardly a Porsche. What wives think is too expensive and what actually *is* too expensive can be two different things. I speak from experience."

"Champagne isn't too expensive unless you're on a beer budget. I thought he was worried about losing his job."

"Editor says no."

Maggie set the banana bread on the seat next to her. "He also seems to have been a bit of a sex addict. Are we sure there isn't a mistress lurking in the background?"

"Not unless he had a burner phone as well. The call history we got all seems to be work-related. The digital content manager, the editor, one of the advertising guys. His layout editor—also known as the typesetter even though they haven't used type in a few decades—is a matronly sort with four kids. Besides, then where would Jerry Wilton come in?"

"Maybe the mistress had more than one, um, client?" Jack suggested.

"You," Riley told his partner, "have a nasty mind."

• • •

At her house, the dog again scratching at the slider, the radio tuned to 105, Stephanie Davis dialed a number she had found among her husband's papers. The bastard had started locking that desk months ago, but his hiding places had been as unimaginative as his lovemaking. She'd found the key easily enough . . . not that she'd expected to find anything in it except the bill for whatever he'd bought on impulse recently. But she'd stumbled on something much better.

"It's me," she said into the receiver. "I found some very interesting items in Bob's desk this morning—good thing, too, because the cops showed up an hour later." *Pause.* "Of course not. I moved them." *Pause.* "Well, I think we should talk. Don't you?" *Pause.* "No, Tower City. By the fountain." *Pause.* "Fine. One hour."

She hung up, smiling at nothing until the dog on the other side of the glass caught her eye. "Sorry, baby. We'll go for a walk later, okay? Right now Mommy has the boys' college tuitions to take care of."

She walked down the hallway, singing with the radio.

Chapter 25

Jack and Riley asked Maggie if she would stop at Shania Paulson's apartment with them now that they had a warrant to search it. The girl was still in the wind, either obviously scared or obviously guilty, and they needed any clue they could get as to where to look next.

"We've checked every ex-boyfriend, every gal pal, and every coworker she has. Her mom gave them all up, worried about her baby girl," Riley reported as they looked around the tidy kitchen. Whoever had trashed Jerry Wilton's office had not made it to Shania's place. Unless, of course, it had *been* Shania.

"You went through her whole address book?" Maggie asked.

"Didn't find one."

"I meant on her computer."

"Computer's missing. It's probably in that backpack she's toting."

Jack leaned in the doorway, checking his text messages, as Riley answered her questions. Maggie did a slow circle, peeking into the matching canisters on the counter. "Cell phone?"

"She left it here. Call history doesn't tell us anything except that she talked to her cousin Jerry once in a while, which we already knew."

"That's smart, leaving it here. Car?"

"In her parking space. She's on foot. And," Riley added, "*what* a foot."

"Workplace?"

"Called in sick the morning after Wilton's murder and hasn't been heard from since. We checked all that. Give us a *little* credit."

"Well, I don't know what you expect me to do here."

"Look at the fibers and the dirt on the floor and tell me where she might have gone."

"Seriously? Who do you think I am, Sherlock Holmes?"

Riley and Jack looked at each other, then back at her, and said nearly in unison, "Yes."

Maggie rolled her eyes and left the room.

In the bedroom she opened some drawers and checked out the medicine cabinet. She didn't want to disappoint the two cops, but she wasn't Sherlock Holmes and in any case there wasn't much she could do without a microscope. Feeling a bit like a voyeur, she examined Shania Paulson's jewelry (understated but quality), reading material (mostly nonfiction, about proper muscle maintenance, the collapse of the economy, investment advice for women, and the occasional bodice-ripper), and clothing (quite a bit bolder than Maggie dared, but from the photos around the room, Shania Paulson had the figure for it). The bathroom held the usual million-and-one accoutrements that women needed to face the world every day, hair items, makeup items, a large tray of nail polishes and files. Maggie paused to admire a few of the shades, then got back to work. The cabinet held an array of vitamins and supplements, but no prescription medication; Shania must have been a healthy young woman. Or, Maggie corrected herself, *is* a healthy young woman.

She took another look at the photos around the room and the clothes in the drawers. Then she pulled a duffel bag out of the bottom of the closet.

Jack had wandered to the doorway. It trapped her inside, but that didn't bother her so much anymore. Perhaps she had grown accustomed to hanging around with a prolific serial killer. Perhaps they were both focused on other things at the moment.

"Are you finding us someplace to look? Based on cat hair and plaster dust?" he asked.

"That doesn't work for everyone."

"Only me."

She frowned at him, but clearly Riley stood nowhere in earshot, so she let it go. "She doesn't spend a lot of time in homes with pets, but she does hang out with a couple of smokers. She likes scratch-off lottery tickets, but nothing indicates that she goes to the casino. She had a cold a few months ago and can't settle on a favorite hand lotion. She goes to the beach in the summer."

"It's not summer."

"Don't I know it. And, you might have noticed, she has neither a Rottweiler nor a willow tree."

"I meant anything that might help us—"

"It's impossible. If I were her, I would pick someone obscure, someone it would take you weeks to work through her social tree to find. A second cousin, my childhood best friend, a sorority sister. But she might be panicked enough to go someplace familiar, someplace she's comfortable but can be unnoticed. Someplace with showers and lockers and a snack bar." Maggie pulled a plastic badge from the bottom of the duffel bag. "Have you checked her gym?"

Chapter 26

Dr. Caitlyn Michaels looked exactly like one expected a psychiatrist to look, but her office appeared to have been lifted straight out of a frat house. Michaels had black hair pulled into a neat bun, cappuccino-colored skin, long eyelashes, and conservative but flattering clothes. Her desk held books, papers, and medical journals in heaps that indicated an all-night cram session, the end table could not fit one more used coffee cup, and the bookshelves had been filled not according to size or subject but whim and convenience. A troll doll peeked from the top of the most recent *Diagnostic and Statistical Manual of Mental Disorders*. An autographed basketball threatened to burst from its cavity between slumping magazines and worn textbooks stacked horizontally instead of vertically and with no regulation of size.

The shelves didn't look too sturdy to begin with and bulged at places where the contents had expanded beyond the available space. Maggie had to clean magazines, an afghan, and a toy football from the couch to find space to sit. The window had some trinket or knickknack sitting on each frame or hanging from the latch or stuck to nearly every inch. The entire place ought to have smelled like a boy's locker room; instead, Maggie caught only a pleasant whiff of lemon-grass.

"I'm glad you could find the time to see me," the doctor began. She sat in a worn leather armchair perfectly sized for her Junoesque body, legs delicately crossed, steno pad on lap. If she sensed any sort of disconnect with her surroundings, she hid it well. Perhaps, Maggie thought, that was the point. She could probably tell a lot about her patients from the way they reacted to her office.

She saw the hazard of speaking to a psychiatrist—the attempt to guess what they were trying to guess and how they were trying to guess it. Did her comment mean that she knew Maggie had been dodging her? That she felt, as a doctor, her time should take priority and she shouldn't have to chase her patients down? Did she think by pointing out that she'd had to wait, it would make Maggie feel guilty and thus work harder to give the doctor what she wanted, which was access to Maggie's soul and innermost thoughts, so that the doctor would feel better and like her? Because surely everyone wanted to be liked.

Did Jack want to be liked?

Dr. Caitlyn still waited for Maggie to make some response, to acknowledge that they were even in a room together. Now she felt even more guilty—

Maggie gave up. Truthful and professional, no second-guessing, that's how she would handle this. Tell her everything except, of course, what she couldn't tell anyone. "You're welcome. I'm sorry it's taken so long. I know I was supposed to report within the first four days."

The doctor waved a casual hand, her gaze never leaving Maggie's face. "That's a guideline, not a rule. What's important is that you're here now. Let me go over some vitals first, so I'm sure I have the right information. Okay?"

Without referring to a file or report—perhaps she'd jotted notes on her steno pad—the doctor confirmed Maggie's age, marital status, how long she'd been working for the department, civilian job category, and general health.

She reaffirmed that her purpose was to provide a safe outlet and emotional support for Maggie, "or just a friendly ear if that's all that's needed." This Maggie believed. She was a little bit of a hero for the department; the powers that be had no desire to discredit or downplay any of her testimony. The mandatory counseling had been decreed because of a genuine concern for her health and welfare, and more importantly, because they were required by the GO—General Orders—for all staff. Even civilians.

She also reiterated that all their sessions were confidential, and that while she would be making a report to say she had no qualms about Maggie working in the field and/or concerns about Maggie posing a danger to herself or others, the details of their discussions would be forever locked away and never, ever revealed. This Maggie did not believe. She highly doubted that Dr. Michaels, despite her integrity as a psychiatrist, would not tell her employers that their serial killer still roamed the city at large and by the way he's one of your officers. Maggie wouldn't even expect her to—*she* wouldn't, if their roles were reversed. Medical ethics were all well and good, but surely preventing future murders took priority. There would be many things she would not be sharing with the good doctor.

"Tell me about yourself, Maggie," the doctor began.

I murdered a woman a few weeks ago. Things like that.

"Um . . ."

Dr. Michaels smiled, a warm, caring smile that probably disarmed most of her patients and did a number on Maggie, too. She had to fight the urge to pull her knees up to her chin and fidget. It was okay to be a little nervous, but if she let her inner basket case show, that would only prolong the number of sessions. Calm. Professional. Go.

She went over her childhood, her loving parents—a chemical engineer and a part-time music teacher—and her adorable and exasperating older brother, Alex. Alex's wife, Daisy, and their two kids. Maggie's college years, her love of forensics, her coworkers. She covered all that in about four minutes flat and felt it a good job.

But then the doctor moved on to more recent events.

"I'm really tired of talking about that," Maggie said, and thought it sounded reasonable. It shouldn't be a story she'd want to tell again and again.

The doctor sympathized but didn't let her off the hook. Dillon Shaw had come close to killing her. Michaels didn't actually state that Maggie needed to talk about it, but it felt implied. Strongly.

She tried to describe the cacophony of emotions that encounter had produced.

"How did that make you feel?"

Maggie goggled. "Seriously?"

"I know. You're thinking, how do you freakin' *think* it made me feel, you moron? But I'm serious."

"You want to know what it *felt* like to have someone try to plunge a knife into my heart?"

"I want to know what it feels like now. Now that he's dead and you know you're safe, now that the urgency and the panic and the terror are over. What is the first emotion that comes to mind when you think of it?"

Maggie tucked one leg under herself without

realizing that she'd done it, that she'd begun pulling herself in for added security. "Hurt."

"In pain?"

"No, hurt. Like my feelings are hurt." She felt herself looking at Dr. Michaels with what she knew must be surprise. "Isn't that stupid?"

"Feelings are never stupid. Inconsistent, illogical, contradictory, but never stupid. Has anyone ever tried to seriously hurt you before, either physically or emotionally?"

"No."

"You've always gotten along with people."

"I wouldn't go that far." She'd conflicted with plenty of teachers, coworkers, superiors, and one incompetent veterinarian in her time. But what was it Jack said? She always had to be the good girl? "No, I've never been attacked like . . . like it was really me they hated."

"Don't take this the wrong way, but what you're feeling is completely normal."

"I'm not crazy?"

She smiled. "Not even a little bit, though I don't like words like *crazy*. . . . I actually don't like words like *normal* either, since I don't believe there is such a thing. What I mean by that is *typical,* but that word has come to be sort of an insult, so that doesn't work so well either."

Maggie smiled back. So psychiatry sessions weren't a walk in the park for the psychiatrist, either.

"Then this vigilante killer returned."

"Yes."

"And killed Shaw."

"Yes."

"And how did *that* make you feel?"

"Really, really glad." Maggie slid her leg out, put her foot flat on the floor. She had to stop moving, every twitch of her toes probably telegraphed information to Dr. Michaels's steno pad. "Is that typical?"

The doctor nodded in a sage and comforting way. "Under those circumstances, yes. I'd say absolutely. And then you followed this vigilante to another location because you believed he planned to kill again."

"And did," Maggie said. *Sort of.*

"You didn't call the police—"

"He took my phone."

"Or stop at the station."

"There wasn't time." Very true statements, delivered unequivocally.

"You went to stop him. By yourself. Unarmed, untrained. You knew he had a gun."

"So?" Maggie demanded.

"I'm not questioning your decision. I just want to talk about what led you to it."

Maggie felt the wrinkle between her brows form. "I don't understand. I just told you what led to it. I didn't see any other option."

"We were talking about typical. Chasing

down this man on your own is not exactly typical."

She tried to smooth out her forehead, without much success. "What does that mean, that I have some sort of death wish or something? Besides, how do you know it's not a typical reaction? How many people find themselves in circumstances like that?"

"True, it's a small sample pool. But—"

"How come when a man does something like that, he's brave, but when a woman does it, she's mentally unstable?"

"I hear you," said the other female in the room.

Maggie saw the real question that the doctor didn't even know she was asking. Would Maggie have run to the building on East 40th and confronted Jack if Jack had been a total stranger? If she had never seen him before he shot Dillon Shaw, if she hadn't spoken to him and worked with him and ridden in a car with him, would she have ventured into that dark house knowing that he was armed and quite dangerous?

Had she counted on his acquaintance with her? Or had she simply reasoned that if he hadn't killed her before, he wouldn't then?

Would she have been so self-sacrificing if she hadn't had that knowledge?

She'd like to think so. But the scenario had been so bizarre to begin with, it felt impossible to calculate an alternate ending. Things were what they were.

A more relevant question now might be: Would Ronald Soltis still be alive if she hadn't been previously acquainted with the murdering vigilante?

Dr. Michaels broke into her reverie. "What are you thinking about?"

Maggie looked at her watch, and said, "I think we're out of time."

"I don't have a patient next hour. We have all the time we need."

"I'm sorry, but I don't. I have a meeting that . . . it was nice talking to you. I'm sorry it took so long to get here, but I feel this was helpful. . . ."

Dr. Michaels stood, gentle and implacable, and with a smile said, "That's quite all right. We'll table that for our next session."

Maggie paused mid-rise. "Next session?"

"Oh, yes." Gentle, implacable. "I'm sure there's much more that you need to tell me, Maggie Gardiner."

Chapter 27

After they dropped Maggie back at the Justice Center, the two cops postponed a trip to Shania's fitness center and returned to the *Herald* building, where Jack studied the white points on the waves of the lake through the windows of Jerry Wilton's office. A few intrepid fishermen braved the brisk spring air to try their luck, and an ore ship maneuvered its way toward the mouth of the Cuyahoga. He wished the windows would open because the police IT tech he'd brought with him wore way too much body spray. He apparently believed the commercials that showed hot girls throwing themselves at any male who liberally spritzed. So far that didn't seem to be true, because the hot girl who had escorted them to Wilton's office hadn't given the kid a second look.

"Finding anything?" Jack asked him, for the third time in the past forty minutes.

"No. At least—no. I don't know. I'm usually looking for kiddie porn or threatening e-mails. This is all about sales figures and advertising rates and where to get lunch today. Really helps if you tell me what you're looking for, dude."

"Something someone would kill him over."

The tech made a not very happy sound, and

Jack couldn't blame him. He wasn't feeling too happy himself. Roth would not let the cops take the computer with them. He felt bad about Jerry, but they still had a paper to get out, etc. etc. And besides, the hard disks belonged to the *Herald*, not to Jerry. If they wanted it they would have to get a seizure warrant, so instead of arguing with Roth it seemed faster to seal the door with evidence tape to prevent any tampering with said computer and bring the tech to it. Faster, that is, for everyone except the tech.

"Stocks," Jack said. "Look for mentions of stocks."

"Tons of that. This guy received memos and memos about stocks. Apparently that's a really big deal here."

"It would be, yes." Keeping the stockholders happy kept everyone in their jobs, kept the newsprint going out on the trucks, kept the true believers in print journalism holding off utter despair for one more day.

Riley appeared in the doorway, a bundle of energy, the trauma of climbing over fences the previous night completely gone. He waved a sheaf of papers with one hand. "Got it!"

"Got what?"

"Sprint finally came through. I've got the call history for Davis's phone. Nothing from Verizon yet, but I'll keep on them."

"Don't make the poor girl cry again."

"I can't make any guarantees. So . . . Davis's phone. Just glancing at it I can see three numbers he called quite a bit. His wife runs a distant fourth . . . which might explain her lack of broken-upedness. So, let's find out who's at the other end of these calls." He picked up the phone on Wilton's desk, shuffling past Jack, who took the spot in the doorway. The office might have a nice view, but not much in the way of elbow room. Riley dialed.

"Won't do you no good," the IT tech said. "It'll be burners."

"Junior's vote of no-confidence notwith-standing," Riley said, and listened. "Ringing. Ringing. Ri—automated voice mail, no ID of the recipient."

"Told you," the tech said.

"Shut up. Second-most-popular number." He dialed.

Jack, leaning on the doorjamb of Wilton's office, heard the tinny notes of Van Halen trilling from the next room. He ignored it.

"Ringing," Riley said. "Ringing. Ringing—oh, this is Tyler, leave a message. Hello, Tyler, this is Detective Riley of the Cleveland Police Department, please call me back." He hung up but continued to speak. "Lot of men in this case. I was hoping to reach a mistress—"

"You didn't leave him your number," the IT tech pointed out.

"Crap," Riley said, then redialed.

Again, "Hot for Teacher" sounded from the adjacent space. This time, Jack jerked his head at his partner, and they moved over to where a door labeled 184 stood open. A carbon copy of Wilton's office, except it had a different motivational poster on the wall, a collection of shot glasses on the windowsill, and a bright blue cell phone on the corner of the desk piping away.

A voice behind them said, "Looking for me?"

Tyler Truss had pale skin, dark hair, and a slightly Asian quality to his features. Tall but slender, he wore a blue dress shirt missing a collar button and carried a steaming mug with a tea tag hanging from the rim. He seemed unconcerned to find two detectives on his doorstep, even after they explained their arrival.

"Oh yeah. Bob Davis called me all the time." His voice sounded like a verbal eye-roll.

"Why?" Jack asked.

Truss moved around to the back of his desk. "Have a seat, please. Just toss that stuff over—um, there."

Riley picked up a stack of paper with two iPads perched precariously on the top. "What is it you do here, Mr. Truss?"

"I'm the digital content editor." At their blank looks, he added, "That means I handle the web part of the newspaper."

Riley said, as if he hadn't just learned of its existence, "The online edition."

"Yes, but . . . so much more. People think we just take the stuff that's in the paper and cut and paste it into a website. That's not it at all. We're taking two-dimensional items and exploding them into three dimensions—stories aren't told only in words and pictures anymore. There's video, there's sound, there's moving items, there's links with affiliates that have to be constantly monitored and maintained. And that's just the content. The advertising is a new world. Target-driven, click-through compiled, focused on local sensibilities."

"So everything is peachy in your universe," Riley summed.

Truss snorted and ran hands through his very short hair. "Hardly! Technology is constantly evolving, billing—look, ads pay for a paper, but with the Internet, advertisers have too many options, cheaper options. We can't charge rates that give us a high rate of return the way a few column inches did. It's like eBooks—suddenly there's this product, a great product, but no one knows what to charge for it. That can paralyze. Then there's local versus national—most advertising is local. National companies use national media like *USA Today* or cable TV. Those rates are too exorbitant for locals, especially with the economy still down. So every day is an experiment, throwing spaghetti at the wall to see what sticks. We're moving forward, but on shifting sands."

He must have realized that the pep in his pitch had flagged, because he went on. "Exciting, yes, don't get me wrong—online isn't just a version or a feature of the newspaper. Online will soon *be* the newspaper. That will change everything, once we finally shake off the ball and chain of a physical paper. Printing presses, rolls of paper, ink, people to run all those machines, people to pack the paper onto trucks that break down and use gas and have to be insured and maintained, to take the papers to paper boxes that can freeze shut or merchants who have to stop what they're doing and take delivery—just like nearly every other industry, when you don't have physical product, that eliminates a glacier of costs."

"And a glacier of jobs," Riley pointed out.

Truss looked concerned. "Yes. Unfortunately, yes. A lot of people's jobs will be eliminated. Just like blacksmiths when the automobile was invented, just like telegraph operators, elevator operators, telephone operators, and the steno pool. Times change, and change is hard. But you can't stop it."

"Why was Robert Davis calling you twice every day? On average?" Jack asked, having heard all he ever wanted to hear about the decline of print journalism.

The eye-roll again. "Oh, that."

"Yes," Riley said. "That."

Tyler Truss sat forward, giving them his full and solemn attention. "Bob Davis was a copy editor. You know what they do?"

"We've been informed."

"A copy editor checks over the stories, approves which stories go in, and does the layout—with the layout editor, but the copy editor has final say."

"Yes, we've—"

"One of the very few advantages of print newspapers, other than being able to wrap your potato peelings in them, is that when you pick up a paper, where is the biggest story going to be?"

He waited until they figured out this was not a rhetorical question. "Page one?" Riley guessed.

"Exactly. Page one will have the story about the school shooting. Page two will have the international economic summit. Page B-10 will have the schedule for resurfacing the potholes in Euclid Avenue. Everybody knows that. You don't have to explain it. But on a digital site, it's not that easy. The stories are mostly listed as links, and people click through to read only the ones they want. It's harder for them to get a sense of ranking. A large part of a copy editor's job, you see, is telling the readers what is important."

"So Robert Davis—"

"Wanted to help me with this task. He wanted

to coach me on ranking story importance and finding a way to convey that online. Thing was, I didn't need his help, and he knew nothing about digital layout. First thing he'd do every morning is go to the website, then call me with all sorts of suggestions about what to put where and how to play up this or that story, none of which made any sense to me. I started ignoring his phone calls, but that didn't help, he'd just redial. Poor guy. I'm sympathetic, I am, but what Robert Davis really wanted was to move himself into the digital side so he'd still have a job when print goes the way of the stagecoach. And I couldn't give him that. The *Herald* of the future will need people a lot more digital media savvy than Bob Davis was."

Riley consulted his printout. "A lot of these calls were in the evening."

"Yeah, all hours of the day and night. Drove me nuts."

"Did you know Davis personally? I mean, outside of your work here?"

"Nope."

"Didn't have beers now and then? Get the families together?"

"No," he said.

Riley gave Jack that exasperated look, which said they'd just spent fifteen minutes being lectured by this bozo and learned exactly nothing. Robert Davis had been worried about his job, just like every other employee at the newspaper. But Jack wasn't so sure. Tyler Truss talked a little too much.

"What about your neighbor, Wilton?" he asked the man. "Know him at all?"

"Yeah, we're friendly. We *do* have beers now and then—did, I mean."

"Any reason why he and Robert Davis would be the ones murdered?"

Tyler Truss's animated face slowed to a freeze. "Jerry was *murdered?*"

Chapter 28

Stephanie Davis sat on the edge of the dancing water fountain at the south end of the Tower City mall's three stories plus of gleaming white terrazzo and glass. She perched on the edge because she would look ridiculous if the water sloshed and soaked her bottom. She had dressed as though for a job interview, which in a very obscure way, it was. She was interviewing for Bob's old position. But not the one as copy editor. And the people in charge had better not turn her down.

She picked Tower City since it was brightly lit and full of people. She felt safe, her target should feel safe, and the running water should interfere with any listening devices in case her target had the police after him. She had seen that in a movie.

A nicely turned-out mother and child went into The Children's Place store. She had never been able to afford their clothes . . . though her boys would have revolted if she had tried to drag them into a place labeled *children*. They had more bravado and hormones than could be good for her nerves, but the thought of them made her smile.

Clear panels formed the roof of the mall, and the sunlight made the whiteness even brighter. It could hurt the eyes, but the city got too many cloudy days for anyone to complain. Indeed, some people paused and tilted their faces upward, as if they could get a start on their tan through the glass.

Someone came and sat down next to her, also perching on the edge. The face seemed vaguely familiar. She guessed the baseball cap and sunglasses were meant to protect against the mall's video surveillance. But why would anyone ever look at the video? Their cloak-and-dagger stuff was stupid, she knew, but if it made both of them feel better, where was the harm?

She cleared her throat. "I went through Bob's paperwork this morning. I know what you're doing."

The person spoke, quietly. "How?"

"*How?* How did I figure it out, you mean?" Stephanie snorted. "Jeez, you sound just like Bob. I am a store manager. He thought that meant I went around putting sweaters back on hangers, but I manage a concern that generates over a million dollars in sales each month. I know more about business than my husband would ever have known. Frankly"—she snorted again—"your mistake was not coming to me first, instead of him."

"What do you want?"

Two little boys raced by, tiny sneakers squeaking against the floor tile, shouts echoing off the glass skylights. Honestly, the way some people let their children run wild. "I want Bob's share, of course. That's all. I'm not greedy and I don't enjoy blackmailing you. I have two sons who need to go to college on a one-income household. Bob's life insurance will barely pay off that stupid car he bought. Your plan can go ahead without interruption—just give me Bob's share and you'll never hear from me again."

She let this sink in. She had to play it cool, had to be tough, but as had happened so much over the past few days, she found it impossible to stay silent. "If you don't mind me asking"—a phrase that always guaranteed someone *would* mind— "Bob was a copy editor. What did you need him for?"

She thought she wouldn't get an answer, it took so long to arrive. "Bob worked with the printing supervisor, but the printing crew works nights. Execs don't schedule meetings at night."

"You needed someone to verify your print burden—how many papers you actually print as opposed to how many you *tell* people you print."

"Yes."

"That was *all?*"

"They're thorough."

She refrained from snorting again. "Not thorough enough, apparently. When will it be done?"

"Two to three weeks."

"Then how long until I can expect delivery?"

"Quickly. A few days."

"Good." She nodded, more to herself than—

"Do you even care who killed your husband?"

The question surprised her, even shocked her. Somehow she had not connected the two situations and fear flooded her from her scalp to her toes, leaving a tingling, quavering feeling in her skin. She spoke without thinking. "Was it you?"

"No!"

She tamped the feelings down and said, ridiculously, "Good, then. I mean . . . of course I care. But Bob—poor guy—is dead and my boys still have a future. They're my priority now. Get me that money and everything can proceed as planned." She stood up, hoping to look firm and determined. "You know where to find me."

She walked off without looking back. Tough. Determined. She didn't let herself draw a deep breath until she got to the elevator. As the doors closed she tried to put this plan into perspective, but her mind ping-ponged all over the place. How should she ask them to deliverthe money? Cashier's check? That could be traced. Cash would be best. Anything else left a paper trail she'd rather not leave. But what to do with it? She couldn't just drop it in a savings account. It would be safe, but the IRS might notice when her 1099-INT took an exponential leap.

She exited the elevator and went to find her car. The sunlight outside seemed blinding compared to the dank parking garage.

She couldn't leave it in a box in the basement,

either. Suppose the house should be robbed, or burn down? Insurance doesn't cover cash, and the last thing she would want to do was have to explain its existence to someone. Like her children.

Where was her car? She had put it next to one of the short supporting walls for easier locating—there. She could probably get a new one, or take over Bob's, but maybe not. It wouldn't be wise to start throwing money around during the early days of her widowhood. On the other hand, she could explain it as life insurance money—no, she'd sell Bob's stupid car and keep her practical one.

A safe deposit box would be her best option. No one would know what was inside, she'd have access to it, nothing reported, no taxes paid. Probably parcel it out to a few different banks. Robbers these days like to rip out all the deposit boxes. She'd seen that in a movie, too.

Stephanie pulled her keys out of her purse. Yes, she'd handled that perfectly. Just the right combination of threat and reasonableness. No reason for them to try to block her out.

She stepped up to her car door.

Setting up the meeting in a brightly lit and populated place had been an excellent idea. What she had forgotten to think through, however, was that to *get* to the brightly lit and populated location, she had to park her car in a place that was neither brightly lit nor populated.

Nor safe.

Chapter 29

Jack and Riley visited again with Janelle, the layout editor, who didn't even look up from her screen as she answered their questions, the mouse under her palm rotating all over the desk blotter. She also ignored the general soup of activity going on around them in the vast oval of the reporters' bullpen. She had to get the next day's paper set for print with only herself and the assistant copy editor, Bennet, to do the job formerly performed by the perfectionist Davis.

Jack regarded Bennet, now so poised to take over his superior's job. Bennet barely seemed old enough to drive, with visible pimples, wisps of an attempted mustache, and arms too thin to strangle his baby cousin, much less a strapping man like Davis. Jack promptly eliminated him from the suspect pool. Janelle would make a more likely murderer, and Janelle probably couldn't bring herself to swat flies.

Though she could, without blinking, hack a story until it bled.

"He's got to drop a paragraph," she told Bennet.

"He's already cut fifty words."

"It's not going to fit. Do we really need all this stuff about the sun rising over the rapid transit station?"

"It's local color."

"Locals already know what the sun rising over the rapid station looks like. It's not vital to the story. Tell him to cut."

Bennet gulped but went off to face the soon-to-be unhappy reporter.

Janelle still hadn't looked up from her screen. "Can I help you, gentlemen?"

"We'd like to ask if there is anything else about Robert Davis's personal life that you haven't told us."

"No. As in, there isn't."

She was courteous but in a hurry and under pressure. Directness would be reciprocated here. Jack snagged Bennet's chair from the next desk and leaned toward her, keeping his voice low. Around them reporters made phone calls, typed faster than humanly possible, and argued with one another.

"Look, his wife doesn't seem real broken up about his death. We're wondering why that is. Did he have an affair? Sleep with someone here? Discover that he was gay? Embezzle from the petty cash? Take payoffs to keep some politician off the front page?"

"No, no, I wouldn't know, no, and no. To the best of my knowledge. Bob and I just arranged the layout. We weren't confidants. Though"—she broke off to give Jack a quick grin—"I'm pretty sure I would know if he had been fooling around with anyone here. This place is a seething cauldron of professional busybodies."

"Okay, so not love. That leaves money. He come into any lately?"

"No . . . he bought that car, but he got a loan like any other schlub. I remember talking about interest rates."

"How about hate?"

The mouse hadn't stilled. On the screen, Jack could see that she had finished one page and moved on to another. "No one particularly liked Bob, but no one *hated* him, either. Except Roger Correa maybe, but he hates everyone. No one else, you see, is capable of his standard of journalistic purity."

"Bob?"

"Roger."

"Janelle!" A man brushed past Riley to stand at the edge of her desk, on the other side of Jack. He stood about six feet and had the kind of tanone got in a studio. Right now it seemed deeper than might be healthy, but only in his face.

"It's just one paragr—oh."

"Yes, oh! I understand you're to thank for this!" He held up the Local section of that day's paper. Front and center, the headline read, CITY PROP MGR OVERBILLS COUNTY.

"Are you Mr. Martin?" Janelle asked, before Jack could.

"I am. I am the Martin who you described as, let me see, 'Made himself a small fortune by conspiring with building managers throughout the county to overbill businesses for ad space rental.' You called me a criminal conspirator. In *print!*" He took a step closer to her. Jack closed in, ready to grab him should an errant fist fly.

"I did no such thing. Not to pass the buck, because this paper stands behind what it prints, but the reporter's name is—"

"Roger Correa, yes, I know! But I heard that he was under control until you guys let him off the leash and approved printing this kind of drivel—"

Janelle, Jack thought next, would have made a good cop. Because she jumped on the telling phrase in his statement. "Heard from whom?"

"If this isn't libel, then—what?"

"Heard from whom? Who told you that I approved this story?"

The pimply Bennet had returned and surprised Jack by also closing in. "It was me. Who approved it." He gulped as Martin's irate gaze swung toward him and couldn't stop himself from adding, "Technically."

Martin leapt on the change in topics. "Fine, then I'll sue you, too. There are laws to protect people like me from malicious slander!"

"Libel," Janelle corrected. "And it isn't either of those things if it's true."

"Don't be so—"

Roger Correa appeared behind Janelle. "I heard we had a visitor."

If County Property Manager Martin had been flushed before, now he turned a dangerous shade of eggplant. "You!" He tried to climb over Jack, Bennet, Janelle, and her ergonomic desk chair to get to the reporter.

Jack and Riley put a stop to his progression. Janelle stood in front of her flat-screen, high-definition monitor with her arms out as if more than willing to take a bullet for it, or perhaps for the news copy she had just spent two hours arranging. Bennet's Adam's apple bobbed as if in a rough ocean and he slumped to the abandoned chair, managing to maintain only partial consciousness. Roger Correa watched the commotion with folded arms and a satisfied expression that said, clearly, he must be doing something right.

"That sort of thing happen often around here?" Jack asked the managing editor, Franklin Roth, after Riley had led the irate Martin off in handcuffs. Janelle had gone back to arranging the next day's layout, Bennet had hustled to the men's room, and even Tyler Truss had come down from his office, instead of viewing the commotion from the walkway above, and gazed around as if deciding which angles would best fit viewing on an iPad. Correa stood at the head of half a dozen reporters—including Lori Russo—drawn to the drama like sharks to a few cells of fresh tissue in the waves. Some seemed admiring of Correa; others—including Lori Russo—seemed to suspect it had all been a carefully scripted performance.

Roth said, "It's not the first time in our history. Certainly not the first time for *him*."

"We're here to be a watchdog press," Correa said, with an air of superiority that made Jack want to knock a few teeth out.

Apparently Roth felt the same way. "Oh my yes, Roger—you're the only one who cares about journalistic integrity anymore. You're the only one with the courage to write it as you see it. You're the only one who remembers what it means to be a reporter. Did I leave anything out?"

"Yeah," Roger said, and straightened up, balancing his weight evenly. With other reporters at his back, perhaps he felt bold. Or perhaps he simply felt he had waited long enough. "I'm the only one who seems to have noticed you're about to sell the paper to TransMedia."

His words were a verbal grenade with the pin pulled. A dangerous stillness filled the air. Even Janelle's hand stilled over her mouse and she turned to look at the managing editor as if he were one of her kids who had come home in the back of a cop car. Jack heard the hushed wind as the reporters, in unison, sucked in a shocked breath.

The grenade went off.

"You're going to *what?*"

"How many of us lose our jobs, tell me that!"

"They'll eliminate the State news, you know they will!" said a skinny man with a skinny tie. His entire body quavered from either fear of losing his job or the terror of confronting his legendary editor.

"When were you planning to *tell* us?"

"Is it a done deal?"

"The union will—"

"How can you *do* that?" Janelle asked, her stricken look more damning than the various obscenities that crept into the reporters' words.

Roth held up a hand, his neck turning red with an unhealthy flush. "That's not true."

Correa had been ready for a denial. "You mean you had lunch last week with Jon Tamerlane and Doug Jackson and Karen Saunders because you enjoy their company?"

Before the cacophony could start up again, Roth spoke with a voice of iron. "They requested a meeting, we had lunch. They made an offer, we said no, end of story."

Correa didn't pause. "And the trip to Virginia last week? That was just to say no, too?"

The reporters, Jack, and Janelle swiveled their gaze back to the editor.

Who gave a small grin without the remotest

suggestion of amusement and said, "Are you following me, Roger?"

"Apparently someone should."

"Are you going through my garbage? Reviewing my expense accounts?"

Correa had shaded from triumphant into grim. "And what about the NAA conference last October? A buddy told me you spent most of the weekend closeted with Saunders and their lawyer."

A female reporter said, with forced calm, "If you're going to sell the paper, Frank, you need to tell us. A lot of the people in this room will lose their jobs. You at least owe them some warning."

"There's nothing to warn of."

"Yet," another reporter said, not even pretending to be calm. "Isn't that what you mean? Not *yet?*"

Jack felt the mood tensing his muscles, readying him for another tackle. He hoped it wouldn't be necessary. Holding Martin back was one thing, but with only himself to protect Roth from fifteen newsroom staffers—the odds were not healthy.

He wasn't sure he even wanted to try. This was not calling out one seamy public official. This meant the livelihoods of a few hundred people— and he had learned enough in the past few days to know that journalism wasn't merely a job for more people than only Roger Correa. It was a calling. It was a way of life. Many of the employees would not only *not* work for the *Herald* in the future—they would not work at all.

It took obvious effort for Roth to keep his temper under control. "They keep making offers. We keep turning them down."

"Better brush up our résumés," one person said.

"Lotta good that will do you," said another. "No one's hiring."

"We'll become a McPaper!" a third wailed. Jack didn't know what that meant, but it didn't sound good.

The different female reporter pointed out, "Tamerlane wouldn't fly into town if he wasn't interested in making a deal."

"Of course he's interested." A withering tone crept into Roth's voice. "He's a businessman. He'll always *listen* to an offer, just to show respect if nothing else. They move in a different stratosphere, those types. But he's not about to give up on one hundred and fifty years of history, of this paper being part of the lifeblood of this city. He has to be practical, yes. It may behoove us to join them in an affiliate status—frankly, we could use their resources. But only if we remain completely autonomous, and retain one hundred percent of our staff."

"That would last about five seconds after you sign!"

"So now we've moved from a flat 'no' to 'affiliate'!"

"We're going to be online only, aren't we? Print will disappear," a paunchy blond woman said.

"That was always going to happen," a young man told her. "Eventually. Get used to it."

Another man made the mistake of demanding of Roth, "Do you even care what happens to this paper anymore? Or do you have a buyout arranged for yourself already, like in—"

"Don't you talk to me about caring about a paper!" Roth roared.

The reporters shut up.

"I wrote obits at the *Press* before most of you were born! I learned to write copy at the foot of Louie Seltzer! I got glass in my shoes walking the streets in Hough after the riots! I came to the *Herald* after Sam Hudson drowned off Johnson's Island. I was the one standing here just a couple years ago when we put every corrupt county official on the front page during the cleanup. Don't you forget for one damn minute who you're talking to!"

It had become one of those "pin-drop" moments.

He took a breath, and in a calmer tone said, "No one's going to let this paper go the way of the *Rocky Mountain News*. But we have to be practical. Multimedia is the future and if we don't face that, we *will* die like the *News*, and we have to stay here. The people of this city need a voice, now more than ever. Newspapers have served in a stewardship role in this country for over two hundred years. I'm not about to let that go just so we can print nothing but propaganda and celebrity updates. Now get back to work."

Roth waited and watched as one by one, the reporters did just that. He had rallied the troops. They weren't reassured, the state of their industry remained too grim for that, but they were temporarily mollified. Correa stayed, fixing his boss with a hard glare, but even he saw that he had lost this round and slowly turned away.

Jack relaxed. He hadn't needed to tackle anyone after all.

A voice at his elbow said, "Hi again."

He turned. Lori Russo, looking even better in daylight with a silk blouse and snug pants, stood with a tiny notepad in one hand and a pen tucked behind her ear. She hummed with that restrained energy all reporters seemed to radiate. "Hello."

"I wanted to ask you, who is in charge of the vigilante killer investigation?"

"I'm sorry, what?" Jack asked, although he'd understood her rapid speech.

She repeated herself while Jack thought. Might as well tell her, vacillating wouldn't do any good in the long run, and he couldn't see what it could hurt. He'd always been underwhelmed by Maggie's ex's detective abilities. Setting Lori Russo on him might slow them both down, which could only be good for Jack. "Detective Richard Gardiner. Homicide unit. Just call the main non-emergency number and ask for him."

Lori Russo scribbled the name on her pad, gave him a brilliant smile. "Perfect."

Jack thought so, too, as she turned away. She'd leave a message that Rick wouldn't return, and they'd play phone tag for weeks.

He hoped.

If not . . .

Riley returned from escorting Martin to a waiting patrol car. "What'd I miss?"

"Not much. A near riot and a brief recap of Journalism in America."

"If I hear one more word about Journalism in America," his partner grumbled, "I'm going to puke."

"You and me both," Janelle said.

Jack's phone rang.

Chapter 30

Maggie could see why no one had found the body before it had time to cool to an icehouse chill. The parking garage tucked under Tower City opened to the south, where the sun gleamed and bounced off the Cuyahoga. The interior remained all dim shadows while the openings to the exterior overwhelmed with light. Since shoppers were coming from the elevators and returning home from dinner, they walked in a half-blind daze right past the body of Stephanie Davis.

"I want some halogens," Maggie said to no one in particular. Who knew what might have rolled under Stephanie's weathered Taurus on the right or its neighbor, a bright yellow SUV, on the left? She might find a shoeprint as well in that narrow channel, preferably one that didn't belong to the two patrol officers or the now-slightly-traumatized sales rep who had found the dead woman. Or the hundreds of consumers who moved in and out of this mall every day.

"I have one." The young maintenance man who oversaw the tidiness and repair of the garage spoke up. "And an extension cord. The closest outlet is that pole."

Maggie rewarded him with a smile and said that

would be great. In the meantime she took out her flat light, a foot-long row of tiny LED lamps in a metal housing, designed to strike the floor at an oblique angle perfect for illuminating shoe-prints. But she couldn't find any sections clear enough to be usable, no doubt thanks to the roughness of the concrete and the hundreds of consumers.

She moved closer to the body.

Stephanie Davis lay facedown, head turned to one side. The cheeks were mottled and her tongue protruding from the force used to strangle her, but her eyes remained open, startled and staring. Her hands were free and seemed to be clawing at the concrete, a few of the nails broken. Maggie didn't see any blood or other injuries. Her hands were clean and so were her clothes, a neat blouse and coordinating slacks. A rosy perfume wafted up from her, mingling with the smells of exhaust and oils, discarded food, and the watery breeze from the river outside. Cars zoomed by on the street, but the garage interior remained quiet. Maggie took some photographs, tried to peer under the vehicles on either side, but she had, at most, a two-and-a-half-foot gap to work in, and the body took up most of it.

The keys to the Taurus dangled from the key lock. The fob had a remote, but Stephanie hadn't used it—perhaps the battery had died. She had been about to open her car door the old-fashioned way and once inside she could have shut the door, blown the horn, driven away. She had been that close to safety. But she hadn't even had time to turn the key.

"I don't see a purse," she said.

"Neither did we," one of the patrol officers said. "Figure a robbery?"

Maggie took a picture of the woman's left hand. "A robber would have taken her diamond ring as well."

"It's not very big," he persisted.

She gave him a look. "Who strangles someone just to steal a purse?"

"It's quiet. And this is a busy area. If she had shouted, maybe some Good Samaritan would have come to her aid."

"Maybe they thought they'd just knock her out, not kill her," the other officer suggested.

"The strap is embedded in her throat," Maggie pointed out. "Then they knotted it for good measure. He fully intended to kill this woman. Besides, it would be straining credibility to think this is about a robbery. This is all about the *Herald*."

"The what?"

A blazing beam of pure white hit her face, temporarily paralyzing her.

"I got it!" the maintenance man announced. "Oh, sorry."

She stood up, blinking. "No, that's all right. Really."

"You said you wanted—"

"It's great. A big help." When her vision cleared of white blobs, she straddled the body, staring down at something caught in Stephanie Davis's hair. She lowered herself again, taking care to keep her face turned down instead of toward the halogen.

It was a piece of paper, just a tiny sliver of newsprint. She could make out only two letters, *i* and *n*. She gave the three men strict instructions not to move, and dashed back to her car for glassine paper and a small manila envelope, what her predecessors in the field had called a coin envelope.

She examined the hair and the knot in the strap but didn't find any more. The strap had a number of hairs caught in it, most likely Stephanie's, but it would remain on the body until the pathologist cut it off at the autopsy. There were slight smears on the ends, where the killer would have had his hands. Maggie could only hope that they would turn out to be the killer's skin cells or even blood, but they looked too dark to be either. Maybe oil or just dirt.

The strap seemed to be the same color and construction as the ones used on Robert Davis and Jerry Wilton, but with much shorter ends. The killer hadn't left a long tail, hadn't intended to string up Stephanie to look like suicide or to prepare her for evisceration. He had come prepared for a quick, quiet murder in a semi-occupied place. How did he know she would be there?

She laid a gloved hand on the woman's shoulder. It felt malleable, rigor mortis still a few hours off, but cool. The concrete had sapped the warmth of the woman's body in record time.

She stood again, careful not to brush the sides of the vehicles. She would want to fingerprint both of them—with luck the owner of the banana-yellow car would stay in the mall for dinner and give her time to work . . . and maybe time to clear the scene before they got a look at the black powder covering half their finish. But she couldn't do that until the body had been moved, and she didn't want the body moved until she taped—

"What the hell?" said a voice behind her.

She looked up—mistake, the halogen on its stand blinded her again, and trying to turn around without touching either car or stepping on the body or being able to see made her stumble. She felt a hand grab hers and guide her out of the crevice in which she'd been working.

It was Jack. He looked murderous.

Maggie had seen that look before, and snatched her arm back. He didn't seem to notice, didn't take his eyes off Stephanie Davis's still form. He turned to her.

"Those boys are orphans now," was all he said. But the way he spoke terrified her.

Chapter 31

Several hours later, the body had been transported—carefully, without touching either vehicle—and the area thoroughly searched. The purse had not been located, certainly not the cell phone. They had gone through Stephanie's car and found plenty of crumpled napkins, broken pieces of Transformers, potato chips and a few errant French fries, a permission slip for a field trip to the Museum of Natural History that never made it home for a signature, and a briefcase of paperwork relating to the running of a Kohl's store, from floor space per brand to which items qualify for the 80% off clearance rack. But nothing that pointed to Stephanie Davis's killer.

She had an old and dusty GPS crammed into the glove compartment, but when fired up it showed only her kids' school and a trip to Westlake the previous December. Underneath the body lay the necklace with her sons' birthstones in its charms, broken in the struggle. Crouching between the cars, Maggie gazed at it, thinking over what Jack had said. He had such sympathy for the Davis children. Perhaps he had had sympathy for Ronald Soltis, too, in the end.

He appeared beside her, as if he had noticed the necklace. But instead he asked, "You okay?"

She looked at him in surprise.

"You *were* just talking to her this morning."

She dropped the necklace into an envelope. "I can't say that's something I'm used to." They stood. "If this is all about the *Herald,* where does Stephanie Davis fit in?"

"Obviously she knew more about her husband's work than she claimed."

"Or she didn't know she knew."

"Then what was she doing here?"

"Probably picking out new furniture. Or a comforter set, or dishes. You saw her—she was manic with energy and giddy with freedom. She had the time off work and probably just wanted to get out of the house, away from the neighbors and their condolences and their food. It's not so strange."

They watched Riley supervise one of the patrol officers as he prepared to drive the victim's car to the police impound lot. They had to keep it, in case it somehow turned out to be involved in the murder, but there was no sense in going through the trouble of a tow in such tight quarters.

"You checked the back seat with the ALS?" Jack asked. "Maybe our first guess was the right one. Maybe this is all about somebody kissing somebody else's wife."

"I checked. No one has been having sex in the back of that Taurus. I think one of the kids tossed his cookies there once, though."

"That glows?"

"It smells."

The other patrol officer approached with a dapper young man. "This guy says he's the owner of that SUV. Can he take it now?"

Jack said to the man, "Sure, in a minute. Can you just tell us, when you parked here, was that Taurus—that one, driving away—already parked in this spot?"

"That's my car."

"Yes, I get that. But did you see the driver of the other vehicle at any time?"

The young man, however, only stared in horror at the black dust now marring the bright yellow paint. "What did you *do* to it?"

On their way back to the station, and since they were driving right by it, Riley and Jack found a moment to visit Shania Paulson's gym of choice—the logical place for downtown-area dwellers and habitués, ReZults Fitness Club. It had, as Maggie had suggested, showers and lockers, as well as extensive daily hours. It smelled of rubber and chlorine and annoyingly robust health. The annoyingly slender girl at the reception desk didn't blink when they entered—men in suits were probably a large chunk of their clientele—but did a double take when it registered that they were not carrying gym bags. "Can I help you?" she offered.

Riley seemed too tired to bother with charm. He identified himself and said they were looking for Shania Paulson.

The blonde looked uncertain. "I'm pretty sure our client list is confidential—"

"I'm pretty sure it's not," Riley said. "This is a gym, not a law firm, and Shania is a person of interest in a murder investigation. Is she here now? Yes or no."

The woman's eyes widened. "Murder?"

"Yes or no?"

She tapped at her keyboard, chewing her lip at the same time. "She was in her spinning class—"

Riley and Jack headed for the door to the rest of the facility.

"Whoa, whoa, hold it!" The girl had regained her sense of authority. "She's not there now!"

They turned back. At the same time, a door behind the wide desk opened and another young woman, similarly attired and similarly slender, joined the first.

"Where is she *now?*" Riley asked with exaggerated patience.

"She left. The facility, I mean. About thirty minutes ago."

"Are you sure?"

"She swiped out of that door," she said, as if that made the situation obvious. Jack figured she knew her layout and that meant that Shania was gone—again. The receptionist didn't seem to be covering for her customer and even turned to her coworker to inquire further. "Did you see Shania Paulson leave?"

The other reception desk worker, a girl with black skin and purple hair that somehow looked incredibly sexy on her, said she had. "You were on lunch. I remember she borrowed Jenna's phone, and like ten or fifteen minutes later some guy pulled up outside and picked her up."

The detectives snapped to intense attention at this. "What guy? Did you know him? What kind of car did he drive? Color of car? Color of guy? Did you get a license number?"

She could tell them that it was a nice-looking gray Lexus, but as for the rest—

Neither woman could recall Shania ever getting a ride before, but then they didn't pay much attention to how their customers traveled, only what said customers did in the gym. The membership information they had for Shania matched what the detectives already knew. The phone number matched the Samsung Shania had left in her own kitchen.

They asked to see Jenna, and her phone with the number that Shania had called.

The girls looked at each other. "She went home."

Riley rubbed his forehead.

Chapter 32

"Do we really have to do this right now?" Maggie asked.

"Yes," her ex-husband told her. "Right now."

"But the *Herald* murders—"

"Are Riley's job. Not yours. He can live without forensic support for an hour."

Maggie slumped into a chair across from the man to whom she had been married for four years, trying to mask her discomfort with annoyance. They were in an interrogation room, but it didn't resemble the dank, cold cells seen on TV. It had ivory paint and lightly cushioned metal chairs, and smelled of neither cigarettes nor urine. Rick's partner, Will Dembrowski, also sat across from her, flipping through a few manila folders. She had known Will as long as Rick, and always liked him. A solid family man who kept his thoughts to himself, he seemed unlike Rick in every way. That was probably what made them a successful team. That was also probably why she'd always liked him.

She didn't think a little irritation would seem suspicious. "Why again? We've gone over this, what, three or four times? I gave you a statement, told you everything I know. And I have a lot to do today. We found Robert Davis's wife—"

261

"Yeah, we know," Rick said. "But we need to do a follow-up, see if there's anything that's come back to you now that a few weeks have gone by."

Maggie settled back in her chair. She was one of them, after all, and they would expect her to be cooperative—even if tired, even if busy. Of course she would be cooperative. "Not that I can think of."

Will took over, his gentle voice lulling her to remember. "Let's go through this piece by piece. We know you narrowed down the buildings by the trace evidence on the bodies and then stopped by the one on Johnson Court. You went inside—how did you get inside, by the way? When we arrived, Jack and Riley had propped the door because it locks automatically."

"It was propped when I got there."

"With a brick?"

She and Jack had gone over this. "No, with cardboard wedged in front of the bolt."

"What happened to the cardboard? It isn't on the property sheets."

"I don't know." She let him assume the non-existent item had been overlooked. In an alley it would have appeared to be just another piece of urban debris.

"Then you saw this Dillon Shaw."

She did not have to fake her shudder. "Do we have to go through that again?"

"No," Rick said.

She gave him a grateful smile. He might be childish and selfish, but he had never been cruel. And he had cared for her once.

"No," Will said. "We're more interested in the man who came in and shot Dillon Shaw."

"Okay." She gave the same description she had before—not the same words, but picturing the same man, who, of course, was not Jack Renner. He had suggested that she picture an actor ("not someone famous enough to be recognized just by description, like Brad Pitt or somebody"). She had chosen Michael Ironside, a long-time favorite of hers who never reached the level of fame he deserved. Though she had always wanted to bed him instead of fear him, he had portrayed a number of baddies over the years and could do the role justice.

"And nothing came back on the fingerprints?"

"Nothing—except the victims we already know about. I want to send them to the FBI, but first I have to eliminate our personnel."

"Our guys wear gloves," Rick said.

"People can slip. No offense, but I've had cops touch things and then swear they didn't. Sometimes it's such an automatic reaction that you don't realize you did it. I can't waste the FBI's time running prints we don't need, and they won't even accept them unless I can demonstrate that I made every effort to eliminate unknowns." She wasn't sure this was true, but it sounded reasonable. "I'll get prints on everyone who was at the scene and then send the truly unidentified to the Bureau."

The two detectives accepted this without further question and she felt her shoulders relax a tiny bit. Will moved on. "So the guy shot Dillon Shaw. Then what happened?"

"He came in and looked at him, as if he were making sure he was dead. Then he looked at me." Again, she didn't have to fake the quaver in her voice. For a few moments there, she had been sure that Jack Renner would kill her. And there were a few more such moments at the house on East 40th. "I thought he was going to shoot me, too."

"Are you okay?" Will asked. "Are you having nightmares?"

She nodded uncomfortably. She didn't like showing weakness in front of Rick. But anything that might speed up this interview—

"Why didn't he?" Rick asked. His partner and his ex-wife both stared at him, and he added, "I'm sorry, Maggie, but I have to ask. Why *didn't* he kill you as well? He didn't know you, and you had seen his face."

Her heart pounded, with a steady, hard thumping. "I don't know. I guess he didn't care. That I had seen his face, I mean."

"You've been through every mug shot within the parameters, and he's not in there."

"No, maybe that's why he didn't care if I saw him."

Will said, "All the people he killed were scumbags. It's probably against his code, quote unquote, to kill someone innocent."

Rick persisted. "But he didn't know she was innocent. She might have been Shaw's accomplice."

"Shaw had been about to kill me!"

"I know. I'm sorry, honey," Rick said, the endearment slipping out without much emphasis. "I'm just trying to make this make sense."

"He's a psycho," Will said. "Who knows why he does anything?"

Maggie said, as if she had given this careful thought—and she had, "He thinks of himself as a hero. Killing me would go against the principles he's upholding. Or thinks he's upholding."

"How does someone get that screwed up?" Rick asked.

"I don't know. I wish I did."

Without warning, Rick changed the subject. "So what's up between you and Jack Renner?"

"What?" Rick might not have been very good at guessing her thoughts, but that only meant Maggie had never had to get very good at hiding them. The fact that he had caught her totally off guard had to be painfully obvious. "What do you mean?"

"All of a sudden you're having little private chats all over the place."

"Bro dawg," Will protested, "we're here to talk about a serial killer who's still on the loose, not quiz your ex about her love life."

"What love life! I have no love life!" she protested. She was finally telling the truth, and a kindergartener wouldn't have believed her. Clearly, Will and Rick didn't.

She made herself take a breath. In a less hurried tone, she said, "We've been working together nearly twenty-four hours a day, every day for the past four. Truth be told I'm bloody sick of him. *And* Riley. Don't tell them I said that."

Will chuckled. Rick did not.

She left it at that. The more she argued, the more curious he would get. The door flew open to reveal a rescuer, in the unlikely form of Patty Wildwood. "You guys done in here? We need Maggie for a powwow on these *Herald* murders."

Will stacked up his manila folders. "Yeah, we've got all we need. And good luck with that. I hear the bodies are stacking up."

Rick did not say good-bye to her. He simply sat with his arms folded, gazing sternly at Maggie and her flushed face as she hustled out of the room. He might not know exactly what he suspected, but he sure as hell suspected something.

And that was not welcome news.

Chapter 33

Patty sort of ran the meeting, just as Patty sort of ran the homicide unit, since the chief of the homicide unit spent most of the day in loftier meetings, drinking coffee in the report-writing room and, for some reason, watching his detectives testify in cases taking place in the network of courtrooms throughout the Justice Center. If asked, he would say that he liked to keep in touch with the rank and file and personally witness his people in action, but most of "his people" assumed that he had perfected the art of doing nothing while appearing to be intimately involved. No one really minded that Patty had taken over in his absence, since she tended to be straightforward, fair, sensible, and brisk, all the things the chief was not—and her salary had not gone up one penny for this added but unacknowledged responsibility. Therefore, the other detectives were perfectly okay with it.

"Robert Davis," Patty began. "What do you have?"

Riley duly reported that the man had lots of minor enemies but no major ones, no mysterious sums of money, no lovers, and his cell phone records came back to *Herald* business. He had called Tyler Truss, editor Roth, and a third number that had not yet been identified, probably a burner. He apparently contacted the first two men often in an effort to keep his job, a topic that caused everyone at the *Herald* great concern on a regular basis. The burner, at the moment, seemed their only clue.

"Maggie?" Patty asked.

"Huh?" She had been thinking about Rick. "Oh, Davis. No fingerprints at the scene. On the body, various fibers, including red silk, pollen, and dog hair. Some is from his own dog, but some is not—apparently a mixed breed, possibly Rottweiler."

"The strap?" Riley prompted.

"Clean, cut with a knife, three-ply, I have no idea where it came from. I haven't had time to check hardware stores, marine supplies, or Home Depot." *And I doubt I ever will, if bodies keep turning up.*

"That all?"

"DNA came up empty, but the strap was so long they couldn't be sure exactly where the killer's hands would have been during the strangulation, and the hanging wouldn't have needed the same pressure." Maggie kept her comments as brief as possible, remembering that detectives had short attention spans.

"Jerry Wilton," Patty went on.

Riley said, "No apparent connection to Davis

other than working at the same paper. Wilton was higher up on the organizational chart, but no apparent enemies. Loving family, couple of ex-girlfriends, but no crazy ones. A pal of Truss, who Davis called a lot, but no apparent connection there. No mysterious sums of money, no lovers, etc. We're still checking phone records—Jerry was a popular fellow—but most of them seem to come back to the *Herald*. Possible avenues, he may have been juggling the circulation numbers, and had been buying stock with his cousin. She's in the wind and is either a suspect or a witness."

"This Shania who you can't find?" Patty clarified.

"Do you have to put it like that?" Riley whined. "Way to make me feel even worse than I do already."

"Heard she outran you," Patty's partner, Tim, said with a smirk.

"You heard that from me, nimrod," Riley said, but without rancor. Every meeting required a certain amount of banter, but no one had much time for it today. "Her locker didn't have anything in it except shampoo and three kinds of face cream. And, you know, feminine stuff."

Patty and Maggie stifled giggles. The three men in the room looked disgusted.

"But we've got a line on her, a girl from her gym who loaned her a phone, but said girl didn't go straight home and isn't answering *her* phone, either."

"Suddenly everyone in the city is unavailable. Maggie?" Patty asked.

"Unidentified prints but no hits, same dog hair, same pollen, same red silk, a blue nylon that might be the same as on Davis, or not, I'm not sure. Same strap. Carol says an insufficient amount of DNA on the ends to get a profile."

"Shit," Patty said.

"Yes."

"The knife?" She meant the knife used to disembowel Jerry Wilton, plucked from his own knife block and left at the scene.

"Nothing. I think the guy washed it in the kitchen sink and then put it back by the body."

"Why? Sort of an F-U?"

"Maybe it seemed sensible to him. He wouldn't want to get caught with it or caught trying to dispose of it, but wanted to make sure he hadn't left any of his own DNA on it."

"Why the blood and guts at all? Nothing like that at Davis or Mrs. Davis. What was different about Wilton?"

"He really didn't like Wilton," Riley said.

Maggie said, "He was letting us know that he knew we knew Davis wasn't a suicide."

"Time," Jack said. "Opportunity. He had privacy."

Patty said, "But then he goes back to simple strangling for Mrs. Davis."

Jack said, "Neither time nor opportunity. He was in a public place."

Maggie said, "The first two, he found the victims in their natural habitat. But he didn't attack Stephanie in her home, even though she was alone there. Somehow—"

"He got her to come to him," Jack finished.

Patty *hmmed,* they all thought on this and then she moved on. "And now we have Stephanie Davis to add to your workload. What do you have on her?"

Riley said, "Normal mom, liked at work, no mysterious sums of money, no lovers that we can see. Things weren't hunky-dory with her and the hubby, but why the killer would care, I don't know. Purse is missing."

"So we'd think this is a mugging?" Tim suggested.

"Then he wouldn't have used his signature strap. No, he probably wanted to collect her cell phone and didn't want to stand there in the parking garage rooting around in her bag for it."

"Maggie?"

"Same dog, no red silk, no pollen, same possible blue nylon. Same strap. DNA is working on it now."

"Autopsy?"

"Strangled. One deep furrow, pure and simple."

"No lump on the head?" Riley asked. They hadn't had a chance to ask about the autopsy.

"No other injuries at all. Bruised toes, probably

from kicking her own car. Scratches at her throat, probably from her own nails. DNA is working on the scrapings. With luck there will be somebody else under there."

"So he didn't feel the need to subdue little Mrs. Davis with a wang to the head first," Riley said. "He's bigger than her."

"Wang?" Tim smirked again.

Riley made a bludgeoning motion with an imaginary weapon. *"Wang."*

"Don't they have kids?" Patty asked. "The Davises?"

Everyone at the table spared a thought of silent sympathy for the two very young men who had just lost both their parents in the same week.

"What's going to happen to them?" Maggie asked. Stephanie had said they didn't have much family. She glanced at Jack, but his face stayed blank. He had his emotions under control.

Riley said, "There's a cousin in Kansas who's going to come and see what she can do. Apparently she's recently divorced. She's already talking about staying here so that the kids can finish high school in familiar surroundings."

"Three murders. And our suspect is a big guy with a dog," Patty summed up.

"And a willow tree," Maggie added. At the bemused looks around the table, she explained, "The pollen. I think it's a weeping willow. Near as I can tell—I can't find anyone who compares pollen anymore. I could send it to the McCrone Institute, but that would take weeks."

"So how did you figure willow?"

Maggie admitted with reluctance, "Google."

"Okay. Any idea how many willows there are around here?"

"They're one of the top ten most common trees in Ohio."

Patty moved on. "Anything else?"

Jack said, "Only that something is going on over at that paper. And no one is talking."

Patty suggested borrowing a few detectives, including herself and Tim, to write warrants for financial records and to conduct interviews at the paper's building. They had a large pool of both suspects and potential victims. "Help is all around if you need it. What's your plan?"

Riley looked at his partner. "I think we're going to have to wang somebody."

Chapter 34

"I'm glad you came back for more," Roger Correa told her.

"I felt like getting out of the office," Maggie said. Between her lack of progress on the murders, her ex-husband's questions, the too-knowing eyes of Dr. Michaels, and one dead and two orphaned boys, she felt ready to spend an hour or two listening to Roger Correa talk about job security and mundane government corruption.

"Me too."

"So I heard."

They sat in his car, again dining on nutritionally bereft fare, but this time they faced a pricey little bar on Euclid Avenue, not too far from the university. The one bad apple, board member Elliott, had pulled open its heavy wooden door and disappeared inside fifteen minutes ago.

"He is, you know," Correa said, almost absently, "going to sell the paper. Our esteemed editor is lying through his teeth."

"How do you know?"

"Because the world has changed, and the old one isn't coming back. Reporters that used to work for the same paper long enough to retire from it with union pensions are the farriers and elevator operators of our time. Reporters are now 'content creators.'"

"What does that mean?"

"Instead of having a beat and reporting on one general topic, like local crime or state politics, we'll have to write a few stories for this paper, maybe a column for another—change to what they call a 'gig' mentality, have a bunch of little jobs instead of one big one. Some forward thinkers insist that this switch to permanent freelancing is 'exciting' and 'freeing' and it's a better time to be a journalist than ever. You know what *freedom* means? It means no money, that's what it means." He leaned toward her, as if the closed interior wasn't already intimate enough. "The ones I really feel sorry for are the print crew—who prints anything on that type of scale anymore? Those guys will never find another job."

It had been a long time since she'd been close enough to a man to identify his aftershave and notice his eyelashes. Maggie backed up an inch and waved her waxed paper cup at the bar. "What are we waiting for, exactly?"

"For a girl," he said, apparently serious. "She'll be here soon. It's the lack of objectivity that really gets me. The future of journalism is online, but there's a different expectation of accuracy for online stuff. If it's printed on a piece of paper for all to see, for someone to clip out and carry into a lawyer's office, it had better damn well be the truth. But online? Well, it's the Internet—what do you expect? They're in such a hurry to be first, to be 'maverick' and bold and daring that they'll print anything. Rumor. Innuendo. They don't care, they'll just say, *we* didn't say that, we just said someone *told* us that. They're *proud* of it. No independent confirmation and nothing's on any kind of record. Online is simply not held to the same standard as print. And I don't believe it ever will be." He turned to gaze at her, dark eyes roaming her face as if memorizing its features.

He said, "On TV, or radio, or in the paper, someone will interview two experts. One says one thing, the other says the polar opposite. The media says, there, we did our job, we presented both sides. But the audience or reader or 'content consumer' has just spent whatever amount of time listening to two people argue and come out with not one iota more information than they had before. The best you can hope for is that they were entertained by the fireworks for a moment or two."

"Sounds kind of scary."

"People want to understand. And with issues today as complicated as they are, they *need* to understand. Instead, news—and I use the term loosely—is intent on making everything as simple as possible. Us versus them. Good versus bad. If we can't trust what we're being told, it's the same as being stuck inside a black hole, cut off from everything, with no idea where to go or what to do—oops, there she is."

Maggie looked up to see a woman with long red hair and a raincoat down to her ankles enter the bar. "Who?"

"Linda. I call her Linda Lou."

"That's nice. Why are we watching Linda Lou visit the Sugar Cane?"

"Because when we walk in, with luck, she will be deep in conversation with Mr. Elliott."

"And that's significant?"

"Well"—he sat back—"that depends on what the conversation is about. We'll give them a few minutes."

"What do you mean, *we'll* walk in?"

"Charming as it is, I didn't ask you here just for the pleasure of your company. You're going to be my beard." At her blank look, he added, "Sort of a disguise. Just something to help me blend in. We enter, everyone will be looking at you, not at me. We can join Elliott before he realizes I'm there."

"I see. A beard."

"And a lovely one at that."

Rick Gardiner had a new girlfriend and a six p.m. dinner reservation, so when the phone on his desk gave an annoying little trill, he considered ignoring it. But Patty's partner, Tim, sat only ten feet away and glanced over. He had already referred to Rick as "lazy as hell" on more than one occasion according to several sources, so Rick figured he'd better not give The Power Couple any more ammunition.

A police department had a great deal of personnel and many different positions in which to place them. Cops who annoyed the higher-ups were punished by involuntary transfers to shifts and departments and responsibilities they didn't want and didn't like. Such punishment could be sold to the public as a reorganization or even a promotion, but every cop knew better. Rick could wind up doing school outreach or something equally torturous. So he picked up the phone and identified himself.

Some chick on the other end said, "Detective Gardiner? This is Lori Russo with the *Herald*. I wanted to talk to you about the vigilante killings."

"That's an open investigation, so as you're well aware, I can't comment."

"Oh, I know—I'm not asking for any new information on the crimes in Cleveland. I wanted to see if you had run across the similar series of murders in Chicago seven years ago."

"I can't comment on any aspect of the investigation," Rick said. He had no idea what she was talking about.

"Five men were murdered there, all shot in the

back of the head with a small caliber, bodies apparently moved, no suspects."

"Chicago has a lot of murders, Miss Russo. It's a big city."

"These men had all been arrested multiple times, brought to trial multiple times, and always got off. Just like our murders here."

"Again, that happens in every city every day. Evidence disappears and witnesses are afraid to testify. It's a sad fact of life, but it is a fact."

"I'm sure you're right." The hack was blowing smoke up his ass, like that was going to help. "I reached out to our affiliate papers in other cities, friends of mine, anyone I had a phone number or e-mail for. There were similar murders in Phoenix."

"As I just said, there are going to be similar murders everywhere. Urban gun violence is hardly new."

"There was a man there who made a habit of buying young illegals from coyotes—boys and girls. He'd keep them in cages in his basement and—"

Rick glanced at his watch. He had ten minutes to get to Lola or his date would order for him—something he loathed, but if he argued with her menu choices he'd be sleeping by himself that night.

"—found him facedown in an arroyo," she finished, as if this proved something.

"Good for him," Rick said, before remembering that he spoke to a newspaper reporter. "I mean, we will continue to investigate every avenue. I can assure you I will get in touch with the Phoenix cops to see if there are any usable ballistics." That ought to get her off the phone. Rick pictured some pudgy do-gooder in Birkenstocks with Nancy Drew fantasies.

"That would be great if you did, because they wouldn't speak with me." Big surprise. "So I called a friend of mine at the *Arizona Republic* and I was telling him about our serial killer and he was trying to look up some stuff for me, and I happened to mention that our guy came to our attention only because his last victim was a woman who ran a horrific, illegal nursing home of sorts—"

"Mm-hmm." Rick straightened up his desk and put his keys in his pocket, preparing to bolt for the door in five more seconds, no matter what. If he didn't, he'd be eating scallops for dinner and they always had sand in them.

"And he said they had a similar case there."

"A vigilante killer?"

"A bunch of elderly victims dead in a house."

Rick stopped looking at his watch. "Huh."

"Yeah, I thought that was kind of weird. He said they never caught the people responsible. Seems like a weird coincidence that we would have both a vigilante killer and a case of extreme elder neglect as well, doesn't it?"

Hmm. Maybe. Maybe not. "Did they investigate some of the murders as a serial vigilante killer?"

A pause, which told him all he needed to know. "No."

"Then they were probably not connected. Crime is a dangerous line of work. Those involved always have a high mortality rate."

"But if you spoke with the Phoenix police—"

He now had five minutes to get to Lola or resign himself to scallops. "Thank you for the input, Miss Russo, but there is an issue here and I have to go." He heard her spluttering as he put the receiver down.

He hustled out the door, thinking that he could call his counterparts in Phoenix, just to look busy, just to see what they had to say. Serial killers on the loose could lead to expense-paid vacations to other states in the name of investigation. But then—Phoenix. He had heard it felt like being on the surface of the sun, too damn hot. If the reporter had contacted police departments in San Diego, or Myrtle Beach, that might be different . . . maybe he would call them.

Maybe not.

Chapter 35

"Let's go," Roger Correa said to Maggie. "Bring the camera."

Maggie got out of the car, digging lip gloss out of her coat pocket in a desperate attempt to, as Correa suggested, blend in. Her heart pounded as if she were about to rob a bank. Playacting had never come easy for her—a game of charades felt like torment. "You realize I am about the worst actress in the world?" The irony of the statement struck her.

"No worries. Just be exactly who you are. Maggie Gardiner, forensic tech and supremely hot chick."

He opened the wooden door, and a blast of music and liquor fumes tumbled out.

"Mockery will get you nowhere," she told him.

"I am never less than accurate," he insisted as he waved her inside. "Stewardship, remember?"

The Sugar Cane worked hard to live up to the motif of its name, with neon flamingos on the walls and a plastic palm tree in one corner. But the ornate and heavy wooden bar said Irish Pub more than Tiki Hut. Clean, softly lit, and if music played she couldn't hear it over the murmurs of conversation. They did blend in, she admitted, herself in neat slacks and Roger in his reporters' uniform of jeans, dress shirt, and loosened tie. For a weeknight, a good amount of people occupied the seats, talking quietly, drinking, eating high-calorie foods, and in the case of one table, arguing over whether or not it would be possible for a "superstorm" to form over Lake Erie. The pro side demonstrated the clash of pressure systems with the salt and pepper shakers, creating an extra cleanup job for the waitress.

Correa put a respectful hand on the small of her back and guided her to a seat at the bar. With only one open he gestured for her to sit down, and he stood at her elbow where the counter made a ninety-degree turn. She kept her large Nikon tucked under one arm; she had no place to conceal it—with a 10mm lens it would never fit in her purse, which she had left tucked under the car seat.

Maggie located Elliott and the woman named Linda at a booth on the other side of the bar. They chatted over beers. It didn't seem like a super-friendly conversation, but at least they weren't throwing the shakers.

"Can you get a picture of them from here?" Correa asked her. "Without the flash, obviously."

"If I had a tripod and my shutter cable. And if they sat real still."

"Do what you can," he said, one arm along the back of her chair, the other leaning on the bar—either playing a man possessive of his date, or trying to shield the Nikon from view. She set it on the counter, adjusting the settings for low light. When someone at the superstorm topic table burst out with a loud exclamation and all heads turned toward him, she lifted the camera long enough to focus on Elliott and click. She set it back down before normal conversation resumed.

The barmaid appeared, didn't even glance at the camera, and took their order, a beer and a tonic water. The couple next to Maggie talked about the tax implications of 401(k)s versus IRAs, and on the other side of them, two intoxicated men noisily conversed in a long series of non sequiturs.

Maggie pressed the shutter button a few times, then asked Correa, "Now what?"

He kept his face turned to her instead of toward their target, his nose nearly brushing her hair. "Now we wait. Shouldn't be long. Is he looking this way?"

"No. Yes."

He pressed in even closer. "Then this is when I kiss you to keep from blowing our cover."

"Try it and you'll lose a finger."

He seemed to stifle a chuckle. "Damn. That always works on TV."

"What are we—hey."

He remained outwardly captivated by her jawline. "What?"

"A young man just sat down with them."

"Yep." He moved his mouth to no more than a centimeter from her ear. "Take some more pictures."

"Who is that?"

"My unpaid colleague, Brandon. He is pretending to be an unofficial lobbyist who can get a board member at Rehabilitation and Correction to sign off on New Horizons, keep Barkley's little cash cow going so Elliott can keep getting his milk. Can you do a video on that thing?"

Maggie adjusted the dial and pressed her shutter button, thinking she should push Correa away, but, in truth, his body heat felt good. She only had a sweater for outerwear and had gotten chilled sitting in the car. She also wondered how one scheduled drinks with a corrupt county official. "So he came here to meet Brandon?"

"Yep."

"Does a halfway house really bring in that much money?"

"It's not the money, the funding, so much. It's the jobs it creates. Political corruption has always been about jobs. Ask Andrew Jackson."

"Who's he?"

He gave her a look. "The seventh president of the United States."

"Oh, for—goes back that far, does it?"

"The spoils system? Goes back to the Roman Empire, I'm sure. Maybe the Mongols and the

Sumerians. One of those inevitable facts of life."

"Okay, fast forward to now. Where does Linda Lou fit in?"

"She set up the meeting, and vouched for Brandon."

"Why did she do that?"

"Because I asked her to."

Maggie turned to him in surprise.

"I can be quite charming when I want to be."

She ignored that. "So you're setting this guy up?"

"Brandon offers a price for keeping New Horizons in the budget, Elliott agrees to pay it, maybe throws in another trip to Vegas. All while he's surrounded by witnesses."

The video timed out. "Then what?"

"We publish a transcript of the conversation on the front page. Oh, and we'll give a copy of the audio tape to the cops, just to show my heart's in the right place. I want you to be proud of me."

"You're taping him?"

"Brandon's got it tucked into that smart suit coat he's wearing."

She leaned back to see Correa more clearly. "Is that even legal?"

"Absolutely. Brandon knows he's recording and for good measure, so does Linda. Perfectly legitimate anywhere in the state of Ohio. We've watched it happen, as well, so our testimony counts for something. I tried to get Lori Russo to come along tonight, too—two paid, professional reporters are always more credible than one—but she's not answering her phone."

"A defense attorney will get it thrown out."

"Of criminal court, probably. Of the court of public opinion, never. We can even post your video with the audio on the website, have some of that multimedia that Truss is always going on about. See? I told you I'm not a Luddite."

"They're leaving. Elliott's leaving."

"Then I really will have to kiss you."

And only because it had been so long since anyone had, she felt tempted to let him. Just a little tempted. Just enough not to back away—

Someone grabbed Correa's shoulder and spun him around. They hadn't blended enough, and Toberlene demanded, "Aren't you that catshit reporter who said—"

His eye fell on Maggie's camera; then he turned to see Brandon, halfway across the floor, and Linda, both watching with horror and guilt, and all seemed to become clear to board member Toberlene. "What are you doing here? Is this some kind of setup?"

"Why would you need to be set up?" Correa asked. "Is there anything in your current history you'd like to share with our readers?"

Apparently Toberlene only desired to share with Correa himself, in the form of a right hook of surprising speed. Maggie had Correa in her lap before she even heard the smack. It would have been worse had Toberlene taken the time to wind up, but still the force knocked Maggie into the 401(k) supporter to her right.

Said 401(k) fan told Maggie, "I wouldn't mind if I weren't with my wife."

Correa righted himself and went after Toberlene. They grappled, evenly matched and doing more damage to the superstorm group's table than to each other. Brandon grabbed Toberlene around the waist from behind and called to Maggie to grab Correa.

"I will not," she said. She'd sooner get in between a pair of dogs, feeling that people who engaged in bar brawls deserved whatever injuries they received as a result. If someone grabbed a bottle or produced a weapon, then she might interfere.

Correa punched Toberlene in the gut, and Toberlene responded with another shot to the jaw. Patrons gasped, screamed, and did not appreciate the jostling.

Linda came forward with her glass of ice water, also perhaps seeing the similarity to canines, and tried to pour it over their heads. She succeeded only in dousing one of the intoxicated men to Maggie's far left, who took quite some time to notice. Undaunted, Linda snatched up a rum and coke from the superstorm's table and dashed it in Toberlene's face.

Movement halted. The board member wiped his eyes and looked fairly ridiculous, and not even Roger Correa would strike a man under such circumstances. Maggie stood by at a safe distance, monitoring the situation until her phone rang. She moved to the hostess station to get some napkins for Toberlene as she answered it.

"Where are you?" her brother asked.

"At the fights. Where are you?"

"You despise fighting."

"This isn't exactly official. What's up? Where are you?"

"At your apartment."

She choked. "Oh . . . really?"

"Had a seven-hour layover between Atlanta and Sioux Falls. I came to find out what it is you're not telling me."

Chapter 36

"You have no food in this place," Alex complained as soon as she entered her kitchen.

"That's not true! I have ice cream, Gala apples, and fat-free hot dogs. What else could I need?"

She studied him—light brown hair, short but unruly, eyes a shade lighter than hers, only a few tiny acne scars to interrupt what she thought were fabulous looks. Then she threw her arms around her brother and hugged him tight. Not spilling every gut she had to him would be outstandingly difficult.

But she would try.

She made cinnamon toast—a childhood favorite of both of them—while he filled her in on Daisy, the kids, the bass player's new girlfriend, and the travails of flying with a guitar. Then he checked his watch and said, "I have four more hours before my next plane leaves out of Hopkins. Spill."

In her family, serious conversations were always had in the kitchen.

"Why are you so insistent that—I can't believe you routed yourself through Cleveland just because you thought—"

He shifted in the hard kitchen chair. "Remember when you broke the basement window playing prison escape with that dorky girl next door?"

"We were escaping from a crashed 747—into the Alaskan tundra, I might add. And Julia wasn't dorky."

"Dad thought it was vandals, but I knew it wasn't, and you moped around for three days before I nagged you into confessing?"

Maggie rolled her eyes.

"And that time Bruce Wagner grabbed your boob in biology class and you got a detention for slamming him in the face with a pan full of dissected frog?"

Maggie said, "But he never did it again."

"Yeah, but you gave Mom some lame-ass story about the detention that wouldn't have fooled anyone except, well, Mom. But I knew."

The memory of splashing a frog's spleen into Tony's nose helped her to laugh as she asked, "Your point?"

"I know when there's something you're not telling me, sis. And you're not telling me something big."

She swallowed the last of her toast with difficulty. Might as well get it over with. "Something happened."

Calmly and competently, she told him about the vigilante murders, the trace evidence she had found and traced to a location, her near rape/ murder at the hands of Dillon Shaw, her desperate dash through the streets of Cleveland to stop a murder, and her failure to do so. She told him everything, in fact, except for the fact that she alone knew who the serial killer was and that she had entered a deeply bizarre and uneasy alliance with him, and all because she had actually been the one who pulled the trigger. And that the serial killer might still be killing, most recently a teenage gangbanger named Ronald Soltis.

His expression changed from horror to fury and back again as she spoke, and she regretted that, too. Surely with a wife, two children, and an unsteady income he had enough on his mind. She assured him that she was fine, unhurt, and the red line on her neck would eventually disappear. All the trauma did at least keep him from realizing that she had held part of the tale back, that there remained a significant chunk she had not relayed.

For now.

"Mags," he breathed when she had finished. "Why didn't you call me?"

"I wasn't ready to talk about it—and this isn't exactly a phone conversation." He continued to gaze at her while she pointed to the clock and said, "Are you taking the rapid to the airport—"

"That's it? Maggie—" He stretched his arm out and gripped her shoulder. "Is there anything else you want to tell me?"

He was thinking, she knew, that perhaps her rescue from Dillon Shaw had not been quite in the nick of time and that she'd been raped. He could think of nothing worse, and wanted to be her comfort and support for everything, every last horrible detail, no matter how it hurt him. It would never enter his mind that the last horrible detail might stretch in a different direction entirely. He'd rather die than see his baby sister hurt. But if his baby sister had hurt someone else . . . her darling Alex would have no idea what to do with that. None at all.

So she looked directly into his eyes and, as solemnly and convincingly as she could, lied to him. "No, that's all of it. Hell, isn't it enough?"

His words stumbled over themselves trying to assure her of benign intentions, then quizzed her about her coworkers' emotional support, department-sponsored counseling, and whether she could take a few weeks off to go to a few gigs with him and the fam. Mercifully, her phone rang.

"Did you get in a fight with Roger Correa?" Jack demanded.

"I did no such thing. I just happened to be present when he got into a fight with someone else."

Alex had recovered enough to mouth "More frog guts?" at her. He could always make her laugh at the most trying of times.

In clipped tones, Jack said, "You do realize that Roger Correa is probably our best suspect in three homicides?"

"Yes."

"Then what the *hell*—"

"What do you need, Jack?"

She heard a sound as if Jack were biting off what he would have preferred to say. "I need you to come here."

"Why? What happened?"

"We found Shania Paulson."

About an hour earlier, Jack had shown up at the tidy doorstep of a tidy apartment in Tremont, not far from the Civilization coffee shop. The apartment had a glossy red door and a welcome mat. It also had only one escape route in case of fire, a window over the back alley with the metal framing to guide an emergency ladder unfurled from inside. Riley now stood in this alley, just in case the tenant or guest decided to lower themselves the three stories to the ground. Jack had offered to switch roles, but Riley refused to admit which of them could run faster. Jack figured his partner itched for a rematch with the fleet-of-foot Ms. Paulson.

He knocked.

No one responded, but shuffling sounds were made behind the door.

He knocked again. He said nothing, did not

identify himself as an officer. Plenty of time for that.

More shuffling, and what sounded like a brief discussion. Then Tyler Truss opened the door, still dressed in his daytime uniform of dress pants, white shirt, and loosened tie.

"Detective," he said, without his usual energy. "You might as well come in."

He didn't seem threatening, either physically or emotionally, but Jack kept a careful watch on him as he stepped inside. The apartment spread out in updated antique glory, original wood floors gleaming and all openings framed with heavy oak moldings. A leather couch faced a big flat-screen television and enough stereo equipment to service a small nightclub. Like many bachelors it seemed that the coffee table was his true ground zero, with video games, movies, junk mail, a water bottle, and a half-eaten bag of chips covering its polished mahogany surface. The kitchen counters weren't nearly as cluttered, and the dining room table was bare except for a wicker basket with a complement of condiments. And Shania Paulson, sitting in one of the straight-back chairs.

"Miss Paulson," Jack said. "I'm afraid I'm going to have to place you under arrest."

"Yeah, I figured that," she said.

Chapter 37

Jack thought it prudent to give Shania Paulson the impression that if she cooperated, they might not have to arrest her at all.

"It was Jenna's phone, wasn't it?" she asked them, when Riley had abandoned the alley. With slight disappointment he gave up the idea of another footrace and sat at the online editor's dining room table to hear why the first one had been necessary.

"Yes," Riley told her now.

"I figured. How did you know to go to the gym?"

The two men, predictably enough, didn't want to admit that it hadn't been their idea, so they hesitated long enough for Shania to go on without waiting for an answer. "I knew enough to leave my phone behind—which sucked—but after I worked out and could think of things calmly . . . I was just tired of running, so I called Tyler." She reached out and patted his hand. She noticed the detectives' glances and added, "I barely know Tyler. We're not *together* or anything."

Tyler Truss's face fell a bit at this.

"But I knew he was a good friend of Jerry's, and I didn't know who else to call. All my friends, family—they all think I'm crazy to be so afraid. But Ty worked with Jerry, so I thought he'd understand."

"Understand what?" Riley asked.

"That whoever killed Jerry, why ever they did it, it had to have something to do with the *Herald*."

"What makes you say that?"

"Because Jerry didn't have any other enemies," she said with irritation. "He wasn't into drugs or gambling or fooling around with other men's wives. All he did was work out, and work."

"Tell us about him, Ms. Paulson."

Shania rubbed her face as if weary. "I'm sorry for running away from you guys, but—anyone can say they're the police, buy a badge on eBay for five bucks."

Riley opened his mouth to protest, then let it go.

"After what happened to Jerry, I wasn't going to take any chances. But we saw you pull up, and Ty said you were the real deal. I was tired of running. It sucks, running." She nibbled on a long nail without tearing it. "And Jerry's funeral is tomorrow. No way am I going to miss that."

"Your mother is beside herself—"

"I spoke with her." She looked from Riley to Jack, both across the table from her. "Is it true, what people said? That he was gutted like a deer?"

"I'm afraid so, yes."

She shuddered, visibly. Tyler Truss put a hand on her shoulder, but she didn't seem to notice. "That's horrible. Who would do something like that—*why?*"

"We were hoping you could help us understand that."

Shania studied her hands. She still didn't want to talk to them, and Jack could guess why.

"Tell us about the stocks," Jack said.

She hesitated. "Jerry had me buying stocks for him. He was paranoid about not having a paper trail between them and him—he'd take cash out from his paycheck every week and bring it to me. I'd deposit it in a separate checking account, use that to buy online. We went through E-Trade. How did you find out about it?"

"We found your e-mails."

She gave a mirthless laugh. "Yeah, even that he hated. *Don't e-mail me! Leave nothing for the SEC to find!* But he didn't always answer his phone, he'd be too busy at the paper, and I couldn't wait all day to make the buy because I had things to do, too—I told him spring gets crazy for me with the training and then the games—" She gasped out a sob, cut it off. "Did I get him killed? Do you think?"

Riley tried to calm her without making any promises. "We don't think so, but there's a lot we don't know yet. How long had this been going on?"

"About four months."

"How much stock did you buy?"

"About forty thousand dollars' worth. Where he got all that money, I don't know—I think he cashed in other things, other stocks, IRAs, maybe some kind of pension plan. He'd bring me stacks of cash, insist on driving me to the bank to make sure I didn't get robbed in the parking lot. He didn't tell me all the details and I didn't ask, because he'd tense up when I did. But I know this—he was damn serious about this, man, serious as death. He stopped going out, broke up with his girlfriend, hadn't bought new clothes in months, wouldn't even go on vacation with the family to Hilton Head like we usually do after New Year's. He told me once, 'I'm putting everything into this. This is the rest of my life we're talking about.' That's why he'd get so hyper about saying anything in an e-mail or even over the phone."

"What stocks was he buying?" Riley asked. "All different types, or a particular fund—"

She frowned at him in surprise. "The *Herald*."

"Only that?"

"Yep, just the *Herald*. I mean, it was easy, since it's pretty much in the toilet. Three-eighty a share at the beginning of the week."

The two partners exchanged a glance. "Obviously he expected that it would go up."

"Duh. I mean, sorry . . . but *duh*. He expected

it to go *way* up. He said when he cashed out, I could have fifteen percent. Agent fees, he called it. Sounded good to me for such easy work. And Jerry"—her eyes again filled with tears—"knew what he was talking about. Anyone else I know, I wouldn't have agreed. But Jerry's always had my six, and I had his. I trusted him more than I trust myself—*especially* where money is concerned."

"Why was he so sure the value of the stock would rise?"

She looked at him with wide, red-rimmed eyes. "I have no idea."

Riley pressed. "He expected to make a killing. He must have known something."

"I'm sure he did," she said with dignity. "He worked there. He had me buy the stock because otherwise it would be insider trading. That's why I didn't ask why. No one would think *I* had inside knowledge; no one would connect me with Jerry. We didn't have the same last name or anything."

"And he never hinted what would cause this leap in price?"

"Nope," she said, solid on that point.

Jack asked the most important question. "Who else knew about this?"

"No one. Just me and Jerry. I mean *no one*. He made that really, really clear. I told you he was paranoid." Another sniff, and she dabbed at her nose with a paper napkin. "I guess he had reason to be."

"You didn't tell anyone about this arrangement, not your mother, not anyone, not even a hint?"

Again, the answer was immediate. "No one. Jerry was a fanatic about that, and he insisted he had never told a soul, either. He said it would all be worth it when it was over."

"When was that going to be?"

"He didn't say, I didn't ask. Lately I've been too busy, and I got so used to making the buys, I didn't even think about it much anymore. But I had the impression it wouldn't be too long. Like a few more months, a year, maybe. That's a guess."

Jack turned to Truss before the guy had time to think and asked, "Did you know about this?"

The man's fair skin reddened. "*No*. This is the first I'm hearing about anything. I didn't even know Jerry owned *Herald* stock."

"Do you?"

"No." As the other three at the table gazed at him, he said, "Not a penny. I hate to say it, but the truth is, no one in their right mind is investing in newspapers at this point. That ship has sailed."

"You work there."

"Yes, in the digital division. I have faith that online news can be made profitable, but history has not yet borne that out. I think it will. I intend to try my hardest. But I'll wait until we have a number of quarters in the black before I invest my IRAs in *Herald* stock." He reconsidered his candor. "Don't tell Roth I said that, though. Seriously, don't."

The cops stared at him. Jack said, "According to you no one in their right mind would invest. But Jerry did. And he seemed in his right mind."

The man crossed his arms. "Yes, he did. Obviously he had a plan he didn't let me in on, or he knew something I don't. I can't explain it."

He spoke openly, without squirming or looking away, but Jack still didn't believe him. Or rather, he did and didn't. Truss sounded a bit outraged when talking about the stock, perhaps annoyed that his friend had seen a sure thing and hadn't let him in on it. But as to Wilton's motives for trying to corner the market . . . it seemed that Truss might have some solid theories on what his friend had been thinking. Dots had begun to connect in his mind.

Under this scrutiny Truss did squirm. "I'm telling you, Jerry and I were friends to have a drink now and then after work, or compare fantasy football picks. But we weren't BFFs. I had only met Shania once or twice before she showed up on my doorstep last night." That comment fell with a thud and he hastened to cover her hand with his own again, speaking to her directly. "But I'm glad you did. Anything I can do to help. My couch is yours as long as you need it."

The gratitude in her smile seemed to make him forget Jerry Wilton and his stock deals. "Thank you. But I'm ready to go home, sleep in my own bed, wash in my own shower—"

"Miss Paulson—" Riley started.

"I don't think you should," Tyler Truss said. "Whoever killed Jerry is still out there. If they knew about this stock deal, they might know about you, too."

"That is a point, Miss Paulson. We think you should come with us. We can provide protective custody for you."

"You can stay here," Truss said.

She appeared to think this through—quite rationally, to judge from her next comments. "How would that benefit the killer, though? It's not like he's going to get access to Jerry's stock. I have a will, if I died all my assets would go to my mom, and after her to my sister Cindy. Unless they want my laptop, figure they could get to the site from my browser history. But they couldn't withdraw from the stock accounts without my password. I suppose maybe a hacker could find it in there—is that possible?"

"I don't know," Riley said, weariness from the long day showing in his voice. "And until we do, you shouldn't be alone."

Shania said, "Okay," to Truss, not to Riley.

"Miss Paulson—"

"It's okay. I'd rather stay here than be stuck in

a hotel room with some cop—no offense. But I wouldn't know them."

Riley visibly struggled with a way to point out that she didn't know Tyler Truss, either, and gave up. "Nothing against Mr. Truss, here, but he is almost a total stranger as well."

"Ty's been great! He brought me right in and—"

"Could we have this discussion in private, please?"

"No, Ty was Jerry's friend, and he didn't know anything about this stock business. I *know* that."

She stood up, arms crossed over her chest, relatively large for her slight frame, and pushed the hair back where it brushed her firm jawline. Whatever else Tyler Truss might be, Jack thought, he wasn't blind. But he by no means had been struck from their list of suspects, either . . . even though he didn't have a Rottweiler or a willow tree, or— "Is that tie silk?"

Truss reacted as if Jack had suddenly spouted words in Swahili, and the other two people in the room stared as well. Truss's chin dipped; he picked up the end of the multicolored tie as if wondering why it sat on his chest, dropped it, and said, "Uh—yeah."

"Okay."

Riley brushed off his partner's odd outburst and pressed on. "Something is going on at your cousin's paper, Miss Paulson, and until we know what it is, everyone who works there is a suspect. Again, we mean no offense to Mr. Truss, but we can't in good conscience leave you here under those circumstances."

"I don't care about your conscience! I—" She snuck an embarrassed glance at Truss, then continued. "I *like* Ty. I trust him, and if he wanted to murder me he could have done it last night when no one knew I was here, or after he picked me up at the gym today. He could have dumped my body—"

"Shania," Truss said, as if ill at ease with the talk of bodies. He was either a really nice guy who had fallen immediately in love with Jerry Wilton's cousin, or he was a really good actor.

"—and gotten completely away with it. You can't tell me what to do."

"We can arrest you as a material witness. On paper, Miss Paulson, you are the most likely suspect in your cousin's murder."

"What?"

"By your own admission you and he shared funds that are now yours alone."

"You're going to put me in cuffs? Just because I won't do what you want? You have no idea how many lawyers I know—"

"Not as many as I do," Riley snapped back.

"Shania," Truss said.

"—and we can sue you for harassment—"

"Shania, they're right," Truss said, and his

capitulation startled her into silence. "You may be in very great danger, and I don't even have a gun. If some knife-wielding, strangling psycho breaks in here, I can't guarantee your safety."

"*I* can," she said, still puffed up with the adrenaline of stress and annoyance.

"You'll be safer with them." He played his last card. "I wouldn't want anything to happen to you."

She gave up. "Okay. Maybe you're right." She rallied long enough to fix Riley with a glare. "It had better be a *nice* hotel."

Riley, wisely, said nothing.

But as Shania Paulson moved around to gather up her backpack, Jack's partner hissed to him, "I could have taken her."

Chapter 38

Too wound up from the night's activities, Maggie went back to her lab. In the cool silence she could reexamine her trace evidence and maybe see something she hadn't before. But then she picked up Jack's fingerprints—his *real* fingerprints—and sat down with all the latents collected from the Johnson Court building and the house on East 40th. She wouldn't have a better opportunity to weed his out without Carol or Denny or Amy seeing her work on a case she wasn't supposed to be working on. Josh wouldn't notice, or care, that she had done half his task for him. Josh had enough to do.

Several prints had been identified as belonging to prior victims such as Marcus Day, but many remained unidentified. Jack had been good about wiping down the table and more permanent structures of his "murder room," like the Plexiglas he had put over the windows, but not the collection of alcoholic beverages or the battered work desk in the corner. She found four that were his, neatly identified three of them as "Det. J. Renner," and put them back in their envelope. They would not be sent on to any federal agency. They would not be sent anywhere. Jack's past would not be exposed, not to the Cleveland

Police Department, and not to her. Jack could go on killing the Ronald Soltises of the world.

And how did she *feel* about that?

The same way she'd felt about it for the past few weeks. She was protecting a murderer, and therefore protecting herself, because she had become a murderer, too. As simple as that. The law said that murder was murder. But it also said that the purpose of people like Jack and herself was to protect citizens. Trying to figure out which declaration took priority ran her around in circles and she had tired of that. Her brain couldn't handle any more calisthenics.

Still she sat there, the fourth latent print under her fingers. What would happen if she sent it on? What if some toiling FBI fingerprint analyst scanned it into their database, let the massive servers compare its tiny ridge endings and divisions to the hundred million sets of people's fingerprints but, more importantly, to the millions of unidentified crime scene prints. The servers churned twenty-four hours per day, seven days per week, every week of every year. Someday they might spit out a match. This match would tie their series of murders to—what? More murders? Crimes even more horrific than a pattern of cold executions?

It wouldn't necessarily incriminate Jack. It would simply tie their unknown vigilante killer to murders in other places, other times, which she knew and everyone else suspected must exist.

Perhaps it would hit on his 10-prints, a set collected long ago before he had crimes to hide. Perhaps it would be filed under his real name. She wondered what that might be.

That still wouldn't lead to the man she knew as Jack Renner, with his fake name and fake prints in the official file. But it might fill in his past for her, tell her exactly whom she was dealing with.

Unless there weren't any other crime scene prints to find. Maybe this had been the first time he hadn't had time to clean up after himself. Maybe he hadn't *left* prints anywhere else.

Unlikely, she knew. People touch more than they think they touch.

It was awfully tempting, to get a glimpse of who Jack Renner had been before he became Jack Renner . . . tempting, but dangerous. For both of them. If the police caught him, the first thing he would do would be to make a deal by giving her up. He owed her nothing, and once his secret became known she had nothing with which to buy his silence.

She labeled the fourth latent and dropped it into the envelope. It wouldn't be going to the FBI. It would stay here, locked in a file, neatly identified and written up and with no reason for any person to ever look at it again.

"What are you doing here?" said a voice at

her elbow, causing her to both die of a massive coronary attack and scatter latent print cards across the floor.

"Sorry," her boss told her.

"Denny! What are you doing to me?"

"I thought you'd hear me walk up. You usually do." The head of the forensic unit wore a thin sweatshirt, what looked suspiciously likepajama bottoms, and a child. Said child slumbered against her father's chest in a soft fabric carrier so comfortable-looking that Maggie had to stifle a feeling of envy. "I guess you were really concentrating."

Maggie rubbed her face before picking the cards up from the floor. "You do realize it's two a.m."

"She wouldn't sleep."

Maggie peeked at the week-old child, slumbering with mouth agape, tiny ebony hands curled into fists. "She sure looks like she's sleeping."

"*Now,* yes. But she won't sleep if anyone else is sleeping. We haven't been able to so much as blink at the same time since she came home. The kids can't stay awake through their classes, and my wife is getting that scary look."

"She's scared?"

"She scares *me.*"

"So you brought the kid to a forensics lab?"

"Look at her—she doesn't care. As long as at least one of her parents is not sleeping she's happy, the sadistic little demon spawn. I thought I'd check my e-mail. Why are *you* here?"

"I couldn't sleep, either."

Denny slumped against Josh's desk, knocking over a battered action figure of Boba Fett, and patted the back of his small offspring. "Has that been every night, or—"

"Come on, Denny, not you too. I've got enough with Carol practically wanting to take my temperature and BP every hour."

He didn't smile. "I know you're tough, okay? Believe me, I know. But—"

"It's not a matter of tough. I'm just not traumatized, at least not that I can figure. Even if I were, there's not much I can do about it. I'm up because I had a late call—cops finally located a suspect and I needed to bring her laptop in. I'm not having night terrors or anything like that."

Although she had. The nightmares came, and often. But she considered that, as Dr. Michaels would say, typical, and not cause for alarm.

"Okay," Denny reassured her. "I just care about you, okay?"

"I thank you. But I'm all right. You seem more strung out than I am right now—no offense."

"I can't take offense to the truth. Did you have your appointment with the counselor?"

"I did. Nice lady. Don't you have e-mail to check?"

"Plenty of time. If I go back to that house

before dawn my wife will construct a barricade. My kids will help her slide the couch in front of the door, and the neighbors would probably pitch in for good measure. How did it go? Your appointment?"

"Just fine. As I said, nice lady." They stared at each other, Maggie feeling at a loss, Denny studying her with those too-observant eyes. "If you're waiting for me to relay my feelings for my mother, you'd be better off pacing the lobby. Your kid's stirring."

Indeed, baby Angel pounded her fist gently against her father's shirt, her hand so slight it didn't make a sound. Denny jumped up as if the desk had caught fire and walked in a circuit around it, weaving past Maggie's for good measure.

But he kept talking. "The department requires it, you know. Liability. So she's nice, but does she seem like she has a clue?"

"Oh, yeah." Uncomfortably so, Maggie thought.

"What did she say?"

"Confidential."

He laughed. "Sorry, I wasn't asking for details. I mean, she didn't make any noises like she'd recommend a leave of absence or anything, did she?"

"No . . . sort of implied that I'd better cooperate or she'd *start* making such noises."

"So you'll—"

"Aren't I always cooperative?"

A small puff of air. "If you say so."

"We got on famously," Maggie assured him. "We chatted for quite a while. I even asked her what she thought the vigilante's motivations were—"

"Wait. You asked *her?* I thought she was supposed to be asking you stuff."

Maggie rubbed the back of her neck, aching after hours with the prints. "I figured since I had to spend time with her, might as well put it to use. She's the one with the PhD in What Makes People Tick. What?"

Her boss swayed from side to side, keeping the baby in soothing motion, so perhaps he only appeared to be shaking his head at her. "Maggie, Maggie, Maggie. You're the only one who would take a therapeutic counseling session and turn it into a research exercise."

"Maybe I find research therapeutic."

He kept up the motion. "With anyone else I wouldn't buy that, but you—so okay, did you learn anything interesting?"

"Just what we'd already guessed. He thinks of himself as a hero. He believes that he's doing the right thing."

"Crazy, in other words."

"Dr. Michaels doesn't like to use words like crazy," Maggie informed him. She had a problem with it herself. Jack struck her as anything but insane . . . except in certain moments, when demons threatened to overtake him, demons he wouldn't admit to having. Was that insanity?

"Anything else? Wait, I've got to have some coffee or I won't make it back home. You want some? You shouldn't have any. You should go home and get some sleep."

"Let me do it. I can't have a sleep-deprived man dangling an infant over a hot plate."

Angel kicked, so Denny kept walking as Maggie got out the filters and the grounds. She could talk to Denny, she knew she could, without worrying that he would store her admissions away to be used against her when he needed a wedge. She trusted him. But there were topics she didn't want to discuss with anyone, not a close friend and certainly not a trained psychiatrist. The trained psychiatrist asked too many uncomfortable questions.

"Do you feel guilty, Maggie?"

"Because he got away? Disappointed. Not guilty."

"I meant because he killed that person and not you?"

The concept had stunned her. Survivor's guilt—no. She had much more immediate factors to feel guilt over. Like pulling the trigger, like committing murder. Like helping Jack cover up his crimes. Like knowing that he could be out there committing more, and all because she had done nothing to stop him.

"That's normal, you know. Or typical, if you prefer."

"Yes," Maggie said, keeping very still in the midst of her personal minefield, not daring to move more than an inch in any direction. "I understand that."

"You might even feel grateful to him."

"Grateful?"

"For not killing you. He spared you—twice. Why do you think he did that?"

"Because killing me would have been against his code," Maggie said, but absently. Her mind had already leapt ahead to her own actions. Is that why she let him go? Because he had saved her from Dillon Shaw and she felt she owed him? Did she kill his final victim so he wouldn't have to? To return a favor by sparing *him?* Or to get herself so enmeshed in the crime that the question of turning him in, or not, simply went away?

If she hadn't pulled that trigger, she would have no reason to protect his identity. She could have told the cops the complete truth. Even Jack had been prepared for that outcome.

But by doing so, the question became not

should she protect him, but what did she need to do to protect herself?

She thought she had done it out of rage, hatred, a desire to step out of her cocoon and take action. Those were selfish reasons. But perhaps her reasons had been even more trivial: to make one tough decision purely in order to avoid another. She didn't want to work against Jack because she appreciated his motives, his urge to protect, and so she made it impossible for herself to do so. She had forced herself into a box, limited her choices. And it had worked very well. Jack walked free. And so did she.

Was she grateful?

Did her simmering anger and discomfort with him stem from the knowledge that she had walked herself into that box?

She heard a coo beside her as Denny's small daughter talked in her sleep. "I think the coffee's done," her boss told her. "You've been staring at the full pot for three circuits now."

"It *is* three o'clock in the morning, you know."

"Believe me, I do." He took the cup she offered, turned his head, and sipped, keeping the hot liquid as far from Angel as he could without dislocating his neck.

She studied the infant, the dark eyelashes, the

teensy fingernails. "Let me know if you need someone to spell you and Angel's mom. Walking around in a circle—even I could handle that."

"Not tonight, missy. Finish up and get out of here. You're falling asleep on your feet."

"Okay, boss. Maybe you're right," she told him . . . though her mind roiled too strongly for sleep to be an option. Not tonight. Maybe not ever again.

Chapter 39

"Zoe," Maggie said. "Jack. Jack, Zoe."

"Good evening," he said. In the lowered light of the electronic evidence room, the forensic computer tech studied him before returning the greeting. "Are you getting anywhere?"

"No," both women said in unison.

Maggie summed up. "We've spent all day getting Shania's e-mails, bank accounts, the online trading account. Everything seems to be just as she told you. She e-mailed Jerry Wilton and he e-mailed her. No one else. All her other communications deal with dinner, shopping, family gossip, and the Indians' spring schedule. She didn't talk to anyone else about the stocks, at least not via e-mail."

Zoe added, "Unless she's got some secret code worked into the price of sports bras at Macy's and her new nephew's birth weight. I never understand why people tell you how much a baby weighed when it was born. What do I care? And isn't that a violation of privacy anyway? The kid's got the rest of his life to be obsessed with weight, does it have to be his label from day one?" Noting their stares, she said, "Oops. Sore subject with me, I guess."

Jack asked, "Did she communicate with anyone else from the *Herald*? This Tyler Truss, for instance?"

"Nope. Unless she used smoke signals, or, you know, snail mail—"

"Or actually talked to them," Maggie said.

"Yeah, barbaric stuff like that; otherwise, no."

An officer appeared in the doorway and told Zoe he had a phone to submit. She told him, "Forget it. It's way past quitting time."

He said, "But you're still here."

"Yeah, what *is* up with that?" She gave Maggie a good solid glare before pulling herself out of her chair, leaving Jack and Maggie alone. When the sound of her footsteps in the hall faded away, Jack said, "You look tired."

She knew it, although she had grabbed a few hours at home to the point of coming in late that morning. But the day had become an endless cycle of evidence processing, computer analysis with Zoe, more caffeine, and wondering when Alex would begin to suspect there might be more to her story. "Never tell a woman that. You might as well say I look like crap and get it over with."

"Okay. You look like crap. What's happening with those fingerprints?"

"From Johnson Court? So, you are a little concerned."

"No . . . just . . . did you pull any prints of mine?"

"All taken care of."

"What if you missed one?"

"I didn't." She wondered why he seemed so worried about it. Somewhere out there must lay one hell of a crime spree, its latents humming along in the FBI's unsolved files—or else he wouldn't care. She felt a twinge of regret for not giving in to temptation and sending one from Johnson Court along . . . then stomped on that twinge. This wasn't a game she was playing. This could put her in jail for the rest of her life.

Jack sat back. He did not look reassured, but put it aside to muse aloud on the *Herald* murders.

"So Jerry is doing a little insider trading. But what does that have to do with Robert and Stephanie Davis? They didn't have funds to invest and all of their paychecks went to bills."

"Maybe Jerry's stocks have nothing to do with it," Maggie said.

"Maybe we have two murderers."

"That would complicate things," Maggie understated. "If there are other people trying to get the inside edge, how could we ever find them? You can't subpoena the financial records of everyone who works at the *Herald*—"

"And that wouldn't even have caught Wilton. He used Shania to conceal his purchases."

"And they're not about to fess up. Insider trading is a crime, isn't it?"

"Why do it at all? What made Jerry Wilton believe that the stock price would increase?"

320

Maggie said, "An impending sale to TransMedia, of course. That would raise the stock price, and everyone there seems to think it's in the offing."

"Riley and I should talk to TransMedia—they're in the catbird seat, maybe they'd feel free to be honest. But I have no idea who to approach, and Roth won't even admit they're in negotiations."

Maggie thought of something. "Ask Roger. You said he's been keeping tabs on the editor's lunch dates. He'd know their names."

Jack raised one eyebrow. "Roger?"

"Yes."

"You shouldn't hang around that guy."

The absurdity of *him* telling her that made her laugh, and she considered asking him again whether or not he had killed Ronald Soltis. She decided not to—whether he had or not, she doubted his answer would change.

"He's been remarkably educational. He could probably give you the TransMedia guy's phone number and arrange an introduction."

"He's our best suspect."

"All the more reason to listen to anything he says."

"Hmm," Jack said. "I'd ask the same question of TransMedia that I'd like to ask Jerry Wilton. His coworkers thought a sale would finish the paper for good. Why did he think the stock price was going to skyrocket in an industry that's pure doom and gloom, and he believed it so much that he sunk every penny he had into it."

"Good question. According to Roger, before the ink is dry on the contract, they'll cut back all spending at the paper, lay off most of the staff, and get by with a skeleton crew. They'll coast for a few months on the backs of the habitual readers, farm out the best writers and managers to jobs in other concerns, find buyers for the physical stuff including the presses and the building. Then they'll announce that the paper's problems were too profound for them to overcome and shut down."

"Assuming Correa is playing for your sympathy, what *else* would make them want to buy the *Herald*?"

"TransMedia would want a high profit margin. Low cost, steady income. They have to be able to sustain the kind of ROIs to which their shareholders have become accustomed."

"ROI?"

"Return on investment."

He considered her. "You got a secret MBA, Maggie?"

"I knew a lot of business majors in college."

"According to everything we've been told, the *Herald*'s profit margin is not all that enticing."

Something occurred to her. "Jerry Wilton was juggling the circulation numbers."

Jack's stare told her that he had forgotten about

that. "Yes, making it seem like the paper had more print readers than it does. Why?"

"Circulation is what brings in advertisers. Advertisers produce profit. High profit margin equals good investment."

"Yes. But would that be enough? Enough for Jerry to invest every penny he had?"

"Why not? Even a small increase could—wait a minute." She leaned forward. "You're right, it's not enough, because print is only part of the equation. Even Roger admits that the number of print readers is never going to grow. It's a habit of earlier generations, which young people have never formed. If a newspaper is to survive at all, it will be as a largely digital publication."

Now Jack leaned forward, his face intense and lit by the glow of Zoe's computer screen. "Wilton had to know that just increasing the print circ numbers wouldn't be enough. Digital readership would have to increase even more."

"But he couldn't fake that, could he?"

"I'll bet his buddy Tyler could, though."

Again, a shadow appeared in the doorway. "What are you two doing sitting in the dark?" Riley asked.

"Waiting for Zoe," Maggie said.

"We need to talk to Truss again," Jack told his partner.

"That," Riley said, "is going to be difficult."

Chapter 40

It should have given her a feeling of déjà vu, to be met in the lobby by Printing Supervisor Kevin Harding. But this time the chipper personality that had seen him through the surprise of Robert Davis's death had fled, leaving a haunted expression of shock. He stared at Maggie, Jack, and Riley as if he had never seen them before.

"Kevin?" Maggie asked.

"It's awful," he told her, but straightened up and led the three people through the building. As before, rooms were largely empty. A lone reporter sat at a desk and barely glanced up as they walked by, too far away to hear Kevin Harding's account of finding the body.

"We had started the printing, so the sheets and rolls room was empty. Me and my two guys were monitoring the rollers and the folder, of course . . . then the rolls started getting low, so I went to put another on the shoe. Our lights—the lights are on motion sensors to, you know, save money. So I didn't see anything in the . . . dimness . . . but I heard a little splash."

He glanced down at his feet. Maggie saw flecks of dried, dark liquid along the tops of the brown leather, and knew that whatever they were going to see would be, indeed, awful.

"I thought one of the ink tanks had leaked, one of the pipes got a hole in it—it's happened before, made a terrific mess and wrecked the whole run—so right away I went to the tank to shut down the valves. Then the lights came on. And I saw . . . it wasn't ink."

He led them past the room with the aluminum sheets, into the pen of huge paper rolls.

Beyond them, the rollers were still. The run hadn't finished—continuous streams of newsprint formed their spiderweb from one to another and into the next room. They hung in midair as if under a magic spell. She caught a glimpse of Roger Correa's byline and a story about New Horizons . . . just a few paragraphs, a taste of what would come. The deafening cacophony of the moving rollers would have been preferable to the blanket of eerie silence that now lay across the space.

The overhead lights sprang into action, bathing the room in an unforgiving glare. Infected by Kevin Harding's sense of horror, the cops and Maggie moved slowly past the rolls of paper. They seemed almost sentient to her, waiting, watching for a command to come to life. Past them she saw the red that wasn't ink, spread across the concrete.

Tyler Truss lay next to a roll that had been

placed on its side, as several others in the space had been in preparation for loading onto a shoe. His arms were flung wide, the roll still resting on his left hand, and his body caved in from shoulders to knees. The limbs remained connected, but that was the best Maggie could say for them. His chest looked as if someone had taken a fist to a bag of chips. Some of his small intestines lay piled to one side, having burst out of not only his abdomen but his shirt as well. His clothes had soaked in fits and starts, not a solid stain but a spreading patchwork of red.

A roll had obviously gone right over him. But had he just lain there and waited to be crushed?

"They weigh nineteen hundred pounds," Kevin murmured from behind them, as if facts and figures would explain what they saw. "Unrolled, one will stretch for 8.4 miles."

"Then who did this?" Riley demanded, his voice strangled. "The Incredible Hulk?"

"They're not that hard to push," Kevin said. "Maggie could probably push one across the room once she got it moving, and since we were halfway through the run he had space in here to get some speed up."

"He?" Jack asked.

"Whoever," Kevin said.

Jack turned to him. "And no one saw anything?"

"Once the rolls are lined up, we're done in here. No reason to . . . come back . . ."

"And he could have screamed his head off without anyone hearing it over the printing," Riley finished for him.

They could hear murmurs from the loading dock area around the corner and past the roller towers. At least Truss got a measure of privacy from curious coworkers. Maggie felt sure this would not make him feel a whole lot better.

She moved closer, mindful of the tacky puddle on the concrete. She would have to get some plastic steps to be able to work around the body. The blood had spattered as far as the roller towers, leaving a fine mist across the concrete and up the machinery frame.

The dead man's feet and head were soaked with it, but otherwise unscathed. He stared out at the roller towers without expression, the laces on his shoes still neatly tied. Somehow that seemed more horrifying, and more sad, than the dripping entrails and drenched paper.

"How do you know this is Tyler Truss?" she asked Harding.

He pointed to the crushed torso, where an ID tag still clung to the pocket of a formerly blue dress shirt. It said TYLER TRUSS and bore the photo of a smiling young man Maggie had never met.

Jack grasped her arm. She turned to see that

look again, the one that frightened her. She had grown more accustomed to him in the past few days, able to forget the past long enough to fit him into a normal part of her workday. Now all that hard-won relaxation dried up as if it had never been.

"Gutting Wilton was bad enough," he said, his voice so low she could barely make out the words. "Making the Davis boys into orphans was bad enough. But this—"

She couldn't come up with a response. No one killed like this over a business deal, and yet this killer wasn't crazy. As the scent of Tyler Truss's last drop of blood wafted up to her nose, she knew—this was *evil*.

She agreed with Jack on that.

She only feared what he might do about it.

Maggie turned to the three men. In a level voice she said, "I need to get some stuff out of my car."

Chapter 41

She didn't start out with high hopes for the crime scene, as far as fingerprints went. Every inch of machinery in the place required a great deal of oiling and lubricants that coated the surface and were then overlaid by the handling of a few dozen print crew workers and especially the dust. Even fresh paper had tiny fibers that abraded with each movement, each pivot, each fold, each cut, and turned into an incredibly fine dust that settled on every surface in the printing area.

In fact, vacuums collected the dust from various points in the process and transferred it to a large metal box the size of several refrigerators put together, next to the ink tanks. Every so often it gave a shuddering *clang* that took several months off Maggie's life, despite Kevin Harding's warning that the huge filter within had to be shaken now and then to make the tiny particles fall off it to the bin at the bottom. For all the noise it didn't do a good enough job to suit her, because everything she examined seemed to be coated with a fingerprint-preventing coating of the stuff.

Riley and Jack had gone to canvas the loading dock area, to find out who had been present when and what they might have seen. Kevin Harding, an ashen cast over his dark skin, returned with the Medical Examiner's investigator. He then hovered, approaching them, getting a glimpse of the body, turning a little green and then retreating to the roller towers. Perhaps compelled by loyalty to his coworker, he would wander back until accidentally catching sight of the body. He didn't want to stay but would feel ashamed if he left—Maggie had seen it before. He was in her crime scene, but that was all right. The alien landscape prompted a lot of questions, and it saved time to have him present to answer them.

The ME investigator, still statuesque and still very pregnant, took in the scene with one glance. "That's not something you see every day."

"Tell me about it," Maggie said.

They placed plastic sheets over the blood puddles—Maggie had inspected them as best she could with shoe coverings and halogen lights and found nothing of interest. The ME investigator also found nothing that surprised her on Tyler Truss's body. His torso made a crackling sound whenever she touched it, the noise of broken bones grating against one another. She also retrieved his wallet and a set of keys.

"No phone," Maggie said aloud. "The killer always takes the phones. But what happened before the crushing—did Truss just hand over his phone and then lie obediently on the concrete?"

"I doubt it," the investigator said, her hands in the silky black hair. "He's got a lump back here and maybe, a chip of bone. Someone hit him pretty hard."

"That fits the pattern as well," Maggie said. "And explains a lot. He must have been unconscious—"

"Then why are his eyes open?"

"I-I don't know. Do you think—"

"I think he woke up at a very inopportune moment," the investigator said, leaving Maggie with a mental image she tried hard to dispel. Instead, she looked around for more clues.

The killer had nearly twenty-five feet of vacated space to get the roll of paper up to sufficient speed to go over Truss's body instead of merely pinching one side of it. She crouched down and held her flashlight at a forty-five-degree angle to the floor that hadn't been stained with his blood. Dust, a myriad of shoeprints, paper shavings, a dead fly sprang into view. A few hairs, which she collected in a glassine paper fold. A tuft of something dark—she took a quick look with a loupe, trying not to breathe and blow away the lightweight fibers or fuzz or feather down that made it up.

She turned her attention to a lump of what looked like dried mud. Nothing seemed helpful. The killer almost certainly worked in the building, and thus could easily explain away any trace he might have left in the crime scene. Even if his fingerprints appeared on the paper roll—her best bet, once she could remove the outer covering and get it back to the lab to be plied with ninhydrin—it might not necessarily prove anything. The printing area wasn't exactly locked down. Traffic was discouraged for reasons of safety, not security, and the loading dock area had a number of vending machines that any employee might decide to access.

Along one wall sat a row of paper rolls, still on their ends instead of their sides. They couldn't have been moved without the aid of heavy equipment, so she ignored them and turned to the other wall. The tanks of ink—which must have held at least eight or nine hundred gallons each—stood with pipes and spigots coming out of them. A heavy adjustable wrench sat on an electrical box next to one of them.

She used the flashlight to take a closer look, saw a black hair caught in its teeth.

"I put that there," Kevin Harding admitted, suddenly at her elbow.

"What? Why?"

"Because I thought the red tank was leaking. I thought I'd have to turn the valve off and it's old. But by the time I reached the tank the lights had come on, I looked down, and realized there wasn't any ink in front of the tank. I turned around and saw—him." He didn't reenact this part, keeping his back to his dead coworker.

"So you set the wrench here?" She gestured.

"Yes."

"Where did it come from?"

He blinked. "From—here. The electrical box. That's where it usually is."

"So you picked it up from here and then put it back down?"

"Uh-huh, once I realized I wasn't going to need it. Then I turned and—"

"Yeah, I got that." She picked up the wrench with two fingers at its neck and dropped it into a bag. If the killer had used it to disable Tyler Truss, he had put it back in its proper place afterward. Why? To keep her from thinking it had anything to do with the death? Perhaps he didn't wear gloves and worried about fingerprints, not realizing that she could get them much more easily from the paper around the roll than from a dirty, rough tool handle?

Or from force of habit, because he worked in this area often and needed tools to be put back where they belonged?

Kevin again retreated to the roller towers, and Maggie looked more closely at the electrical box and the ink tanks. One small screw in the side of the box held a clump of blue fibers. With a loupe and a flashlight she decided that they didn't have the same layer of paper dust than every other surface in the area. Maybe they belonged to the killer's pants. Of course, maybe they belonged to Kevin Harding's pants. Hell, maybe they belonged to *her* pants—humans came into contact with so many more surfaces during the course of a day than they believed. Nevertheless, she collected them.

What did the killer do next? He had to get out of the building and she and Rebecca had disabled his escape route. The fire door would have sounded its alarm. Jack had said he would check all the other fire doors to make sure he hadn't set up a new one for himself. If all the contacts remained intact, then the killer had to be on camera leaving the building. The print run began at about the same time every night. The time crunch would narrow their suspects a great deal.

Unless, of course, he was still in the building.

Maggie collected swabs from various areas, an exercise in futility because surely all the blood belonged to Truss. Body snatchers Deion and Tony arrived, again escorted by Kevin Harding. They had the same reaction as the investigator. A raised eyebrow from Tony and a "What the hell is *with* this place?" from Deion.

"Yeah, not what I wanted to be doing tonight, either," the investigator grumbled.

Maggie said, "This is probably even worse for you."

"Nah. My mother was right—the first three months are the worst. If this happened during my first trimester, I'd be puking right now. And for the next hour."

"I'm okay with you not doing that."

"So am I."

Deion and Tony laid out a plastic body bag and clean white sheet on a steel gurney. With gloves on, they pushed the murder weapon off the victim's left hand. The roll *wasn't* that hard to push, Maggie saw.

Once the blond investigator zipped the remains of Tyler Truss into his clean white bag, Kevin Harding approached. He had stayed at a distance throughout the process and looked as if he didn't need to be pregnant to start vomiting.

"I don't even know how to ask this," he said to Maggie. "But—what about the paper?"

"The paper?"

He gestured at the roller towers. "We . . . we have to get the paper out. But the paper rolls are all bloody and the day crew is gone, so . . ."

Maggie surveyed the damage. "You'll have to just sell what you've got. We can't release this area yet, and even if we could, the whole place is one big biohazard."

He exhaled through his teeth. "As if our circulation hasn't fallen enough."

Chapter 42

By the time Maggie had done all she could possibly do in the printing center, everyone had scattered and left her alone. Jack and Riley had gone to clear the building and eventually inform editor Roth that he had lost another employee, Printing Supervisor Harding disappeared, and the bustling loading dock workers and drivers had departed. That end of the area was dark and silent. The mini-forklifts were lined up against the wall, the large overhead doors were pulled down and locked, and the un-bloodied newspapers were on their morning trip across the city.

Quiet had descended, the calm after a tough job well done—at least for one more day. She could hear only a steady hum from the vending machines dispensing Fritos and Dr Pepper, and the only light came from that source as well. She found herself standing in a forty-by-fifty-foot area, its edges lost in shadow, with a concrete floor, the stacking and binding machineries, and three Formica-topped tables littered by used coffee cups. She had only glanced at this area before; it made one bookend for two of her four crime scenes, but had been full of people during both murders. The room itself had an alibi.

It contained no lockers, but one wall had been

completely given over to industrial shelving. Most of the items on these shelves related to vehicle maintenance—oil, washer fluid, parts from fan belts to headlights. Then there were supplies for the binding mechanism, the plastic straps fused by the binder to hold the stacks together until the drivers got them to where they were going. Each delivery person or carrier would have a box cutter to cut the straps off so the papers could be put in a vending box, or folded and tucked into someone's mailbox or tossed in their driveway.

It was a long process, from writing words on a screen to deciding which words got used to putting them all on a page, to printing that page, to getting it to people's homes in time for their six a.m. coffee. And they did exactly that every day. It was amazing now that, for the first time, she could see the process in her mind from start to finish. She could see why the people in that process didn't want to see it lost.

Next to the crates sat another box, on the bottom shelf, a dusty, worn, misshapen cardboard structure with something white peeking out the top of it. She pulled on the white shape, glowing vaguely in the dimness. It spooled out of the battered cardboard like a string of handkerchiefs from a magician's sleeve.

A white mesh strap, about an inch wide.

Her murder weapon.

"Huh," she said to herself. Not exactly earth-shattering news. She had always believed the strap would prove too generic to positively identify the killer even if they found him with it, and its presence here simply pointed to someone inside the *Herald*, where the investigation had been pointing all along. As a clue, then, not particularly helpful. All their suspects—if they could even be sure of their list of suspects—had access to this room, and even if they didn't it would be no trouble to enter through the open overhead doors during loading hours.

All the same, it could be one loose end—no pun intended—tied up, the goal in every investigation. You never knew what tiny detail could become a huge stumbling block during the trial phase. She should collect the end of this strap right now, to compare it to the cut ends found on Stephanie Davis.

She heard a sound behind her.

She straightened and turned. She saw no one, but somehow the shadows seemed deeper than they had before. The vending machines were to her left, against the interior wall; now their illumination seemed to blind her, turning the north half of the space into a black hole.

She did not move.

She thought she could hear someone breathing, but surely that had to be her imagination. Whoever had murdered Truss could still be in the building, but he—or she—had no reason to attack her—she didn't work for the *Herald*. While she might have discovered the source of their mesh straps, it brought her no closer to the killer's identity.

The blackness beyond the vending machines' illumination shifted and separated. Someone was there, a dark figure. She heard the faint whisper of cloth against moving skin and picked up the slightest waft of human sweat. It could be her own, since her heart had begun to pound against the inside of her rib cage.

The compressor in the Coke machine kicked on. The split-second glance she threw its way ruined her vision all over again and the figure disappeared. Still rooted in front of the shelves, she scanned the area and saw nothing—except shadows that moved and drifted—

And then he was there.

Strong fingers grabbed her elbow and she jerked away.

"Maggie!"

In the light from the Coke machine the dark figure became Kevin Harding, looking ordinary and professional and very tall. And she had nothing but a mesh strap.

"What are you doing here?" he asked. The friendly tour guide of her first visit had disappeared.

It took a moment for her to find her voice. "Just looking around."

"You have to be careful in here. Our machinery can be dangerous."

"So I've seen."

"What do you have there?"

She still held the end of the white strap. "I think I found our murder weapon. From some of the deaths, anyway."

He frowned. "That? We—I didn't know we even had that."

"Why do you? Have it?" she asked without moving. She would not back up, even as he leaned his large frame over her to examine the box.

"They tie it to the door handles. The overhead doors—here on the dock, and on the trucks. Gives them something to grab to pull them back down again. That's all."

"Your editor said the paper didn't use straps like this."

Harding snorted. "He's never loaded a truck in his life."

"You didn't like Robert Davis." She didn't make it a question.

"No one did."

"Or Tyler Truss?"

Now he seemed to catch the drift of her thoughts. "I've run into Tyler Truss maybe five times in as many years. I just feel . . . I mean, he worked here . . ."

He had been stooping to look at the box, and

so they were eye to eye. "Do you have a dog?" she asked.

She heard a *click*. She looked down to see a box cutter in his hand, blade out.

"Dog? No." He moved the blade toward her. "Allergies."

"What are you—"

"I figured you'd want to cut a piece off." He rotated the box cutter so that he could hand it to her handle-first. "Why are you asking about dogs?"

"No reason." She took the cutter, turned her back on him, and cut off a length of the strap, tying a knot in the cut end so that she would know which end to compare with the pieces used in the murders. She *snicked* the blade back into its holder.

Kevin Harding held out his hand.

Don't hand a weapon back to a suspect just because he asks for it. That should be a rule in the cop handbook somewhere. Or at least the common sense handbook.

But because she didn't know what else to do, and because she knew if he really wanted to take it away from her, he could, she held out the cutter.

In one smooth move he took it and dropped it into the pocket of his khakis, then gave her a tired grin. "Want a Coke? I've got change."

Just like that, her fear evanesced and left chagrin in its place. "No, thanks anyway."

"Come on, I'll escort you to your car."

They walked away from the dim area, back into the well-lit place with the print rollers, taking a side hallway to avoid the paper roll warehouse. Only half its lights were on, but she no longer felt afraid. She asked where the cops were. Harding didn't know.

"You think whoever hung Davis took the strap from the loading dock?"

"It would make sense."

"Huh," he said, pausing in the midst of the reporters' bullpen. "You know what's weird?"

"What?"

"Strapline is something a copy editor would write."

"So I heard."

He took another step, noticed that she did not. "You want me to walk you to your car?"

She noticed a light on upstairs. "No," she told him. "I'm staying."

Chapter 43

Maggie wandered onto the second floor, the ring of offices looking down on the reporters' bullpen. From above, the desks looked as chaotic as always, especially Roger Correa's. For an industry with a purely digital future, it didn't seem ready to let go of the tactile feel of paper anytime soon. Blotters were scattered with notes and printouts, clippings, photos, as if a strong wind had whipped through the space. But the wind had stopped and the building sat silent and abandoned. It seemed that the churning stream of newsprint truly represented the lifeblood of the *Herald*, and without it, everything and everyone else had died.

She heard a sound, a soft *clunk,* from one of the offices up ahead.

The office at the very tip of the oval had a light on, and the door stood open. She moved toward it.

Franklin Roth sat behind his desk, staring at a bookshelf against one wall of his office. The other had been hung with framed photos of himself with local and national celebrities, various journalism awards, and a few front pages from the *Herald*'s history. Behind him windows spread wide so that he could watch the sun rise over the eastern half of the city every morning.

He'd been on the phone, finishing with: "Just

tell Mrs. Russo to call me as soon as you hear from her. We do still have a paper to get out, even if it doesn't feel that way." He hung up the receiver, rubbed his forehead, and caught sight of Maggie standing in his doorway.

He gazed at her without recognition. He seemed to have aged at least twenty years since their first meeting, his skin pasty, thin hair flat on his scalp, too many lines in the flesh under his eyes.

"Mr. Roth?"

His absent stare cleared. "Miss Gardiner. Are you finished with the print room?"

"Yes, but I'm afraid it won't be operable anytime soon. You'll have to have it cleaned—"

"Yeah, I get it. It doesn't matter. A day or two offline will hardly make a difference at this point."

She moved inside. "Why is that?"

He blinked, as if surprised at her interest—or her naïveté. His mouth opened once or twice to formulate an answer, before he said, "Sit down."

She did, taking one of the two armchairs across the desk from him. It was leather, soft and comfortable, and it felt good to sit. She'd been on her feet for hours.

He leaned over and opened a lower desk drawer, out of her sight, then produced a bottle. "You drink bourbon?"

She lied about her liquor preferences for the second time that week. "Sure."

"I hardly ever drink this—I think this bottle has been down there for at least ten years—but felt I had to have it. You know, the booze in the desk drawer. It goes with being an editor. Some traditions have to be maintained. Guess I watched too many movies as a kid. We all watch too many movies as kids. They teach us what to want, drill it into our heads, and we won't give it up, even when we know better. Could you get those two glasses there, on the shelf?"

Franklin Roth, Maggie decided, was in shock. She stood again, found two cut-glass tumblers on a matching tray in front of a matching series of textbooks on journalistic ethics. The tray sat next to a framed photo of a younger Franklin Roth and an attractive blond woman.

She held a wriggling black puppy.

"This your wife?" she asked, picking up the frame.

"Yes. She passed away—eleven years ago, now."

"Do you still have the dog?"

"Louie? Fourteen now, still going strong. You like dogs?"

"Sure." She set the glasses down gently on the blotter in front of him. "He's a Rottweiler, right?"

"You know your breeds." He spoke absently, his mind too full of what had happened to his paper to wonder at her curiosity about his pet. He plucked a tissue from a box on his windowsill and polished the glasses. Maggie retook her seat, staring at his tie and wondering if it were made of silk.

She took the glass he pushed at her and let him talk. She felt more than a little afraid to be alone with him, but even more afraid to leave. If she waited, Jack or Riley would find them there. Wouldn't they?

Franklin looked spent. But then, someone had crushed Tyler Truss under a paper roll. Someone who could move through the *Herald* offices unnoticed. Someone he would turn his back on. Someone familiar.

But she could not quite believe it had been this man.

He sipped. "I say it doesn't make a difference because we're on death watch here. The paper. The industry. The business of news as a whole, and maybe with it, democracy itself, if I can be a little melodramatic. People have more information than ever, and it's more useless than ever. Without information, *relevant* information, how can people know what the hell their leaders are doing?"

"That's what Roger says."

Roth gave a mirthless chuckle. "I'll bet he does. The paper is supposed to be a watchdog. News, as an entity, used to be considered so vital to democracy that the FCC *required* television channels to have a certain amount of public service content . . . as if they recognized right away what a time suck television was going to be. That's why TV news existed in the first place. When I was a kid you had three networks, they all had the news on at seven, and you had no choice but to watch it. But ratings weren't great—let's face it, no one in this country has ever been as big on staying informed as we would like to think. So in the late sixties broadcasters discovered market-driven journalism. Fluff, in other words. Feel-good stories, lost puppies, recipe ideas, and of course, the secret lives of celebrities. It raised ratings and still satisfied the FCC code. But then came cable, and people started watching reruns of *The Mary Tyler Moore Show* instead of Dan Rather. Now we have entire channels of news, quote unquote, that isn't remotely news. Magazines are the same—they're probably the only industry in America that's even worse off than newspapers. Ever wonder why you can stop renewing a magazine and they keep sending it to you for another couple years? Because subscriptions don't pay for it. Advertisers pay for it, and they want to see high circulation numbers. And corporations want to see profit. Lots and lots of profit. Sure you don't want a refill?"

"Maybe I will," she said, and passed her glass over the largely clean desk. Perhaps bourbon wasn't so bad after all.

"You see, in the sixties and seventies the

printing process changed. It began to require more skilled labor, more sophisticated machines. Small-town, family-owned papers were overwhelmed. The chains came in like carpetbaggers."

Maggie couldn't hear a sound from the rest of the building. She wondered if she and Roth were the only two left in it. She wondered where Jack had gone, and what he might be doing while she drank bourbon with Franklin Roth.

"Gannett, Knight Ridder, Tribune, McClatchy threw money at the families who were pained but relieved to sell out. By 1977, ten percent of newspaper corporations owned two thirds of the papers in this country. Meanwhile they not only bought up papers, they drove the ones they hadn't bought out of business—lied to advertisers, spread rumors that the other paper would soon be out of business so don't bother renewing your ad contract with them, they sold advertising space at a loss just to steal customers. Of course, once the other paper folded, rates went up and up and up, because once local concerns had no other options for ad space, they could charge whatever they wanted. I'm not making this up, young lady—"

"I didn't think you were," she said.

"—and this isn't industry rumor or innuendo. These are documented cases, lawsuits, proven violations of antitrust laws. Check out the Salem *Community Press*, the *Santa Fe Reporter*, the

Detroit News, the Green Bay *News-Chronicle*. Just to name a few. But what they hadn't figured out was that readership had fallen steadily, continued to, and no one had yet faced up to it. And there's no point in having a monopoly on a product no one is buying. That's why in the nineties all the newspapers started to get really creative with circulation numbers."

Now Maggie heard the slight scrape of a footstep in the hall. "Jerry Wilton handled that for you, didn't he?"

Roth drained his glass. "That was part of his job. But all circulation numbers are independently verified."

"Right, Media Audit. But that's only once or twice a year, isn't it?"

She felt rather than heard a shift in the air and figured Jack was standing in the doorway behind her. He was the only large man she knew who could walk that quietly. The sudden widening of Roth's eyes confirmed it.

"Wilton was cooking your numbers," he said to Roth. "You knew that."

The man's lips twisted, but he nodded.

"Because of TransMedia?"

"Every paper cooks their numbers," Roth burst out. "If they say they don't, they're lying. We were just trying to ensure a sale. TransMedia has to buy the *Herald*. If it doesn't, we're done. All of us."

Maggie heard Jack move, and he dropped himself into the chair next to her. She kept her gaze on Roth.

"And Truss?" Jack said. "He had the digital component of the paper. TransMedia would want to see strong online readership numbers, wouldn't they?"

Roth made a sweeping but listless toast with his glass. "Digital is the future."

"And they're both dead, Mr. Roth."

All three people in the room stayed completely still.

"Why is that?" Jack asked.

Roth set the glass down, carefully, as if it might break. Then he stopped being a legend and went back to being a man. "It was only to get a good price from TransMedia," he told them. "That's all we wanted."

Chapter 44

"We need to be bought," Roth started. "That's not in question. If we're not, the *Herald* will be in Chapter eleven by next year. We need TransMedia to save us."

"So the circulation numbers—"

"Had to look good. It's a business investment and TransMedia is very much a business concern. They want low costs and high income. They don't give a crap about public service or journalistic integrity. It's all numbers, and we only have six weeks before the NAA audits our figures."

"So you put some sawdust in the engine to make it sound smooth," Jack said. "Slapped on a coat of wax."

"That's it. Everyone does it."

"Sell out to the carpetbaggers?" Maggie asked.

Roth looked about ready to cry. "Wilde said, 'Each man kills the thing he loves.' Maybe it's more that each man becomes the thing he hates."

"But what happens after the sale?" Maggie asked.

The wet in Roth's eyes disappeared with one blink. He toyed with the empty tumbler.

Jack said, "Yeah, that's the problem, isn't it? What happens when this big corporation comes in, takes over, and somehow the circulation turns out to be a fraction of what they thought they were buying. They come looking for you. But you didn't plan to be here, did you?"

"I told them I was okay with taking retirement and letting a TransMedia guy assume the editorship."

"Of course you're okay with it. Because otherwise, board meetings would have gotten a little awkward, wouldn't they?"

Roth said nothing. Maggie waited, still.

"What about Wilton and Truss and—where did Davis fit in?"

For a moment Maggie thought Roth wouldn't answer.

"He worked with the printing crew. He'd know how many papers we were putting out, regardless of what Jerry reported. We had to bring him in, and he was more than willing. He had expensive tastes."

"How do you see this playing out?" Jack pressed. "You think we'll keep your little secret— after all, corporate espionage is a civil matter, not a job for cops. Maybe you can still pull this deal off. Or has it finally penetrated that the members of your little conspiracy have been picked off one by one, leaving . . . you. Which either makes you the killer or the next victim."

"I didn't kill anyone!" He looked from Jack to Maggie. "I had no reason to, and I would . . . I would never have done that."

"So you're next."

The man's shoulders sagged. "Yes, probably. I don't know."

Jack said, "Expensive tastes? Why does that figure in?"

"I'm just saying . . . Bob couldn't afford to lose his job. . . ."

Maggie heard Jack exhale as he made the leap. "You were going to get a kickback. TransMedia was going to pay you off to put this deal through."

Roth said nothing. He seemed to be holding his breath.

"You weren't looking for a savior out of the goodness of your heart. You were doing it for a fee. The *Herald* could—"

Roth banged the glass on his desk. "Don't tell me about my heart! I put my heart into this paper for twenty-five years, and into other papers before that! Of course I care about the *Herald*. Why do you think I did all this just to save it? But . . . I needed to save me, too. I'm too old to start over and I don't want to. So I wanted to pad my pension a bit. The objective didn't change."

"The objective? You really have become a businessman."

Maggie asked, "How was TransMedia going to pay you to lie to them?"

"Not to them," Roth admitted. "It—look—it was a deal. They buy the paper; I help smooth their way. That was all. The paper has to be bought or it's going to die, but they're tired of swooping in to save people's asses and being greeted with pitchforks and torches as if they're the devil. I convince the people here to take the buyout without all the drama, the paper continues, everyone wins."

"Except TransMedia, which buys a lame horse," Jack said.

"And your employees, whose jobs are slashed and their equipment harvested," Maggie said.

"Or we go into Chapter eleven by next year," Roth reminded them. "There are no good choices here, don't you get it? The good old days are not coming back. Unbiased, online news might survive if publicly subsidized, because it will never pay for itself. News*papers* aren't going to survive at all."

"Fascinating," Jack said. "But we still got a lot of dead people here, whose deadness has not yet been explained. Who else knew about this?"

"That's it. Just the four of us."

Maggie didn't believe him. He had just confessed to a crime, despite all his justifications. He might be trying to protect his last partner—or partners.

Or he wanted to keep those partners free and unencumbered so that he could take care of them, just as he'd taken care of Truss and Wilton. But why? Surely the buyout wouldn't happen now. He could not possibly keep the truth from

TransMedia, unless he killed both Jack and Maggie right then and there.

Jack pressed. "There had to be other people. Assistants. IT guys. Secretaries."

"No one! We never even talked about it here, only when we'd meet at Great Lakes Brewing. We'd even get a private area there. Everything was oral. No memos, no e-mails, no phone calls."

"Davis made a lot of phone calls, especially to Truss."

"Davis was an idiot."

"What about your publisher?" Jack asked.

Roth made a sound that sounded both relieved and derogatory. "Him? He has no clue what goes on here. He would sign anything I handed him."

"Low cost, high income," Maggie said. "Truss and Wilton bumped up the income. Who did you get to lowball your costs?"

"Nobody."

Jack said in a warning tone, "Roth—"

"Me, okay? I told you, editors have been doing the publisher's job for probably twenty years now. I handle the business end, spend more time on it than the journalism side. I shaved the costs."

"*Shaved*. I like that," Jack said.

"I estimated bids for paper and ink that were more optimistic than what we would probably end up with."

"Bully for you. Still not buying it, though, that

the trail ends here. If there's another conspirator on the loose—"

"Stop saying that. We're not *conspirators*."

"I hate to be the one to point this out, but conspirator is exactly what you are. I'm sure TransMedia would agree."

"And the SEC," Maggie added.

"Yes, regarding the stocks."

Roth gazed blankly across the desk. "Stocks?"

Jack told him, "Wilton had been buying up *Herald* stock, assuming the price would take a leap after the TransMedia sale."

Roth's eyes narrowed. "That was stupid. That's the kind of thing that lands you in court. . . ."

"He had someone else buy it for him."

"Oh. Well . . ."

"Now you're only sorry you didn't think of it yourself, aren't you?" Jack asked. "What about Stephanie Davis?"

Roth's face, which had been pasty, whitened further.

"That wasn't my fault," he said.

Chapter 45

"I didn't kill her!" he still insisted ten minutes later. "I didn't kill anyone!"

Jack said, "You just told us you went to Tower City to meet with her, where she proceeded to blackmail you."

"Bob had made notes about the number of papers printed that he got from Harding and how much we should increase it to look competitive with other papers. Idiot." Suddenly Maggie saw past the old-school reporter and caught a glimpse of the hard businessman, with nothing but contempt for an underling who couldn't follow a simple order. "All he had to do was back up whatever we said when the TransMedia goons asked him for confirmation."

"Annoying. You figured a squirrelly guy like him would never hold up under questioning or through the storm that would flatten this place once the ink dried on the deal with TransMedia. Oh wait, you didn't intend to still be here when that storm hit. You and the others would have taken your blood money and skedaddled." Jack's voice grew even harsher. "What happened when Bob's little wife figured out what was going on? Did she demand an explanation? Or a cut?"

"Both," Roth said, slumping back in his chair.

"You agree to meet, tell her whatever she wants to hear so that she leaves quietly and then catch up with her in the parking garage."

"No! I told her she could have his cut, no problem. I-I didn't care by that point, just wanted to get the sale done and over with. And she did have two kids to raise."

"What about now?" Jack said, his voice low. "You intending to pass Bob's money along to his orphaned children? That would be mighty nice of you, man."

Roth stared at them both. "I'm sorry for his kids. But I didn't kill Bob and I didn't kill Stephanie. I don't know who did."

"Who else here would have picked out these three particular guys to off? Is that pure coincidence?"

"I don't know! All I know is that I didn't kill anyone!"

Jack stood. "Mr. Roth, I have a feeling I'll be seeing you again before long."

The man's face went slack, elongating every wrinkle and worry line until he seemed to age before their eyes. She could see him try to rally, to inject a bit of bravado as he stated: "I'll be here. Tomorrow's paper still has to get to the streets."

But his voice quavered, and again his eyes filled with tears.

Maggie followed Jack to Rebecca's office. The young security guard seemed as weary and shell-shocked as Maggie felt. Maggie curled up on a worn couch with holes in the cushions that Rebecca had salvaged from a laid-off Features editor, and tried not to fall asleep. It was only nine-thirty p.m., but it felt like the wee hours of a cold morning.

Jack sat on one of the task chairs. Riley was off obtaining an arrest warrant for Franklin Roth. After listening to Jack's summary of Roth's statement, both cops agreed that it would be the logical next step.

Though neither, Maggie thought, seemed completely convinced of the man's guilt.

Rebecca skipped through the video coverage as quickly as she could without missing any quick movements. The quality of the video had not improved in the day or two since Maggie had last viewed it, though Rebecca had gotten a cleaning crew around to take care of the spiderwebs. But the resolution limits and low light after sunset kept the system's abilities in check. To make the images worse, it had been drizzling rain off and on all evening, so many employees of the *Herald* approached the doors under umbrellas or raincoat hoods, as effective as a ski mask for concealing face, hair length and color, sometimes even gender. Rebecca did what she could to guess at the identities, but only in a few cases that showed a distinctive car or coat could she be sure.

"I'm not liking it." Jack spoke to no one in particular after ten minutes in deep thought. "Why would Roth kill off his coconspirators before the deal went through? He needed them to rope in TransMedia."

"They really are going to buy us?" Rebecca asked, trying to catch up. Her job would be at stake as much as anyone else's.

Maggie said, "Don't know. TransMedia might step back and rethink investing in a place with a series of murders."

"This is a newspaper," Rebecca reminded her. "If it bleeds, it leads. I heard that our circulation spiked over the past week. One more murder will probably seal the deal."

"Maybe not once they find out all the stats that Roth and company fed them were lies. They'll have to start over from scratch, have every penny independently verified."

"I guess you'll see how much they want this paper," Jack told Rebecca. "And we'll see whether the killer nixed the deal or saved it."

Maggie said, "And which did they intend to do? I still think it's more likely to scare TransMedia away. Either way we're left with: Who *knew?* Roth says no one else. Who would Stephanie Davis have told about her blackmail plot? She had no confidantes here, and she said she hardly had family."

Jack said, "So he lied. He's protecting the fifth

member, the one who's stayed under the radar until now."

"If the TransMedia deal falls through, there's nothing to protect. They'd be unlikely to be prosecuted for attempted fraud—it wouldn't be worth TransMedia's time. Plus you made it clear to Roth that you intend to arrest him for murder. If he could steer us toward another suspect, don't you think he would?"

"Depends on how much he cares for number five, and how good he thinks our chances of a conviction are. With what we've got, his lawyer will get him out on bond. Then all he has to do is alibi for one of the murders and he can walk."

"True, but—"

"There's Ty coming in," Rebecca said.

They looked at the screens. The tall man arrived during a break in the rain and had hustled up to staff entrance number three, flashed his ID card at the scanner, and turned the latch. Jack made a note of the time.

Maggie finished her thought. "But what if he isn't the killer and neither is number five, if number five exists? What if someone *did* want to kill the deal? Someone was aware of this conspiracy the whole time, but Roth didn't know it."

"Who?"

Maggie rubbed her forehead. "That's the question. Kevin Harding might have somehow found out that Davis reported more papers printed than he knew to be true. Roger Correa was already keeping tabs on Roth. Jerry Wilton felt confident enough to invest in stock—who knows how else he had tried to capitalize on the situation? Truss . . ."

"This is a big place. Could be anybody, and they're not going to speak up now. No reason to," Jack said.

"But they were careful. They wouldn't have involved anyone they didn't need."

"There's Roger," Rebecca commented to the room at large.

Looking at the screen, Maggie saw a large man shuffling along in a blue windbreaker, the hood obscuring the face. "That's him?"

"Yeah, I recognize the tie. He's got some wild ties."

It looked like a blur of various shades of gray to Maggie, but then the younger woman spent a lot of time viewing her coworker through this particular lens.

"I think I need to talk with Mr. Correa," Jack said. "Now."

"I'll come with you," Maggie said.

Chapter 46

Jack protested, of course—Maggie had no business accompanying him on a suspect interview. She was neither trained nor authorized, and it would be a mess to explain in court. But she convinced him that her presence would put Correa at ease. She could say they stopped by only to drop off the photo disk with his pictures and video of Elliott at the bar. Besides, she did not entirely trust Jack to be alone with someone he might think had rolled a 1900-pound weight over Tyler Truss. Not entirely . . . actually, not at all.

"I don't think he did it," she told Jack as he drove.

"For logical reasons? Or are you thinking with another part of your anatomy?"

It seemed to surprise him when she laughed. "For emotional reasons—but his emotions. Roger thinks newsprint is a sacred trust. His life is that paper, and half the city won't receive their copy today because there's guts all over the paper rolls."

"But what a story it will make for tomorrow's paper. Rebecca said if it bleeds, it leads."

"I'm not sure Rebecca can recognize a tie from a fuzzy video either."

"She sees those people through that fuzzy video every day."

"Yes . . . and knows who's coming and who's going . . ."

"We're suspecting the security guard now? You really think little Rebecca could strangle a guy with nothing but her hands and a mesh strap?"

"It's all about leverage," Maggie reminded him. "But no, honestly, I don't. She had no reason to feel desperate—there will always be jobs in security. But for that matter, what happened to the whole rope thing? Truss wasn't strangled like the other three. And what was the digital guy doing in the print room?"

Jack pulled into Roger Correa's driveway and Maggie took in the house. A real-estate agent would refer to the bungalow as "classic" when everyone else would have said "old-fashioned." She had expected either a trendy loft or a seedy apartment over a bar, and wondered if Correa had inherited the home. But she recognized the car in front of the detached garage, which sagged under the long branches of a weeping willow.

She noted the tree. But, of course, it was one of the top ten most common in Ohio. During her childhood her neighbors had an entire row. It meant nothing.

Jack knocked on the side door. A series of barks was emitted from the house, and someone came to open the door. But it wasn't Roger Correa. Instead, a young man with shaggy hair and an easygoing smile greeted them, rubbing his eyes like a child.

"Nice to see you awake," Jack said to him.

Maggie had no idea what that meant. Past the kid, through the doorway, she saw a young black man with a Bluetooth headset typing on a laptop and glimpsed a girl with long dark hair. She seemed to be pinning something to the wall, just out of sight.

The boy said, "I work weird hours. Roger isn't here, he's out with Chaz somewhere."

"His car's here," Maggie said.

"They're on her bike. What can I do for you? The dogs are going to keep going nuts as long as someone's standing here."

Maggie noticed the logo embroidered on the kid's black shirt.

Jack noticed something else.

"Dogs?" he asked the kid. "As in plural?"

"Um, yeah."

"We need to see them."

"What, the dogs?"

"Jack—" Maggie said, thinking about the Great Lakes Brewing logo on the kid's shirt. Perhaps he knew something about the conspirators' secret meetings at the eatery.

"Yes, the dogs." Jack pulled out his badge. "Right now."

"Dude, seriously? Why do you need to look at the guy's *dogs?*"

"Jack—"

"We're coming in, and we are going to see those dogs."

"I don't care if you have a badge, I know you still need, like, a warrant to enter premises—"

Maggie interrupted. "What kind of dogs are they?"

This shut both men up. Then the kid said, "Um, Max is a German shepherd and Olaf is a Rottweiler, I guess. I mean, he's got that shape and coloring. I never asked for their pedigree—"

"I didn't see the Rottweiler when I was here," Jack said, making this sound like an accusation.

"He's old, spends most of the day sleeping in Roger's bedroom. What the hell is going on that you're here asking about dogs?" The animals had, anticlimactically, finally grown bored with the barking and quieted down.

Maggie got the significance of the Rottweiler fur and moved on to the next topic. "You work at Great Lakes Brewing?"

"Yeeeah."

Now Jack peered at her and back at the kid, plugging in another piece of the puzzle. "You overheard Roth and the others talking about the deal, and reported back to Correa."

The kid's eyes grew wide, and he stepped backward and tried to shut the door. Jack kept it from closing with one hand, his gaze boring into the kid through the glass, and reluctantly the boy let it open again.

"That's not illegal. There's nothing illegal about it," he insisted.

"Then you're not in any trouble. Right?" Jack pointed out.

This didn't seem to reassure him. "But is Roger?"

"Roger can take care of himself. You provided table service for Roth's meetings and listened to their discussion. What did you tell Correa about what they said?"

The kid looked from Jack to Maggie and back again. "I think I'd better talk to Roger before I tell you anything."

Jack lacked the patience for this. "He's not an attorney, and nothing you heard or repeated is privileged. You have to tell me."

"I'm a source. He can protect his sources."

"Not if we already know who you are, nimrod. There's nothing Correa can do at this point. Four people are dead and we're trying to prevent a fifth. So talk."

He shuffled his feet as a show of reluctance before giving in. "Sometimes I'd overhear business stuff."

"Such as?"

"About how they wanted TransMedia to buy the paper, and they'd all get—"

He broke off as a motorcycle zoomed up the drive. Roger Correa drove up with a girl clinging to his back. They both stared at the two visitors. The girl stepped off. She wore all black, from her leather jacket with feather fringe to her high-tops, and looked about as welcoming as a thornbush. Correa stayed on the bike, not surprised to see them but not concerned.

The girl opened her mouth to say something, and Correa gunned the engine, turned the wheel, and sped away.

Jack ran for the car, and after one startled second, Maggie followed, jumping into the passenger seat and pulling the door shut just in time to avoid clipping the girl in black, who stood in the driveway with her mouth still open.

"You think he did it?" Maggie asked, struggling to get her seat belt buckled as the car bounced over a pothole.

Jack seemed to notice her presence. "What the hell, Maggie? What are you doing?"

"Coming with you."

"You can't be here. We don't know if he's armed or what. This could go bad—"

Roger Correa turned onto Chester and ran a red light. Jack hit the red and blue flashers and Maggie closed her eyes as they entered the intersection, tensing for the crunch of twisted metal. No one hit them. Correa picked up speed, but Jack didn't.

"Aren't you going to lose him?" she asked.

"He's on a motorcycle. I don't want him goosed more than he already is—if he hits a pebble he might spin out of control."

Indeed, Correa's speed stabilized, and he stuck to Chester. If he was trying to lose them he wasn't doing a very good job of it.

She lost track of where they were, unfamiliar with this neck of the woods, and Correa must have seen the train before they did. But she felt the rumble.

"Jack," she warned, without even knowing what she warned of.

The red lights flashed, the white arms of the crossing gate lowered. From her right she glimpsed movement between the houses and trees, a giant being with a white light glowing like an eye, illuminating the track ahead and across the road. Jack took his foot off the accelerator.

Correa did not. He swerved into the other lane and sped around the lowered crossing gate arm. Onto the tracks, just as the train appeared.

Maggie shouted, *"No!"*

Jack hit the brakes.

They watched the taillight of Chaz's motorcycle dodge past the other gate, just before the engine clattered across the road, splitting the night with one outraged horn blast.

"He made it," Maggie said, wonderingly.

"And we're stuck," Jack snapped, letting the car coast to the crossing and then stomping on the brakes with irritated force. He calmed enough to add, "But I can guess where he's going."

Maggie shuddered. "Me too."

Chapter 47

Correa had disappeared into the night by the time the train rumbled past and the gates reopened, but at least, Maggie reflected, pieces of him were not scattered across the asphalt. Jack hit the accelerator and they shot forward. Maggie grasped the door handle through the rough and much too fast ride. Jack had used the wait time to call his partner and explain that he might need some backup, when and if he located Roger Correa.

"*Might* need backup?" Maggie asked when Jack hung up. "I'd say you definitely need it."

"We don't know he's at the *Herald*. I'm not calling out troops until I'm sure I need them."

"You shouldn't go after him alone," Maggie said evenly, meaning, *I don't trust you with him alone.*

"Don't worry."

She worried. Jack had been in a fury at Truss's grisly end, and especially at the sad orphaning of the two Davis kids. She knew if he wanted to continue his old habits he would have to find a new technique. Shot while trying to escape would work, and Correa had certainly tried to escape—he had Maggie to verify that.

When they arrived at the *Herald* building, it seemed to have already been sold, gutted, and

371

shuttered. Windows were dark and the delivery trucks already gone. No one worked on the docks, and only a few scattered vehicles remained in the lot. This didn't surprise her—the workers had probably dispersed the reduced amount of papers printed. No more could be produced until arrangements could be made to clean and decontaminate the cutting mechanism, and the police had sealed it off as a crime scene. Roth and any remaining employees had probably gone home.

Chaz's motorcycle sat parked, neatly within the lines, outside the north employee entrance.

Which created a problem. Correa had a key card to get inside—they did not.

"Stay here," Jack said as he bailed out of the driver's side.

Maggie, of course, did not listen and joined him as he pounded up the sidewalk to the door. He raised one arm to hammer at it—pointlessly—before noticing that it sat ajar, by no more than a quarter inch.

They both stopped dead, staring at the sliver of blackness along its edge, the hint of a deep and unknown interior.

Jack unholstered his weapon.

"Stay here," he said again.

"No," she answered, tone still even.

"I am not shitting, Maggie!" He kept his voice low, but forceful. "This is police business. You have no authority to interfere."

"I'm not interfering. I'll stay behind you. I'll stay out of the way."

"This is not your choice."

"You've made it my choice."

Then he got it. His expression changed from rage to such exasperation that she thought he might push her out of the way.

"Oh, for God's sakes, Maggie—I'm not going to *kill* him!"

As if that settled it, he pointed his gun at the door and pulled out a flashlight. He nodded at her, and she pulled open the door as fast as she could, tensing for the shot and protected by the brick wall. Jack swept the inside of the entranceway with the light, apparently saw nothing, and went in. A smooth operation.

She followed him.

Inside, the hall and stairwell were lit only by an emergency light on the next landing, filling the space with a ghostly blue glow. The opening ahead led into the reporters' bullpen. It didn't appear any more illuminated than the dark stairwell. Jack doused his flashlight and crept ahead silently.

Until he realized she was still behind him.

"Maggie!" he hissed.

"Let me talk to him. He likes me."

Jack poked his head into the cavernous room, surveyed, and retreated in one motion. He kept his voice near a whisper, but it made a furious sound all the same. "You think because he has the hots for you he's going to give himself up on four counts of murder?"

"I think he wants to tell a story—he's been telling it to me all week. That's what this is all about, the story."

"Are you trained in hostage negotiation?"

"Huh? No."

With a hand on her stomach he pushed her back against the wall. "Then stay here and shut up." With that he stepped into the open area, gun raised and pointed high.

"Freeze, Correa!" he shouted, in a boom that filled the canyon. "Step away from him!"

She heard Roger Correa's voice, easy, mocking. "Glad you finally got here, Detective. We've been waiting for you. Where's Maggie?"

Chapter 48

She watched Jack step into the darkness, gun raised and aimed. "Just me," he called to Correa, not as loudly as before. "Step away from him."

"All I have to do is push and he goes over. So I think you ought to put the gun down."

"Not going to happen."

"You can't hit me from there, and you know it. Not without going through him."

Maggie took two silent steps forward.

"Only one way to find out," Jack warned. But this didn't work, Correa must have feinted somehow, because Jack gave a startled twitch and held the gun away from himself in a gesture of capitulation.

"Okay, okay. Gun is down. What do you want?"

Maggie could stand it no longer. She crept to the corner, only three feet from Jack, and risked a peek into the bullpen, hoping that the shadows would hide her. It sounded as if Jack was right—the situation was bad, Correa had a hostage, and she could not help in these circumstances. Best to stay out of the way and leave it to the professionals.

But she had to have a look first. Then she could leave the building and call Riley, let him know to send the SWAT team and what they could expect.

Jack faced the east end of the building. On the second floor, in the hallway right outside Franklin Roth's office and backlit by its fluorescents, Roger Correa had tied a noose around the editor's neck and marched him up to the dangerously low Plexiglas barrier. He had tied the loose end off to the round, clear railing . . . and yes, all he had to do was give the man a hard shove and the last of the conspirators would die, dangling over the newsroom he had sworn to protect. Of course then Jack would shoot Correa, but she didn't think the reporter cared much about that at this point. He couldn't have made his own confession more plainly than this standoff.

The shadows did not do their job.

"There she is!" Roger Correa crowed. "Hello, Maggie."

She jumped back—too late, of course.

"What do you want?" Jack asked him again, after shooting a look of pure rage at her.

To her surprise, Correa said, "I want Maggie."

Jack couldn't help a startled glance in her direction before saying, "Not going to happen."

"That's what you said about putting the gun down."

"Not. Going. To—"

"Oh, relax, I'm not going to abscond with her. I simply want her to take dictation. Maggie, come on out. Let her come out—I don't have a gun, I'm completely unarmed. I can't do anything to her, or you, and I don't want to. The only person in danger here tonight is our esteemed editor."

Maggie didn't move from her place against the wall, deciding, perhaps too late, that she would defer to the professional officer. Even if that professional officer was simply waiting for Roger Correa to leave him enough room for a kill shot. There were only so many circumstances she could affect, and she had no way to determine if Jack would be a cop or a killer tonight. She would have to trust him.

That would not be easy.

He looked at her, considered. Then nodded.

She stepped out into the space. Correa still stood behind Roth, using him as a human shield. The editor's hands were tied behind his back, leaving him helpless. She couldn't see his expression, but his body stayed still. At that distance he barely seemed to be breathing.

"Great, there you are," Correa said.

This didn't seem to require a response.

"This is what I want—Maggie, I assume you can type?"

"What?"

"Type? Like, words? Even if it's hunt-and-peck—"

"Yes, I can type."

"Excellent. Would you grab my laptop—it's on my desk—third from the end there—"

She didn't move.

"Just come toward me, I'll tell you when you get there."

She didn't move.

His sigh reached the ends of the cavern. "Get the laptop and bring it up here. We're going to write and file my story. Franklin here can fact-check any details for us. All I want you to do is type and hit *Send*. That's it. Then we can all go home. Well, *you* can go home, and this worthless asshole here can go home. I assume Detective Renner and I will be taking a ride in a squad car."

"That's the deal?" Jack asked. "You file your story and then you'll let Roth go?"

"I give you my word as a newspaperman. Don't judge by our esteemed editor—those words still mean something to me."

Jack looked at her, and she told him, "I can do it."

He said to Correa, "She comes up there, I come, too."

"No need for that."

"Not negotiable."

"I can't do anything to her but dictate. I have no weapons other than our editor's weak neck."

"Not negotiable."

"You'd rather see me toss said editor's body off the landing?"

"Go ahead," Jack said with such finality that Maggie watched, terrified, fully expecting the editor to fall and die in one muffled *snap*.

Correa considered, then folded. "No closer than ten feet. Both of you."

Jack accompanied her to the desk where the laptop charged its battery. She pulled the power cord out of the back. If it ran out of battery life, so much the better, it would give them more time to think of something.

They took the elevator. Correa didn't protest, since it only went to two floors and both stops were visible to him. Maggie expected Jack to spend the brief trip lambasting her for not leaving when he told her to, but instead he called Riley and gave his partner a brief but comprehensive layout of the problem, speaking so fast she could barely understand him.

Ding.

For the second time he shoved her against the wall next to him, so that they would not be clearly visible to Roger Correa. Just in case he'd been lying about his lack of weapons.

The doors slid open. Maggie held her breath.

"I'm still not armed, Detective." Correa's voice floated into the space. "You can come out."

Jack stepped into the opening, and Maggie followed him as he turned left to circle the open atria. They passed Jerry Wilton's and Tyler Truss's offices. Maggie reminded herself to breathe.

"Ten feet," Jack spoke in a near whisper. "Don't you get any closer than that, no matter what he says, *no matter what happens.* If things go bad, you run like hell. Got it?"

"Got it."

"We're trying to save Roth, but our safety comes first. That's how this works."

"Right."

He glanced at her, as if second-, third-, and fourth-guessing his decision to let Correa call the shots and involve her. The expression on her face evidently did not reassure him. She realized, too late, that she must have looked scared as hell. "Roth is not your responsibility, so don't—"

"I'll do exactly what you tell me," she said. And mostly meant it. This didn't seem to reassure him either, but they had run out of hallway and come within ten feet of Roger Correa and Franklin Roth and, therefore, run out of time for further discussion.

Correa, his silk tie loosened, his hair going every which way from the motorcycle ride, watched them with gleeful excitement. He had turned his hostage to face them, maximizing the use of him as a barrier, and stuck close to the man's back. His head shifted to the right and left and back again, never giving Jack a steady target.

A stream of blood matted the editor's thin hair, just behind his right ear. It made a spot on his shirt collar but seemed to have partly dried. Maggie said to Correa, "What did you hit him with? I thought you said you had no weapons."

"A chair. I don't believe office furniture counts as a weapon."

"An adjustable wrench might, though. Under the right circumstances."

Correa's jaw tightened, but he said nothing.

Franklin Roth didn't seem so still up close. His thighs trembled, and circles of perspiration darkened the dress shirt under his arms. He smelled of fear but said nothing, his jaw tightened with a determination to stay strong and hang on to his dignity until the bitter end. For his sake, she hoped he could do it.

"Sorry I don't have a desk for you, Maggie," Correa said.

In response she sat down on the carpet, crossed her legs, and opened the laptop. Jack stood next to her, watching for an opening. Watching and waiting. She could feel the heat from his body radiating toward her like an electric current. The rest of the building sat around them, silent and lifeless.

"Okay," she told Correa. "Go ahead."

Chapter 49

A half hour later, she was still typing, fingers beginning to cramp as she struggled to keep up with his rapid-fire prose. Outside, she knew, Riley and other Cleveland police officers would be massing, waiting for Jack's cue before breaching the center of the building.

"In a series of secret meetings in a quiet location, these four men plotted—no, laid the plans to cut the throat of the Cleveland *Herald* and step quickly away, clutching their money before the blood it bought could splash onto their shoes. No, stain their shoes. That's better."

Maggie finished typing the sentence and waited for him to continue. Correa's voice had not begun to flag or grow short of breath. He paused only to consider his phrasing. He stayed behind his editor, but not as carefully as before. Jack kept the gun at his side and seemed to be willing to stick to the deal, so Correa grew more casual with his hostage. Roth, meanwhile, seemed about to wilt, resting one thigh against the Plexiglas to relieve the quaking in his knees. Maggie wondered if the weakness came from fear or simply from standing in one place for what must seem like a lifetime.

Jack, she could swear, hadn't moved at all. She couldn't tell he even breathed.

Correa started up again. "Jerry Wilton, the circulation manager—"

"You already said he was circulation manager," Roth said. Once an editor, always an editor.

"I did?"

Maggie checked the previous pages. "Yes, you did."

"Okay, just 'Wilton' then. Wilton not only betrayed his readers and his coworkers, but his fellow conspirators as well by secretly and illegally buying up *Herald* stock, expecting the price to jump—no, skyrocket—once news of the sale reached the public. What's a little insider trading when you're already on your way to the ninth circle of hell?"

Roth made a sound.

"What's that, esteemed managing editor?" Correa asked him.

"A little melodramatic, don't you think?"

Correa gave him a little shove, no more than a minor shifting of his bulk, but against the flimsy barrier it seemed that Roth wavered dangerously over open space. The editor's face reflected his fear. Correa said, "I write color, not play-by-play."

Maggie interrupted. "How did you know?"

Reporter and editor stared at her.

"About Wilton and the stock. How did you know he was doing that?"

"The more you interrupt, Maggie, the longer this is going to take."

"But how did you know?"

Correa blinked. "You told me."

"Me!"

"The police department, I mean. I have sources there, one called me yesterday."

"So you didn't know about the stocks when you killed him," she clarified. "Only about the kickbacks to sell the paper."

He cocked his head at her. "And that's not enough?"

It was as close to a confession as she'd gotten from him. She pressed on. "Why did you take their phones? Davis's, Wilton's—"

"To see who they were talking to, of course. And texting. Truss was really into texting. Digital guy, so I guess it figures. Our editor here, not so much. An old-fashioned man about everything but ethics."

"Is that how you found out about the meetings at Great Lakes? Through—"

"No, no, Austin noticed them months ago and alerted me. A reporter needs to have contacts everywhere. Or spies, if you prefer."

"What about Stephanie Davis?"

His head uncocked, and his expression flattened. "What about her?"

"Why did you kill her? She didn't have anything to do with the sale—"

His voice chilled about ten degrees. "But she still wanted to profit from it. She found out about the murder of public information and did nothing but blackmail the crooks for her cut of it. No one will shed any tears for that little snake."

Beside her, Jack stirred. Maggie thought she could hear the rumble of his anger below the surface as he said, "No one but her two kids."

"But how did you know about her?" Roth asked his captor, as if the question had just occurred to him. "She said she hadn't told anyone else before she met with me at Tower City, and then she . . . she was found in the parking—"

"Parabolic mike," Correa said, a bit of his insouciance returning with his dimples. "The running water made it a pain in the ass, but I could still catch the conversation. You know, that archaic equipment we still have lying around from when we used to be able to do real investigative journalism?"

Roth approached the end of his figurative tether, if not his actual one. "That's what you think this is? Journalism?"

"Exposing corruption that works against the public interest? Yes! That's exactly what I think it is!"

Roth twisted to look behind him. "Writing a story about it is journalism. Killing your subjects off is insanity!"

Correa shifted his weight, pushing the man into the Plexiglas—a slight move, but the clear partition bowed out enough to make Maggie gasp and Roth lean back, trying to backpedal. Correa held him there as he hissed, "It *was* self-defense. You four were trying to kill the thing that gives the rest of us a reason to live. You four versus one hundred and fifty, versus the 1.2 million people who live in this county and need to know more than just who wore what to the Oscars. You're the villain of this piece, Roth—don't forget it. Continue, Maggie. 'But the tragedy at the *Herald* is a story that has already been written thousands of times across the country in cities large and small, as newspapers have been shuttered, swallowed, and driven out of business by owners' greed—no, the greed of their owners and the apathy of their readers. The real tragedy is yet to come, when a celebrity's shoe size will be the only accurate fact a citizen can glean from the corporate machine referred to as news, quote unquote.' I mean actually put the quotation marks in—"

"I got it," Maggie told him.

"On that day, democracy as a function will have truly ceased to exist."

He stopped.

Maggie looked up. "Is that it?"

"Yeah," he said, as if this came as a surprise. "I think that's it. Put a thirty at the bottom. Hyphen, three zero, hyphen."

She did so. He gave her instructions for submitting it not only to the *Herald* site but to all the major news outlets, from the Associated Press to *The Huffington Post*. She didn't try to fool him; Maggie didn't care if the story went out. Why not—it was all true. She didn't care about saving the *Herald*'s reputation, or the memory of the victims. She only cared about saving Franklin Roth from the hangman's noose. However—

"We're done," Jack said, his voice landing like a stone in Correa's puddle of Pulitzer fantasies. "Let Roth and Maggie walk out of here, and then you and I can take a ride."

"Jack—" Maggie stood up, still holding the laptop. She didn't dare leave Jack alone with Correa.

"Maggie can go as soon as she hits *Post* on that screen. I have no interest in hurting Maggie." If Correa meant this to sound reassuring, it didn't.

"And Roth," Jack said.

"Seriously?" Correa said, his arm on the editor's shoulder as threatening as a gun to the head. All it would take was one shove, easily done. Of course Jack would then have a clear shot at Correa, but only after Roth dangled from the end of the strap. With his hands bound Roth could do nothing to save himself. "You think he deserves to live?"

Maggie moved to the Plexiglas railing.

"I think if he doesn't walk out of there, you won't either," Jack said.

"I can see my own future and—Maggie!"

His voice had the edge of true panic, and all three men stared at her as she held Roger Correa's laptop out over the railing, only her two hands keeping it from plummeting through thirty feet of space to the hard floor below.

"I haven't hit *Post* yet," she explained to Correa, willing her voice to sound calm and cool and only partially succeeding. "If I drop this, your story disappears."

Correa said nothing. He seemed to be sorting through options while holding his breath. Roth stayed still as well, aware that his life hung at the edge of a precipice both literal and figurative.

"Untie Roth and I'll hit the button," she said.

"Maggie, haven't you been listening to anything I said? I thought you cared about—"

"I have no problem with filing the story. I think people *should* know. But I also think there's been enough murder and I'm not about to let you kill this man in cold blood."

"There's nothing cold about it!"

"Let him go, or the story dies."

She thought she could see the hint of a smile at a corner of Jack's mouth. He turned back to Correa and said, "I'd listen to her. She doesn't care for compromise."

Correa hesitated, but not for long. His story trumped all other considerations. With a sigh and a glare he loosened the noose from Franklin Roth's neck and let it drop to the floor. The editor's relief showed in the heavy hiss of air from his lungs and the slow collapse of his shoulders.

"And his hands," Maggie said.

"Show me that you posted it first."

Still at the railing, she moved toward them, but Jack stretched out an arm. "That's close enough."

Balancing the laptop on the unsteady railing, she clicked on the *Post* button, then turned the screen so Correa could see the confirmation that the story had been sent. His mannerisms echoed the relief of his editor. It was done. He had finished his story.

He shoved Roth aside with both hands.

With his arms still bound, the man could do nothing but tumble helplessly into the clear barrier. It might have stopped him, he might have been able to catch onto it with his feet or legs, but it tore away from its moorings as if it had been made out of cardboard. The railing sections came apart and the whole thing flopped open, creating a slide straight into open space. Roth went over the edge of it with only a strangled cry.

Jack leapt forward, colliding with Correa, who aimed to either stop Jack or make sure Roth completed his fall. Their weight fell on the section of already bowed out Plexiglas. A snapping sound rent the air.

Maggie never remembered dropping the laptop and stumbling forward, reaching for Jack. She did remember that some sensible, calmer voice in the back of her head had already begun to calculate the distance to the floor below, estimate injuries depending on whether he landed on a desk or on the floor, if he landed on his feet or his torso or his head. Thirty feet, maybe twenty-five, acceleration due to gravity—he could probably survive the fall with just broken bones.

Probably.

But maybe not.

Her hand caught his.

She had already been in a crouch so she didn't have quite as far to go when his weight snapped her to the floor, the not-clean industrial carpeting digging into her cheek. An explosion of pain in her right shoulder made her vision turn to bright white. The searing agony reverberated to her toes and back again. She would have screamed had she been able to draw in any air. The universe condensed to one single thought: *Hang on.*

And one other: *Don't let them pull you over.*

But her body lay on an open area, with nothing to use as an anchor except the railing supports, and she had just seen how well they worked.

Her vision cleared enough for her to see Jack below her, hanging on to her hand with an odd expression on his face, as if he could not determine how he had come to be there. Below him, Roger Correa had both arms wrapped around Jack's left leg. She had two large men dangling from her arm. No wonder it hurt.

Though hurt was an understatement. Her arm would be ripped away from her body if she didn't—

Jack raised his free leg, and with thoughtful aim kicked Roger Correa in the face.

The reporter fell away, and Maggie watched him slam into a reporter's desk, half on, half off, his spine catching the edge with an audible crack. Then he quaked, rolled, and landed on the floor next to the supine editor. She didn't calculate his odds of survival. She no longer cared whether Roger Correa or Franklin Roth still lived. She almost didn't care if Jack did. She just wanted the pain to stop.

Jack gave one strong tug to her arm—and now she *did* scream—to get one hand, then the other, up on the walkway edge. Somehow he pulled himself up, climbing over her, the weight of his body crushing the breath from her lungs. Then he turned her over. When she thought over the mass of sensations later she realized he'd been trying to be gentle, but it didn't make a difference. Her vision went white again.

When it cleared, she heard him calling for an ambulance and then updating the situation for the entry team. He snapped the phone shut.

"Are you okay?" he asked her.

She couldn't answer. She was too busy trying to breathe.

Chapter 50

Rick Gardiner rubbed one eye and watched his ex-wife's coworker—Josh, the kid's name was Josh—brush black powder all over the piece of Plexiglas that had fallen from the second floor. Neither he nor Josh saw the purpose in it, both had made clear to the other, since all their suspects were (a) dead and (b) worked in this building, so their prints on the railing would prove exactly nothing. But both he and Josh knew that their respective butts would be chewed if that box on the solvability checklist hadn't been colored in, so the kid threw powder and Rick watched. At least until Patty Wildwood figured out some other grunt task for him to do since, as usual, she had put herself in unofficial charge. He could be at the hospital asking his ex-wife how she had come to be in the middle of this, how very, very physically she had been in the middle of it, and how that bastard Renner had jerked her arm out of its socket—

"Detective Gardiner?"

He turned. The reporters, who had a grapevine that rivaled the cops', had returned to their roost despite the late hour and Patty had let them, provided they stayed on the other side of the yellow tape strung across the bullpen. She hoped

392

that they might talk now that their boss had died and open up without circumspection within sight of his blood on the floor. Rick wondered how that was working out for her. Then he wondered who was this blond hottie who knew his name.

"That's me."

She smiled, white teeth above an elfin chin and really healthy boobs. "I'm Lori Russo. We spoke on the phone."

"We did? Oh—the vigilante killings."

"Yes."

He'd blown her off, but here she was tossing her hair over one shoulder at him. Hot and not above using it to get what she wanted. She had a wedding band on her left hand, but who the hell cared about that nowadays? He straightened his jacket. "How's your story coming?"

"I've found out some interesting things from my contact in Phoenix. I'd love to talk to you about it."

"So would I," Rick said, and meant it.

Jack sat in an uncomfortable chair against the wall of ER room 8 at Metro General, watching Maggie Gardiner sleep. The two doctors on duty had been occupied with a cardiac arrest, so a physician's assistant had given her a shot of morphine to hold her over until one freed up—but then one of them found a few minutes to maneuver her arm back into its socket anyway.

Now Maggie had both morphine and a relocated arm and looked more comfortable than she had on the floor of the *Herald* building.

She should have let me go, Jack realized. *She should have just opened her hand and released me into the air, or better yet, never grabbed me in the first place.* No one would have blamed her— he still couldn't believe he hadn't pulled her over the side. The fall might not have killed him, and if he survived she'd have had a perfect explanation for her actions. No one would have known her true reasoning except him, and he could hardly explain their background to another living soul without hanging himself. He wondered if that alternative future had occurred to her, or would when the morphine wore off and she woke up with a throbbing shoulder.

If he died, her secret died with him. Maggie Gardiner could have gone through the rest of her life with that burden lifted, could have left behind the constant fear that a few words from him could put her in jail. She'd be free.

Then he thought, he should have let go of her. Let his body fall, let the darkness overtake him, leave this screwed-up world and his own paltry efforts to improve it. He had done what he could. He couldn't do it forever and told himself he had no desire to try. He should have just let go.

But surprise surprise, when the opportunity arose, he wasn't quite ready to shuffle off this mortal coil—instead, he pulled Maggie's arm out of its socket rather than take the chance that he might. He had clung to life just as fiercely as those clients of his with their voracious evil, who spread nothing but pain and death, as fiercely as they would have clung to theirs had he ever given them the opportunity to do so.

This didn't make him feel guilty for ending their lives. On the contrary, he felt proud of himself for saving them from those panicked, agonizing minutes before the crash, that feeling of utter and complete desperation. He had spared the world from their violence as he had spared them from that instinctual terror. He'd been kind. Much kinder than Roger Correa had been to any of his victims.

Both Roth and Correa were dead. Each might have lived if their landings had been a bit softer. Roth's body had pivoted just enough that the floor caught his head first, causing an internal bleeding that the doctors couldn't fix in time to save him. A desk had snapped Correa's spine. It might have left him paralyzed but had managed to kill him instead. Jack couldn't decide which option he preferred, but thought he could guess the choice Correa would have made.

Maggie stirred, turned her head, and caught sight of him. "Are you here to hold my hand?"

"Making sure you don't talk in your sleep."

She gave a tiny but amused snort.

"How are you feeling?" he found himself asking, not sure why. In another life, another world, he used to say things like that. He might as well stay in practice.

"Peachy. At least until that hypodermic wears off." She blinked at him, once, lashes sweeping lazily over sky-blue eyes. "Good stuff. Unfortunately they won't let me take it home in a six-pack."

"They'll give you meds."

A not-amused snort. "They won't be any stronger than Tylenol. Prescription drug addicts have ruined pain meds for everyone. Don'tcha hate that?"

He didn't return her smile. "You could have just let me go."

Okay, *this* wasn't practice he needed to stay in, this heart-to-heart crap.

"Yeah," she said. "I could have. I wonder what Dr. Michaels will make of *that*."

"Why didn't you"—*Stop talking, Jack*—"let me go? It would have seriously uncomplicated your life."

"Yeah," she said again, as if pondering a mildly interesting phenomenon. "But I didn't want to."

She should have let him die, but didn't. She was a good person, was Maggie Gardiner. It almost made him feel guilty for lying to her about Ronnie Soltis. Also known as Reign.

Almost.

"I guess . . ." Maggie was saying, staring at the small dots on the ceiling tiles.

"Guess what?"

"I guess I think we make a pretty good team. Sometimes. In a way."

"We're not a team, Maggie," he said. But her eyes had already closed.

Acknowledgments

First, I'd like to thank Phillip Baker at the Fort Myers *News-Press* for giving me two tours of the printing plant along with all sorts of information and for helping me fix one of the murders in this book. Also Melissa Montoya-Ocampo and Tony Rybarczyk at the *News-Press* and Sgt. Dana Coston at the Cape Coral Police Department, who put me in touch with all these interesting people. Visiting the *News-Press* was a huge help to me since I couldn't get time to spend at Cleveland's *The Plain Dealer.* (P.S. The motto "Give Light and the People Will Find Their Own Way" was actually the motto of the *New Mexico State Tribune* in Albuquerque, and later all Scripps newspapers.)

I would like to thank the authors of the following fascinating books:

Brock, George. *Out of Print: Newspapers, Journalism and the Business of News in the Digital Age.* Kogan Page, Philadelphia, PA: 2013.

Doctor, Ken. *Newsonomics: Twelve New Trends That Will Shape the News You Get.* St. Martin's Press, New York: 2010.

Jones, Alex S. *Losing the News: The Future*

of the News That Feeds Democracy. Oxford University Press, New York: 2009.

Manjoo, Farhad. *True Enough: Learning to Live in a Post-Fact Society*. Wiley, Hoboken, NJ: 2008.

McChesney, Robert W., and John Nichols. *The Death and Life of American Journalism*. Nation Books, Philadelphia, PA: 2010.

McCord, Richard. *The Chain Gang: One Newspaper Versus the Gannett Empire*. University of Missouri Press, Columbia, MO: 2001.

O'Shea, James. *The Deal From Hell: How Moguls and Wall Street Plundered Great American Newspapers*. Public Affairs, New York: 2011.

Teachout, Zephyr. *Corruption in America: From Benjamin Franklin's Snuff Box to Citizens United*. Harvard University Press, Cambridge, MA: 2014.

Thanks as always to my sister Mary, who is always there for a medical question. And my sister Susan, who is a one-woman PR force.

I want to thank Michaela Hamilton for her tireless editing of this manuscript, as well as Morgan Elwell and the rest of the great team at Kensington Publishing.

And of course, my agent, Vicky Bijur, and her group at the Vicky Bijur Literary Agency for their continuing belief in me.

Center Point Large Print
600 Brooks Road / PO Box 1
Thorndike, ME 04986-0001 USA

(207) 568-3717

US & Canada:
1 800 929-9108
www.centerpointlargeprint.com